THE *lifestyle* PUZZLE

WHO WE ARE IN THE *21st century*

THE *lifestyle* PUZZLE

WHO WE ARE IN THE *21st century*

HENRIK VEJLGAARD

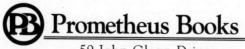 **Prometheus Books**

59 John Glenn Drive
Amherst, New York 14228-2119

Published 2010 by Prometheus Books

Inquiries should be addressed to
Prometheus Books
59 John Glenn Drive
Amherst, New York 14228–2119
VOICE: 716–691–0133
FAX: 716–691–0137
WWW.PROMETHEUSBOOKS.COM

14 13 12 11 10   5 4 3 2 1

Library of Congress Cataloging-in-Publication Data

Vejlgaard, Henrik.
    The lifestyle puzzle : who we are in the 21st century / by Henrik Vejlgaard.
        p. cm.
    Includes bibliographical references and index.
    ISBN 978–1–61614–185–1 (pbk.)
    1. Social change. 2. Identity (Philosophical concept). 3. Lifestyles. 4. Popular culture. I. Title.

HM831.V445 2010
306.0973'0905—dc22

2010013079

Printed in the United States of America

To my mother and to the
memory of my father

CONTENTS

Introduction

PATTERNS AND GENERALIZATIONS

*L*abeling and classifying people—putting people into boxes—is what this book is about. It is something that almost all people do; some keep it to themselves that they do it while others are open about it. We also label and categorize ourselves—that is part of creating our identity. How and why will be revealed in the chapters that follow.

When we label and classify other people, we often run the risk of making generalizations, especially when dealing with whole groups or categories of people. Making generalizations is the goal of much analysis. We typically want to see the clearest picture and not focus on all the exceptions and deviations. Of course, when someone makes generalizations that do *not* reflect the characteristics of the majority of a group, we have to be critical because then we are dealing with bias or prejudice. When prejudiced generalizations are negative, derogatory, or hateful, we are beyond facts and are dealing with bigotry, which has nothing to do with lifestyle analysis.

That said, generalizations of the descriptive kind are unavoidable when trying to identify patterns in how we live. *Patterns*—a reliable sample of traits, actions, and other observable features characterizing a group—is a term or principle that is sometimes misinterpreted as reinforcing stereotypes. This is something I learned with the publication of my book *Anatomy of a Trend*,[1] which was about identifying patterns in the social process that takes place when we see changes in style and taste. Some groups are more active in this social process than others. In that book I underscored that there is a pattern of overrepresentation of some groups when changes take place in style and taste. I specifically mentioned that not all artists, designers, celebrities, gay men, and young people are alike and that not all in these groups contribute to the early stages of the trend process. But among the reactions I received from some readers were that the book reinforced stereotypes. Stereotypes or not, I reported the patterns that I identified. That some people do not like such patterns is actually an expected pattern when the analysis is about identifying patterns in the lives of people with whom we identify.

I will acknowledge that there is a risk that you do not get all the details out in the open when communicating about patterns. On the other hand, most people are aware that identifying a pattern is not the same as making a generalization about *all* people in a group. Patterns are about identifying and pointing out what is fairly typical among members in a group. This is one of the main themes of this book.

The Lifestyle Puzzle is also about us becoming even more individualistic than we were late in the twentieth century, and there is nothing that twenty-first-century individualists dislike more than being labeled and put into boxes. However, like it or not, many people are in fact individualistic in the same way. So even among present-day individualists we can see group patterns. Of course, not all people are individualists and many people still wholeheartedly embrace being part of groups of all kinds.

My goal here is not just to identify familiar patterns—the focus is actually on new patterns. "New" in this respect is not about being completely new, the never-heard-of-before variety of new. The changes that this book focuses on are social changes that take a long time—often a decade—to emerge, and then a couple more decades to become firmly established components of a new reality. As I am more interested in what is happening in society right now than I am in what may or may not happen with society sometime in the future, this book explains our current common reality and highlights the patterns that will continue to exist for at least a part of the twenty-first century.

While some people think that changes in society are fast and furious, again and again I am struck by how slowly society changes. American society represents more than 300 million individuals with highly different personalities and attitudes toward changes. For the majority of Americans—as for people everywhere—to change is not just a complicated process, it is a time-consuming process. Based on what I know about trends and what this book reveals about the many highly diverse lifestyle groups that form American society, I would estimate that many major changes in society are about thirty years in the making before the changes become real to the majority of people.

No group or generation represents all of society, but the premise in this book is that young people in particular represent the change that is going to take place. However, I will be the first not to be so prejudiced as to say that all young people are alike. They are not. As this book will show, they are actually more diverse than they have ever been before. One point is that they will take this diversity with them as they grow older in the twenty-first century.

Chapter 1

LIVING IN A MILLION WAYS
Laying Out a Jigsaw Puzzle

*O*uter space holds a great deal of fascination for humans and inspires intriguing questions. Many scientists and visionaries want to know if there is (primitive) life on Mars and other planets. While some ponder about what goes on in outer space, most people probably care more about what goes on here on Earth. And with more people populating the planet than ever before and with constant changes in technology and communication, present-day living on Earth can also be viewed as quite puzzling—and complex.

Just how complex was summed up by the *New York Times* in the beginning of the twenty-first century: "It has become harder to read people's status in the clothes they wear, the cars they drive, the votes they cast, the god they worship, the color of their skin."[1] So the question is, how do we read other people's status in the twenty-first century? It is not that clothes, cars, and other designed objects do not reveal anything about who we are. It is just that they do not reveal what they used to reveal, like, for instance, our age or our income.

The next big question is, does this change result in us living random and chaotic lives or are there still recognizable patterns in how we live? When historians describe "the olden days," they identify patterns of the period they study. But now that we are in the twenty-first century, does this mean that there is a new rule that states society is chaotic and in a constant flux? If this were the case, that would certainly be a radical change in the history of humankind because so far in human history there have always been solid patterns in the way we humans have organized our lives. Without a doubt, present-day society is complex, but being complex is not the same as being chaotic. When something is complex, we just have to dig deeper to find the patterns.

Some will ask, does it matter whether or not there are patterns in how we live our lives? Well, if you have a curious mind, it does. For people who like puzzles of all kinds—both the entertaining ones and the serious ones—this is a challenging puzzle. If for no other reason then because it is such a daunting one: figuring out the patterns of how we live is like laying out a gigantic jigsaw puzzle with millions and millions of pieces. Actually more than 300 million pieces, as the United States passed the 300-million-citizens mark in the first decade of this century.[2] The challenge is not only the size of this jigsaw puzzle but also that it is not absolutely clear what the motif—the dominant theme—of the jigsaw puzzle is. We know only that it is about who we are in the twenty-first century.

It may well be that this is a jigsaw puzzle that cannot be laid out. On the other hand, if we can fit just some of the pieces together, then we might not be so, well, puzzled. But for this to be doable we have to believe that there are patterns in present-day human life and that knowing these patterns can enrich our lives. Otherwise it is an aimless task to try to understand the social fabric of human living in the twenty-first century.

Many changes that took place in the twentieth century have had direct influence on how we live in the twenty-first century. By picking just a few random pieces from the entire pile, it is fairly easy to highlight some of these changes. For instance, here is a jigsaw piece that has a couple on it. The man is the actor Billy Bob Thornton, who has been married and divorced five times. That was by the time he was just fifty years old. He has three children: two sons from one of his marriages, and a daughter who was born when he was fifty years old.

Many other jigsaw pieces show families, but many of these families appear to be quite different from each other. Judging from all these jigsaw pieces, a family is not just about a mother and a father with wedding rings on their fingers and two or three kids. Today only 23.5 percent of American households are organized in this way, the traditional family model.[3] Many other jigsaw pieces show different ways of organizing family life. For instance, more than 5 million unmarried couples cohabit. That number has gone up eight times since 1970. Four out of ten children are born to women who are not married.[4] Then there are the families that consist of just one parent—a mother or a father. That was the case of President Barack Obama, who was raised by a single mother.[5] In a growing number of families, the husband is a stay-at-home dad and the mother works outside of the home and is the main provider. According to *Newsweek,* this is the case in about 11 percent of households.[6] In 40 percent of all households the woman is the primary breadwinner.[7] This was also the case in the household of Michelle and Barack Obama for a period before he became president.[8]

More and more families are established late in life. Young people certainly don't marry in their early twenties anymore. In 1970, 65 percent of Americans were married by that age. In 2000, the number was only about 15 percent.[9] Now, some people are establishing their first-time families when they are in their forties. At that same age some other people who were married in their twenties are getting a divorce. In fact, four out of ten marriages end in divorce.[10] And divorces take place in all kinds of families. Here's one example of the high divorce rate: in the 2008 presidential campaign, four out of the five Republican candidates had been married multiple times.[11]

People divorce for many reasons. It can be about emotional issues, but it can also be because people want to organize their lives in different ways. Billy Bob Thornton has explained in an interview why he and his fifth wife, actress Angelina Jolie, divorced: "We had a great relationship. We loved each other the whole time we were together. We just had different ideas about our lives. She has her thing where she is all over the world and that's great. . . . I just want to stay at home. . . . I watch a lot of sports on television. I'm a big baseball freak."[12]

Then there are families like the one Jon and Michael Galluccio have written about in their book, *An American Family*; in this case, the family consists of gay parents with three adopted children.[13] Writing a book about one's family is not common, but the existence of gay families is. Otherwise the cruise ship–vacation company R Family Vacations would not be the success that it is. This cruise ship company specializes in arranging vacations for gay families and their friends. The company was founded by actress and talk show host Rosie O'Donnell and her then significant other Kelli O'Donnell, who have three children themselves.[14] That gay men and lesbians have children is not uncommon anymore: 22 percent of gay male couples have children. For lesbians the amount is 34 percent.[15]

Today, marriage and "coupledom" do not always equal children for heterosexual couples. This got the attention of realtors in the 1980s. They started using acronyms like DINKs (short for Double Income, No Kids) and SINKs (Single Income, No Kids). Also, there are a whole lot of SWANKs (Single Woman And No Kids), another realtor acronym from the 1980s. Single-person households represent more than 27 percent of all households.[16]

The reality is that a growing number of people are not living their lives according to once-familiar patterns. Today there are many options in how we can organize our lives. Being aware of and understanding how we organize our lives certainly has consequences in many ways: in personal relationships—in how we relate to other family members and friends. In short, it affects how we as individuals are "glued together" with some people and not with others.

RELATIVE AGE

Just by looking at the many jigsaw pieces that have people on them, you will sometimes find it difficult to judge how young—or old—the people are. Here is a piece that shows a group of people who are in their forties. Or are they in their fifties—or older? This is hard to tell. This is not so surprising because age is more fluid than ever. Becoming a father at the age of nearly fifty, as Billy Bob Thornton did, is not common, but it is not unheard of either. Only when women start having babies in their sixties can we firmly say something has definitely changed. In 1996 a mother in California became—what was then—the world's oldest mother, aged sixty-three.[17]

Like the concept of family, the concept of age was also something that changed in the late twentieth century. For decades the combination of family life and age was fairly standard: you married and had children when you were young, not when you were old. This pattern was based on biology, convention, and life's circumstances.

These days—as relatively fewer people have jobs that require hard physical labor—fewer people are physically worn out when they reach retirement age. Because many people do not look or feel their perceived biological age, aging is no longer just about biology and is more about a state of mind. Consequently many people feel that they are younger than the age on their birth certificate. For some it is just a few years; for others it can be several decades. One of the first to notice this was Faith Popcorn, the internationally known author and marketing consultant. She called the phenomenon *down-aging*.[18]

Today, age is definitely fluid. The result is that a person's psychological age can be considerably younger than her biological age. A person's biological age may be forty-five years, but her psychological age could be thirty-five—or even younger. I use the term *age elasticity* to describe this phenomenon in which you see yourself as being younger than your biological age.[19] Age elasticity is the difference between

- biological age: the age according to your birth certificate, and
- psychological age: the age at which you perceive yourself.

Figure 1.1 is a graphic illustration of how different biological age and psychological age can be. Someone who is seventy years old can feel like a sixty-year-old, and someone who is fifty years old can feel twenty years younger.

Figure 1.1. Age Elasticity: Two Examples

Physical Age	Psychological Age
70	70
60	60
50	50
40	40
30	30

Age elasticity affects many aspects of our lives. Being a senior citizen used to be about retiring to a nice, quiet life, maybe with grandchildren to take care of. Today not all senior citizens feel that is the way to spend their time. And there are many alternatives to a quiet life at home for senior citizens. When grandparents and other people of a similar age were starting to travel as freely as their grown-up grandchildren, this was a new pattern in the travel industry. In the 1990s people over the age of sixty en masse started trekking in mountains and going on other adventurous and physically demanding travels. They also started participating in endurance sports, like the New York Marathon or the Hawaii Triathlon.

Many more signs indicate that age is becoming relative and that people are letting their psychological age—not their biological age—define their lives. No matter what your age is—as long as you feel fit—you can go roller-skating, travel around the world, or dress in fashionable clothes. The magazine industry understands the changed concept of age and has launched a number of magazine titles that help people aged fifty-plus in organizing a life based on this new reality, for example, *Travel 50 & Beyond* and *Southern California Senior Life*. It makes sense that these and other magazines appear because they help the readers confirm their younger-feeling identity and give them inspiration on how to organize their lives as active senior citizens.

Age elasticity applies to both women and men, but generally men's age elasticity seems to be higher than women's. It is not uncommon for men in their fifties to see themselves as being twenty-five-year-olds, whereas a woman in her fifties is more likely to see herself as a forty-year-old. There are different reasons for men's higher age elasticity, but the main reason is probably that men can father children for more years than women can give birth to children (at least the natural way).

Men's high age elasticity also makes them sensitive to how their girlfriends and wives look. For instance, if a husband and a wife are both fifty years old but the husband feels like a twenty-five-year-old and then looks at his wife and sees a fifty-year-old woman, he may feel there is an imbalance. Though he may himself look like a fifty-year-old, he may be more attracted to someone who is closer to his psychological age. This may explain why after a divorce some men end up marrying women who are younger than their first wives and themselves. (This may also help explain why women are so keen on face creams and plastic surgery—they need to look younger to avoid falling victim to men's high age elasticity.) A new pattern is that of women marrying men much younger than themselves, as in the case of Hollywood couple Demi Moore and Ashton Kutcher. We also have a term for women who are physically attracted to men who are younger than themselves—cougars.

For both sexes it can be disturbing to look in the mirror and see an older person when you feel so young inside. This imbalance prompts some people to take steps to look the age they feel. The solution is cosmetic plastic surgery and antiwrinkle creams.

With high age elasticity, it is difficult to have clear-cut notions about people at certain ages. The consequence is that we cannot expect people with the same biological age to organize their lives in the same way—or to dress the same way. One mother who is forty years old and has teenage daughters can be completely different from another forty-year-old mother who has teenage daughters. Some mothers will think of themselves as being twenty-five years old, some as thirty-seven, and some as forty-five or perhaps older. Those in the first category may dress like their daughters, and in most cases other people will not think this is strange. Age elasticity is one reason why it is harder for us to classify other people.

CLASSIFYING PEOPLE

Classifying people is about how we create distinctions between ourselves and other people and between other people in general. There are some easily observable distinctions between all members of the human race based on biology (having dark skin, being blond, etc.). Then there are cultural distinctions based on history and geography that we are born into (e.g., speech and what we eat). Finally, there is also an abundance of distinctions that are visual: it is easy to spot a cowboy or someone dressed flamboyantly or someone dressed in an understated way. For a first impression—at a distance—our clothes do the talking for us, and other people start classifying us based on how we dress. But as they get to talk to us, our speech and what we say also play an important role in how they classify us.

Speech is a popular way to classify other people because we often can get some clues right away about a person from the way she speaks: it can be about geography (dialects) and education and our social set (what linguists call sociolects), to name three of the most common clues. We have an abundance of dialects, some more pronounced than others, and some more stereotypical than others. It is easy to identify a Southerner because of the use of *y'all*; a New York accent based on *Noo Yawk tawk*; a Bostonian accent with people saying *pahk the cah*. As for sociolects, in Boston the Brahmins, the Old Irish upper class, speak with their own accent, and in New Orleans the local Yat dialect has a distinct working-class sound.[20] However, in the United States sociolects are not as prevalent as in some other countries. Even in the racially divided South before the Civil War, the white plantation owners and the black slaves spoke in the same way. This observation was made by, among others, the English novelist Charles Dickens during a visit to the United States.[21]

Today when someone says, "She ain't been nowhere" or "She done it," most people will automatically start categorizing the speaker based on geography, education, and race. Actually we often go one step further and also assign certain character traits to a person who speaks with a particular dialect or sociolect. When people from New England hear a Southern accent (and vice versa), all kinds of images, character traits, and prejudices may pop up in the minds of the listeners. The character traits can be positive traits, such as hospitality and warmth, or negative traits, such as ignorance and backwardness.

When we speak we not only communicate what we want to say but we also reveal a lot about where we are from and therefore sometimes who we are. But our speech cannot tell (or reveal) everything about us. There are other ways to get clues. Money—as in being rich or poor—certainly qualifies as a much-used way to classify other people. Variation in wealth and income creates social hierarchies. There is literally an abundance of hierarchies in all societies and communities, though they are not always easily identifiable. The Hamptons, a wealthy beach community on Long Island, has its hierarchies with the über-rich CEOs and Hollywood royalty at the very top, according to journalist Bridget Harrison, who spent a summer there reporting on the social scene. "Theirs was a mellow summer of jetting in by private plane, hired caterers for discreet home dinner parties, quiet cocktails served by staff on the deck," she writes in her memoir of being a *New York Post* columnist. "Next on the ladder were the social set—the well-known celebrities and Hamptons-scene regulars who seemed addicted to a weekly round of charity benefits, functions, and fancy parties." Then there was the wealthy-kids set composed of heirs of all ages, and "further down on the strata were the house sharers. The twenty-something generation of New York young bankers, Jewish princesses, and lesser trust-fund kids."[22]

"The working class" in the Hamptons consists of different groups of people, according to Harrison. There is "an army of entrepreneurs" like PR consultants, club promoters, tennis pros, personal trainers, and landscapers earning fifteen times more than the minimum wage an hour. This group could also include the motor yacht crews who work on the yachts of the über rich. Harrison noticed how "the local bars in Sag Harbor would get rowdy with the motor yacht crews— tanned, macho young guys from Australia, New Zealand, South Africa, and Florida—who were permanently drunk, and who sneaked a different girl each night back to the decks of those $50-million yachts. The boys partied nonstop until Friday, when the owners of their boats arrived and they'd be transformed from roguish playboys to uniformed deck boys again until Sunday night."[23]

We can go to other locations where there are different kinds of social hierarchies. For instance, in the middle of the United States there is a different natural—and social—landscape. The Ozarks—the mountainous region that covers a large part of Missouri, parts of Arkansas and Oklahoma, and a little bit of Kansas—is a rural, forested area that has its own social profile: most of the people there are Caucasian, their income level is among the lowest in the country, only about 10 percent of the residents have a college degree, and they get married early and divorce nearly twice as often as the rest of the country. This vast area has also been dubbed the epicenter of conservative Christian fundamentalism or, to use a popular metaphor, the buckle in the Bible Belt.[24]

Hierarchies are not permanent. Or rather, a person's place in a hierarchy is not. But this wasn't always the case. Many histories from many different cultures reveal that being rich or poor *was* a permanent situation, but now it is not unusual to hear stories of how it just takes one generation to change one's economic circumstances dramatically. One who knows what it means to be defined by poverty is Jeannette Walls, who grew up in a family where getting food was often a daily struggle and who was many times labeled "white trash." She wrote about her Dickensian upbringing in her memoir *The Glass Castle*. When the book was published she had an education and a well-paying job as a journalist.[25] Though poverty can be permanent, it was not in the case of Jeannette Walls. One more example of how fluid—how changeable—modern life can be is rapper Jay-Z, who is a multimillionaire several times over, by his own doing. According to the *New York Times*, "Jay-Z's story, as told in million-selling hip-hop albums, is an all-American tale of entrepreneurship: from hustling drugs in the ghetto to rapping about guns and girls to running Roc-a-Fella, a recording company and clothing line."[26] Now, by way of his artistic talents, he has made his own fortune. The rapper and music mogul can afford everything that normally only people with names like Kennedy, Astor, and Vanderbilt could buy. People can be born into poverty and then end up being rich. Or the other way around. During the "Great Recession" in the late 2000s, many people in well-paying jobs were let go. Some lost their entire life savings and some ended up losing everything they owned. The question is, which situation defines them? It is not just our present circumstances that define us. Our past, sad or glorious, is also part of who we are.

We can classify ourselves and other people in numerous ways. We classify people based on their religion, their politics, their furniture, their cars, their pets, the books they read, the music they listen to, what they eat and drink. We call people "snobs," "white trash," "educated," "jet-setters," "fanatics," and many other terms that create distinctions and in one way or another place other people in a certain category that suits us. We typically use language to make the distinctions, either using a descriptive term (like *jet-setter*) or a loaded term (like the derogatory *white trash* or the typically positive *educated*). We classify not only people but also the arts. In literature and movies we talk about "classics," but that is just one way of classifying books and movies. And what is "classic" to one group is "boring," "ridiculous," or "awesome" to another group.

The distinction between descriptive terms and loaded terms reflects that classifying people can be done in different ways: it can be vertical or hierarchical (when something is better than something else) or it can be horizontal when things are just different, but not better or worse than something else. Historically, vertical thinking and social organization has dominated European culture, whereas in the United States horizontal thinking and social organization have been more prevalent—starting with some of the earliest settlers in North America.

IMMIGRANT THINKING

It is a fundamental part of the history of the United States that different communities, regions, and states have their unique ethnic and religious profiles. This pattern goes back to when the earliest settlers arrived from Europe. In 1620 the Pilgrims arrived on the *Mayflower* at Plymouth Rock in what is now called Massachusetts after having left their homes in the northeastern part of England because of religious persecution. After crossing the Atlantic Ocean they found religious freedom.[27]

The name of the area that the Pilgrims arrived in was New England, the name given this "new" land in 1614 by the English captain John Smith (who had come to Chesapeake Bay, Virginia, in 1607 and later in history became famous for having a brief association with Pocahontas, the daughter of Native American chief Powhatan).[28] Probably more than any other group of settlers, the Pilgrims felt like Americans right away. They became Yankees. At least it is worth noting that two of the new states that these and other early settlers settled in bear Native American names: Massachusetts, which in the Algonquin language means "the hill people,"[29] and Connecticut, which originates from the Mohegan word *quinnitukqut*, meaning "place of long tidal river."[30] According to one legend it was the Dutch settlers in New York who started calling the English settlers in Connecticut "Yankees."[31]

The story of the early settlers in the South is different than that of the Yankees. These settlers came from England, Scotland, and Northern Ireland, and they had other motives for settling in America than the settlers in New England and the other Northern states: they came to earn money, and they chose state names that saluted the royal family back in England: Virginia was named after Queen Elizabeth I (the Virgin Queen), North Carolina and South Carolina after King Charles I, Maryland after his wife, and Georgia after King George II.[32] The settlers in the South grew tobacco and cotton, and as cotton production and trade started dominating the South's economy, the need for labor grew, which led to African laborers being "imported" from the West Indies. This led to the horrendous institutionalization of slavery in America.

As the demand for tobacco and cotton grew, a lot of land in what is now Kentucky and Tennessee was turned into plantations.[33] This change of social order made many of the original settlers in these areas move away. Some, like Thomas Lincoln, the father of the future president, ended up moving to Illinois.[34] Others ended up living in the Appalachian Mountains. Referred to as "hillbillies," they spoke a Northern Ireland dialect, smoked their corn pipes, and hunted wild turkeys. At festive occasions they played musical styles such as folk and bluegrass, the roots of country music.[35]

In what later became known as the industrial heartland (New York, Pennsylvania, Ohio, and Michigan, plus New Jersey, Delaware, Maryland, and West Virginia), the settlers were mainly English, German, Dutch, and Swedish. In the 1800s this became the area with the big steel melting pots, and figuratively speaking it was a melting pot as these immigrants assimilated and became American. As industrialization demanded more workers, immigrants from Ireland and later Poland and the Ukraine also arrived in the "industrial belt." They too became part of the American melting pot.

Some new immigrants traveled farther west, to what we today call the Midwest. They encountered the river that the Native Americans called *misi-ziibi* (meaning "Great River"), which ended up being anglicized to the Mississippi River.[36] The first Europeans to settle in this area were originally French immigrants from the East. They used the French word *prairie* to describe the plain, and thus *prairie* ended up becoming part of the American vocabulary.[37] The French also founded St. Louis, named in honor of King Louis XV of France. Many Protestant immigrants from Scandinavia, including Denmark, Norway, and Sweden, also ended up settling in the Midwest.[38]

However, the very first Europeans to come to the prairie were the Spanish, who came from Mexico in 1541.[39] They traveled on horses, and while fighting with the Native Americans, some of the Spaniards' horses got loose, turned wild, and started roaming the Great Plains. The Spaniards called these wild horses *mestenyeno,* which later became *mustang* in English.[40] As the plain's Comanche tribe had learned how to lasso from the Spaniards, they ended up capturing some of the wild horses and learned to ride them with great skill.[41]

For a time the prairie became famously known as the Wild West. Here cowboys and the Native Americans of the plain created a part of American history that is as well known in the United States as it is around the world, though the Wild West era only lasted twenty years, from 1867 to 1887. But even before the Wild West era was over some settlers were on the move again.[42]

In the 1840s word spread among settlers in the Midwest that there was a new "promised land" waiting at the Pacific coast. Soon settlers from the Midwest started heading for the Pacific coast on what became known as the Oregon Trail, passing the Rocky Mountains with their oxen-pulled wagons.[43] Some—the Mormons—settled in the desert near the Great Salt Lake, in what later became Utah. The Mormons wanted to get away from the authorities who did not approve of their polygamy.[44] (The Mormons' leader Brigham Young was married to dozens of women at the same time.)[45]

By the late 1800s many people who held similar religious beliefs and had the same ethnic background had settled together in different parts of the country. Almost all immigrants preferred to settle in clusters of people with the same background to better cling to their customs and traditions. Especially for the strongly religious settlers, being close to like-minded people meant that they could better perfect their version of "the true faith."[46]

At the beginning of the twentieth century the different climate zones of the Pacific coast also ended up attracting people with varying backgrounds. In the northern part, people from northern

Europe settled, as the mild, foggy, and rainy climate reminded them of their homelands. The southern part—Southern California—attracted a different group of people. In the 1920s the producers of moving pictures came to Los Angeles because of the area's strong and reliable sunlight, which was needed in the early pioneering days of filmmaking. Sunny California with the clear skies, the palm trees, and the Pacific coast became the new "promised land" to millions of Americans.[47]

THE MEANING OF *LIFESTYLE*

Based on our knowledge of history, iconic images, television, and movies, we often conjure up visions of how other people live their lives. Most people know from experience that there are patterns in how other people live their lives. Most of us are also well aware of the many well-known ways people organize their lives, but we are unfamiliar with the new patterns.

Especially when talking about new ways of organizing life, we often use the term *lifestyle*. The word *lifestyle* came into the English language in the 1920s, but it was not until sometime after World War II that the word began thriving in the vernacular.[48] One of the first books to have *lifestyle* in its title was *An Alternative Lifestyle: Living & Traveling Full-Time in a Recreational Vehicle*, published in 1955. For several years this was the only "lifestyle book" there was. It wasn't until the 1970s that books with *lifestyle* in their titles were published on a regular basis, as this selection of book titles from that decade shows:

- *Open Marriage: A New Lifestyle for Couples* (1972)
- *Water Squatters: The Houseboat Lifestyle* (1975)
- *It's Your Life: Create a Christian Lifestyle* (1977)
- *The Bisexual Option—Today's Most Surprising New Lifestyle* (1978)
- *Total Health Tennis: A Lifestyle Approach* (1979)[49]

These book titles certainly suggest that the term *lifestyle* encompasses many aspects of modern living, and also that its meaning broadened since the early 1970s when the term *the lifestyle* became synonymous with swinging (that is, having a sexually open relationship). In the 1980s the term *lifestyle* was often about social relations, leisure, and consumption; and then in the 1990s *lifestyle* was often used to refer to dress, style, and design.

Once the term got a prominent position in our language, we started talking about having a lifestyle, lifestyle choices, not approving of certain lifestyles, lifestyle products, lifestyle magazines, and lifestyle television shows. In the beginning of the twenty-first century, journalists started writing about lifestyle medicine, meaning cosmetic dermatology and cosmetic surgery.[50]

Among the reasons for the growing popularity of the word are that it has many meanings, though it is also a term that is rather fluffy to many people. It is quite understandable if people do not always agree on what the term means because it can mean something different to different people. If we listen in on how people use the word in their everyday speech, *lifestyle* can mean different things in different contexts, as these statements illustrate:

- His lifestyle is all about sports. (lifestyle = interest, activity)
- She has a Christian lifestyle. (lifestyle = way of life)
- Americans' lifestyles are changing fast. (lifestyle = life pattern)
- My parents have a whole new lifestyle. (lifestyle = life phase)
- Her glamorous home reflects her lifestyle. (lifestyle = style of living)

The different uses of the term also reflect the fact that *lifestyle* has two very distinct definitions according to dictionaries: (1) Way of life, and (2) Style of living.[51] In order to really come to terms with the meaning of *lifestyle*, we have to dissect what these two different definitions of the word mean in relation to today's society and how they are connected. To better differentiate between the two definitions, this book will use the following differentiation: lifestyle will refer to the way-of-life definition; life*style* will refer to the style-of-living definition.

One of the first books to analyze people's way of life was written by one of the founding fathers of sociology, Max Weber of Germany. In 1904 his groundbreaking study about seventeenth-century Protestant society in Europe was published. In his book he described the differences in the way of life of Catholics and Protestants.[52] To Weber *way of life* meant a systematic organization of everyday life. Systematic organizing in this case means two things: (1) The organizing affects the person 24/7, and (2) The organizing behavior is repeated again and again.

In Weber's study it was religion that was the dominating way of life. The different ways of life of Catholics and Protestants also affected differences in the interior decoration of churches and homes. Anyone who has visited both a Catholic church and a Protestant church built in the 1600s cannot avoid observing the differences in style between the two: Protestant churches have few decorative details, are painted mostly white, and have a stark, simple style. Catholic churches are almost the opposite, with lots of decorative elements, including many paintings and sometimes relics. Historically there has been a certain systematic combination of religious beliefs and style (including art) for each of the two religious groups— which have made them highly distinct.

With this inspiration from Max Weber, we are at the core of what lifestyle is about, namely, how much religion, politics, style, and many other aspects of human life define who we are and how we organize our lives. Lifestyle is about how our individual lives and communities are glued together, not just by personal relations but also by language, signs and symbols, and other means of communication, often as codes.

Originally, codes were devised to keep the content of a message secret to outsiders. Codes have also been used to save space, especially in letters or telegrams. In present-day society, codes play a similar role: we continue to use them to save words. Sometimes it takes too many words to express what we want to express, so then we use codes. For instance, it is often easier to say you like the style of designer Ralph Lauren than explain that you like "a classic, understated clothing style."

In other cases we use codes to disguise what we are saying in order not to appear offensive, derogatory, or arrogant. For instance, "old money" has been a popular code to characterize people who have a long family history, are rich and have been so for several generations, and have large mansions and a life of luxury. "New money" is a code for people with lots of money who do not know the old-school decorum and etiquette. "Old money" will have the highest status in a traditional social hierarchy, and the longer the family history, the higher social standing the family tends to have. This difference in status was played out in the White House during the presidency of Ronald Reagan. The then vice president's wife, Barbara Bush, "a certified old-money East Coast Wasp, looked down her nose at the Reagans," according to friends of former First Lady Nancy Reagan.[53]

We can also save a plethora of words by using signs and symbols. The difference between a sign and a symbol is about our emotional relationship to the object in question. A *sign* is a visual expression; a *symbol* is an emotional expression. The emotional qualities of symbols can be positive or negative, but feelings are involved. The Stars and Stripes, the American flag, can speak volumes and be a thousand times more effective than any words, especially in times of national distress and in times of national celebration, because it is such a strong and positive symbol to us.

Like in all societies, past and present, we use symbols, objects, and names to communicate who we are and to classify ourselves and other people. Language, signs, and symbols are often the glue that binds us together with people who are similar to us. But since people are also different we also create ritualistic, linguistic, and visual distinctions between ourselves. In the twenty-first century the distinctions are more plentiful than ever before.

Chapter 2

WE ARE WHAT WE ARE
Sorting the Jigsaw Pieces

*I*n cities, suburbs, rural towns, and even in the most remote and wild areas, how we live our lives varies enormously. This is reflected not only in the different landscapes but also in varying housing situations. For instance, in Manhattan—or Mannahatta,[1] as the original Lenape Native Americans called the island—brownstones and gigantic high-rises, modest low-rises, and old-style mansions are mixed. On neighboring Long Island the architectural landscape is varied in other ways. In the part of Long Island that is closest to New York City, much of the landscape is marked by masses of identical one-family homes—Levittowns—built in the 1940s and 1950s.[2] In the Hamptons, the wealthy beach community farther away from the city, the architectural styles include nineteenth-century Federal style, Greek Revival style, as well as Shingle style, the latter of which features wood-framed houses hung with weathered shingles and protected by thick hedges.[3]

In Florida you can drive along the central Florida interstate highway and within short distances you can end up in trailer parks, pure ranch land, small towns like Oxford with single-story redbrick houses and auto-repair shops, or in a well-off retirement community (such as the Villages) set behind security gates with artificial lakes and manicured golf courses. As one journalist wrote, "The Villages' 'town square' is a brilliant piece of nostalgia, an idealized small-town midwestern crossroads circa 1954 but actually built in the beginning of the twenty-first century."[4]

The lifestyle puzzle is about how we categorize the people who live in these very different circumstances. When sociologists wanted to categorize people in the twentieth century, they often focused on social hierarchies. They would typically divide us into these seven categories or classes organized hierarchically by income categories and work status:

- Upper Upper
- Lower Upper
- Upper Middle
- Middle Middle
- Lower Middle
- Upper Lower
- Lower Lower[5]

In daily life we rarely use the term *class*. In her memoir *Where I Was From*, author Joan Didion recalls her mother's response when she (as a teenager) asked her what the term *class* meant. Her mother said, "It's not a word we use. It's not the way we think."[6] With growing prosperity and diversity it still seems to be an awkward word to many people. So we use coded terms instead. As the *New York Times* has pointed out, "Episcopalian" has often been a code for upper class, and "fundamentalist" and "Evangelical" has been shorthand for lower class.[7]

Codes are an integrated part of daily communication. They are not just about secret agents and inventive children who communicate using words that nobody else can understand. Traditionally, codes in an everyday context are when words and numbers have hidden meanings other than their face value. One of the most widespread numerical code systems is ZIP codes. Instead of writing—or as a supplement to writing—the city and state, we write a five-digit code. With this system, a letter with the ZIP code 11937 will reach East Hampton and a package with the ZIP code 49015 will be routed to Springfield, in the Ozark region of Missouri.

The actual names of geographic locations can also be coded. In this vein some people will equate the Hamptons with "wealthy," "snobbish," "relaxation," "stylish," or "home." Some will equate the Ozarks with "flyover country," "poor," "hardship," "the heartland of the United States," or "home." So the Hamptons have become code for "wealthy" and the Ozarks have become code for "reduced circumstances." These codes are not artificially invented but are based on what we learn from images we have seen, from stories we have been told by family and friends, from the media, or from traveling. Based on this information we conjure images of places and people just by hearing the name of a geographical location and classify the people who live there. For example, the 1990s television show *Beverly Hills, 90210* did just that.

THE HORIZONTAL STATES

Human nature dictates that we like to classify and put people, places, and products into hierarchies. For instance, we categorize states based on when they joined the Union, how large they are, and how populous they are. But classifying can also be about creating categories that are not about ranking. One well-known example of the latter kind of categorization is how we nickname each of the fifty states: Connecticut is the Constitution State, Florida is the Sunshine State, Washington is the Evergreen State, and South Dakota is the Mount Rushmore State.[8] The characteristics associated with each state in this case are not about ranking the states in a hierarchy but rather about distinguishing them, not only by their name, but also by a key characteristic. It is not possible to rank the states vertically based on these characteristics. Therefore, it is a horizontal classification.

The many early immigrants who came from Europe to the United States left strictly vertically organized societies. Germany, Italy, Ireland, and—perhaps most widely known—England, had strict social hierarchies based on class. Class may be interpreted differently in different countries, but today, class is still something about which many in England are conscious. But the present-day class hierarchy is not based on wealth and occupation.

In her book *Watching the English*, British anthropologist Kate Fox studied class behavior in England in the beginning of the twenty-first century. Her conclusion was that class in England is purely based on "noneconomic indicators, such as speech, manner, taste, and lifestyle choices."[9] This may be surprising to some people, but it does not mean that there is no hierarchy in England. Because there is—only the hierarchy is based on something other than wealth, and in the case of present-day England, it is primarily speech. As Kate Fox writes, "All English people, whether they admit it or not, are fitted with a sort of social Global Positioning Satellite computer that tells us a person's position on the class map as soon as he or she begins to speak."[10] She continues, "a person with an upper-class terminology will be recognized as upper class even if he or she is earning poverty-line wages, doing grubby menial work, and living in a run-down council flat. . . . There are other indicators—such as one's taste in clothes, furniture, decoration, cars, pets, books, hobbies, food, and drink—but speech is the most immediate and most obvious [indicator]."[11]

Though Americans certainly have very different opinions about how appealing different dialects are, the political and economic elite in the United States has consisted of people speaking very different dialects. Not one dialect or sociolect has dominated. Historically, most US presidents have come from the eastern part of the United States,[12] but there has not been a continuous line of presidents with the same accent to set the tone on how an elite person such as the president speaks. There have been presidents speaking with Southern accents (Jimmy Carter and Bill Clinton) and Western accents (Lyndon B. Johnson and George W. Bush). In Europe, kings and queens and assorted princes and princesses have always belonged to more or less the same family, and this has set the tone for how the elite speaks.

The fact that the elite in the United States has not just spoken in one way has been reinforced by the fact that American heroes and icons are a highly varied lot. American elites are lauded on merit that is different from Europe with its long tradition of hereditary privileges. American heroes are primarily the self-made men and women and the regular folk who do extraordinarily good deeds. American icons—the people we look up to—are often from business, Hollywood, and sports. According to Barbara Cady, author of *Icons of the 20th Century*, American icons who came out of the twentieth century were Henry Ford, Charles Lindbergh, Louis Armstrong, Jesse Owens, Walt Disney, John D. Rockefeller, John F. Kennedy, Martin Luther King Jr., Malcolm X, Marilyn Monroe, James Dean, Elvis Presley, Ernest Hemingway, Mohammed Ali, Jacqueline Kennedy, Bill Gates, Andy Warhol, Elizabeth Taylor, and Oprah Winfrey, among others.[13] These American icons spoke or speak in such different ways that there are no unifying patterns to create a speech-based hierarchy as in England. Also, because these icons appeal to so many different groups of people, not all, though some, are unifying national icons.

As noted earlier, however, speech does play an important part in classifying us in the United States, but all the other indicators that Kate Fox mentions—clothes, furniture, decoration—are equally important and play a role in categorizing us (though not so much in hierarchies). When it comes to hierarchies the United States is different from the rest of the world. The United States is a much more horizontally organized society. Americans do not create as many fixed and strict hierarchies and place people in them based solely on the clothes they wear, the cars they drive, or the food they eat. It does not mean that Americans do not make hierarchical distinctions—they do—it's just that most present-day Americans are not as likely to place people in hierarchies as people in other countries. Also, Americans have a history of classifying each other horizontally.

This horizontal thinking is probably due to several factors. First, it is worth noting that few aristocrats from Europe settled in America.[14] The men who became political leaders in the United States were often self-made. Second, race became a defining hierarchy through the evil of slavery.[15] Especially in the South, white people—no matter their station in life or their intelligence level—felt superior to both the Native American population and the black population, whether or not they were slaves. As the historian Alan Taylor has pointed out, "As skin color became the key marker of identity, race obscured the persistent power of class distinctions between the common [white families] and [the wealthy white families]. . . . Newly obsessed with racial difference, . . . whites *felt* more equal despite the growing inequality of their economic circumstances."[16] Third, the many religious and ethnic groups that settled in America turned their newfound home into an ethnic and religious patchwork quilt. Early on, the different religious groups that came to America settled in different areas: the Anglicans settled in Virginia, the Puritan Protestants in Massachusetts, the Jews in New York, the Quakers and the Amish in Pennsylvania, the Catholics in Maryland, the Huguenots (French Protestants) in South Carolina, the Baptists in Virginia and North Carolina, the Lutherans in the Midwest, and the Mormons in Utah. And though the black slaves ended up becoming Christian, they incorporated emotional singing and funeral rituals that celebrated death as a spiritual liberation and restoration to Africa, thus adding another patch to the quilt.[17] Also, several of the Protestant denominations, in particular the Quakers, emphatically tried to dispense with social hierarchies, insisting that all persons are equal before God.[18] Those who were interested in creating hierarchies wanted to base them on religion. This was the case with the Presbyterian Scots who felt superior to the Catholic Irish.[19]

As more and more different nationalities emigrated to the United States, the patchwork quilt got more colorful, though separated by ethnicity and variations of color. With many new immigrants from southern and eastern Europe, especially in the late 1800s and the early 1900s,[20] the United States became a land of residential segregation based on a combination of religion and ethnicity. In the large urban areas, the number of ethnic neighborhoods grew. In Boston the Irish Catholics dominated from the late 1800s. In New York City, Boston, San Francisco, and other cities, there were Chinatowns and Little Italys. In New York City, African-Americans banded together in Harlem, Russian immigrants clustered together in Brighton Beach, Hasidic Jews in Williamsburg, and Puerto Ricans in Spanish Harlem. In Memphis, Tennessee, the Orange Mound district for many years had the largest concentration of African-Americans outside of Harlem.[21] In Los Angeles, the West Side was Anglo and South Central was predominantly black for decades.[22] The South Side in Chicago and Oakland, California, close to San Francisco, was predominantly black. In Miami the Cubans who fled their island nation in the late 1950s and the following decades dominated. And in California, Los Angeles has become home to one of largest Mexican populations outside of Mexico.

The South has its own history of residential segregation. There, racial segregation continued after the Civil War, even with the abolishment of slavery. The South's declining economy was one of the reasons that new immigrants did not settle in the South when the second wave of mass immigration to the United States started in the 1860s.[23] Consequently, the original ethnic division in parts of the South did not change much in the twentieth century. In Wilcox County, Alabama, one of the very poorest stretches of the United States, de facto segregation still appears to be a reality: in the public education system almost all students are black. In the private schools the students are Caucasian.[24]

The patchwork quilt has not been conducive to a strong vertical organization of society based on class because there were both elites and regular folk in all religious and ethnic groups. Importantly, the different elites did not form one unified elite, and the regular folk among the recent immigrants did not mix either. If we look to Europe, which has a majority of countries that historically have been more homogenous than the United States, the elites have been more unified, as have the regular folks. This indicates that Europe has advanced vertically organized societies.

All in all, the unique history of the United States has created a somewhat horizontally organized society. Residential segregation based on ethnicity, religion, moral values, and income is very much the order of the day—but there is not a hierarchy that generally puts one group superior to others. So has nothing changed? Well, before we jump to any conclusions, let's look at not just what we can easily see and identify but also what is generally less observable: our identities. Here we may find some clues not just as to how we define ourselves but also as to how we classify our fellow citizens.

IDENTIFYING IDENTITY

The psychological term for defining who we are is *identity*. Identity is about being able to answer questions such as, who am I? what am I? and where do I belong? Having or feeling identity is a characteristic of what it means to be a human being. As individuals we must be able to answer these questions to feel comfortable in our own skin, so to speak. Though identity is not the only psychological phenomenon to control human behavior, it controls or influences many of the important decisions that we make in life as well as much of our daily behavior.

Identity has always been a significant psychological part of being human, but that does not mean that *what* gives us identity cannot change. It can and it does. In the twenty-first century there are more answers than ever to the question, what gives you identity? The list below represents just some answers from people of different ages and backgrounds.

Identity Givers:

- My family
- My community
- My religion
- The American flag
- My travels to different countries
- My home
- The company that I work for
- Cool brands
- Country and Western music
- Bird watching
- Doctors Without Borders USA
- Motorcycling
- Family heirlooms
- Baseball
- Being a lawyer
- Basketball games
- My favorite charity, Nature Conservancy
- Where I live
- Collecting perfume bottles
- The Dallas Cowboys
- The Republican Party
- Norman Rockwell artwork
- Ralph Lauren
- My sexuality
- The Sierra Club
- The Democratic Party
- History
- The Salvation Army

- Being African-American
- My training as a nurse
- The music on my iPod

It would be a hopeless task to start counting all the different answers to what can give us an identity as individuals; but while there are countless answers, there are also patterns in how identity is construed. When studying all the answers we can conjure about identity, it appears that they all fall into ten fairly distinct identity categories:

- Family
- Geography
- Race/Ethnicity
- History
- Religion
- Politics
- Education/Work
- Leisure
- Style
- Sexuality

In other words, our identity is composed of roughly ten different sources. Though these ten identity categories all are distinct, some are also closely interconnected. For instance, geography, history, and ethnicity are often clustered together and called "culture." Being a homemaker—which is part family, part work—is another example of how two identity categories can be interconnected. Politics and religion can be two sides to the same coin because religion influences how some people vote.

Without a doubt, family—being a parent, a son or daughter, a grandparent, and so on—is one of the strongest identities that we humans can have. One woman in her midthirties, Julie Bennett, said in an interview that she has never considered her work to be part of her identity. For Bennett, her relationships are what give her identity.[25] Family names can play an important part in family identity. This is something President Barack Obama experienced when as a young man he traveled to Kenya, where his father was born. In his memoir *Dreams from My Father* he wrote, "I felt the comfort, the firmness of identity that a name might provide, how it could carry an entire history in other people's memories, so that they might nod and say knowingly, 'Oh, you are so and so's son.'"[26] The identity that is handed down to us through our family is also often emotionally charged because many strong emotions are involved. One of these emotions is love, which—like identity—controls a great deal of human behavior.

As for geography, we can connect to a geographical location on many levels—it can be the neighborhood or the city where we live, a region (for instance, the Rocky Mountains), the state we were born in or now live in, or it can be the whole of the United States of America. *National Geographic Magazine* knows a thing or two about geography. In one of its articles, a retired oil-field worker, Marshall Turnell, from Meetseetse, Wyoming, expressed his joy in living in a small, midwestern town in this way: "We know who we are and where we belong, and we like it this way."[27] Writer D. J. Waldie feels the same way but expresses himself differently about a different place: "Los Angeles . . . is the big city I know best, and its vulgar, lovely, cruel, and touching character . . . forms a large part of my sense of place."[28] A sense of belonging to a geographical location is a very important aspect of most people's sense of well-being.

Nature is an integrated part of geography. We identify with a characteristic landscape, for instance, the Cape Cod coastline, the Grand Canyon, or the open plains. Even though some landscapes can be harsh for people to live in, many who experience these conditions do not want to move. The Inuit people in northern Alaska live in a cold and unwelcoming landscape but have nevertheless been living there for countless generations. The white, snowy landscape is what gives the Inuit people their identity. One reason is that in this icy landscape they can get the food that they are used to and that they like.

Food is altogether an important part of our culture, but food is not just about geography and climate. Food is also about history: the hot dog and the hamburger, for example, are American terms, but both dishes have German origins. The apple pie was perfected by the Pennsylvania Dutch in the nineteenth century. In the early part of twentieth century, being able to afford apple pie for desert became a symbol of prosperity to many American families. Only wealthy families could afford to put dough on top of the pie, creating an upper crust. This difference between poor and rich families was turned into the expression *the upper crust*, as a code for the upper class (elegantly making it possible to avoid using the word *class*). During World War II the apple pie, which was by then a prevalent dessert among all strata of society, became a symbol of American patriotism. When American GIs were asked by foreign journalists what they were fighting for, they answered, "for mom and apple pie." (The actual expression that first became famous was that something could be "as American as motherhood and apple pie.")[29]

Food and the traditions, norms, and rituals surrounding food are part of what we normally call *cultural habits*. Cultural habits also often have another name: *ethnicity*. Ethnicity covers about all the traditions, norms, and rituals that are typical of people from different places, whether a region or a country. We get our ethnicity—or cultural habits—from family, geography, and history while growing up. Ethnicity is different from the related term *race*, which describes physical differences like the color of one's skin—black, brown, yellow, or white—and the many shades in between. (For the record: people do not have "red" skin. The Native Americans who are sometimes described as having red skin were covering themselves with red paint.)[30]

Race in the United States is about the physical characteristics that people have from their immigrant ancestors, from the shape of their eyes to their skin color. Race and ethnicity can be bundled in different ways, as is the case when we talk about "black culture," the subcultural habits that are typical of *some* African-Americans. Though black subculture is far from being static and uniform, it can be about a preference for certain music (for instance, gospel singing); a preference for a certain religious affiliation (for instance, Southern Baptist); and certain speech patterns.

If people live in a residential community where they are surrounded only by the same ethnic group, they are not always conscious of their ethnicity. But if they move away from the geographical location, then they can become aware of it. This is what happened to the writer Edmund White when he moved from Cincinnati to New

York. As he writes in his autobiography, describing himself and a friend, "We were from well-to-do WASP families, a social identity we'd never thought about till we moved to New York."[31]

When ethnic identity is strongly bundled together with geography and history (sometimes also combined with religion), we feel patriotism. Patriotism originates from a strong sense of pride in a country's history, and being a patriot can be a significant part of one's identity—an identity that perhaps is not expressed on a daily basis but can surface in times of national or even personal crisis. When William Reeder Jr. was a young helicopter pilot in Vietnam during the Vietnam War, he was shot down and taken as a prisoner of war. While imprisoned he started thinking about his past: "I got to thinking about American history, my own history, that's what kept me alive, just thinking about that. . . . I realized how little I really knew about my country. And I vowed that once I got out, I would learn all I could. That's what kept me alive, thinking about that."[32] Later in his life, when he was a colonel teaching history at the US Army War College, he attended the annual reenactment of the Battle of Little Big Horn in Montana, where General Custer was defeated by the Cheyenne and the Sioux Native Americans. Participating in the celebration of historical events like this is one way of identifying with history.

For most people, learning about history by reading about it or visiting historical places is the basis of their identity with respect to history. It is about being connected to traditions, customs, and memorable moments that have taken place. Independence Day is, of course, related to the American Revolution. Memorial Day followed the Civil War. Martin Luther King Jr. Day emerged after the civil rights struggle and Dr. King's assassination. History is about symbols, like the Stars and Stripes and "The Star-Spangled Banner," the national anthem. It is about appreciating the Liberty Bell in Philadelphia and the Washington Monument in Washington, DC; and it is about relating to Mount Rushmore and to Iwo Jima—if not the actual victory, then the famous photograph and the monument in the nation's capital.

Last but not least, history is about a common language. Though the ability to speak is universally human, what we say is shaped by history. There is no better illustration of this than American English.

Between the Revolution and the Civil War, American English had changed from the English spoken in England. This is documented by the written accounts of explorers Lewis and Clark, who were commissioned by President Thomas Jefferson to document their discoveries and observations in writing as they went on the first official overland expedition to the Pacific coast. They wrote the way they spoke and spelled accordingly. Scholars have identified about two thousand expressions in their journals that are uniquely American, that capture the vernacular of their time and some that are still in use today.[33]

The first time the expression "the American language" was mentioned in the United States Congress (in a congressional record) was in 1802. In 1855 Charles Astor Bristed published his book *The English Language in America* and documented that American English was developing its own grammar.[34] For instance, he noted that nouns, such as *advocate*, *interview*, *lynch*, *notice*, and *scalp* were used as verbs. Also, completely new words had been invented: *bar*, *bartender*, *cocktail*, and *know-how* are some of the original American words that are now part of the English language everywhere.

Dialects also give us identity. There are scores of dialects in the United States: the broad categories, Southern and Northern accents, and regional and local accents like Appalachian English and Cajun English, the latter spoken in Louisiana. Across the country people not only have different dialects, but they also have unique vernaculars. For instance, in the Smoky Mountain region *airish* means chilly; in New Orleans *alligator pear* is an avocado; in Boston *na-ah* means "no way!"[35] Southerners generally say *dinner* for the meal served at midday, whereas the last meal of the day is called *supper*.[36] In many parts of the South, "*Sir* and *Ma'am* are used by the person speaking to you if there's a remote possibility that you're at least 30 minutes older than they are," according to a Georgia tourist Web site.[37]

All these historic traditions, symbols, and words have shaped the speech of generations and generations of Americans and have created an identity as American—or as Anglo-American, German-American, African-American, Irish-American, Italian-American, and many other hyphenated Americans. However, in the twenty-first century Americans are becoming less hyphenated. In the 2000 US Census, 27 percent could not or would not indicate their ancestry or ethnic origin.

More than 7 percent simply chose the category "American" when choosing their ethnic origin. Ten years earlier the number had been 5 percent.[38] This represents not only a change in individual identity but also a change as a nation.

Like the love for one's country, religion is also about strong emotions. Sometimes these emotions can be as strong as the love between two people. Brother Thomas from Tennessee, a Pentecostal man, told writer Charlie LeDuff, "We believe strongly in our faith. We love the Lord."[39] LeDuff also pointed out that there can be other reasons for religious affiliation than love for a higher being. He wrote in his book *US Guys* about himself having a "need to have religion, a culture, something I can say I belong to."[40]

Politics is also important to many people, but because citizens have to go through the process of being registered to vote, the de facto number of people who vote in the United States is lower than in many other democratic countries.[41] In Europe, where all citizens over a certain age can vote without having to register first, the de facto percentage of the population who votes is generally higher. Another difference between the United States and Europe is that in the United States, income is a poor predictor of party preference.[42] In the United States issues like gun control, the death penalty, school prayer, abortion, and gay marriage are what divide us. In the late twentieth century the divide was literal as the country could be divided into "blue states" and "red states," respective codes for a Democratic or a Republican majority in a state.[43] In the twenty-first century, people also prefer to cluster together with those who are like themselves, in this case with people who share the same values.

Color codes are used not only in politics. When we talk about work there are also two colors that have been popular codes: "blue-collar" and "white-collar"—coded terms for working class and upper middle class, respectively (originally the colors referred to the colors of a person's work clothing). Education and jobs, plain and simple, provide an important part of many people's identity. A degree from an Ivy League university—a symbolic name for some of the oldest and most lauded universities in the United States (Harvard, Yale, and Princeton, among others that originally had ivy growing on their buildings) is code for "elite," which confers a great deal on many people's identity. Degrees from all educational institutions, whether high school or college, also factor into our sense of identity. Most people who have a job get some sense of identity from the job (the function) or the workplace (the company). In her memoir, author Joan Didion writes about how "people in Lakewood, California, had defined their lives as Douglas," referring to the aviation contractor that later merged with Boeing.[44] Similarly, when a person—in this case a man named Jack Turnell—can say, "There is nothing on the face of the earth that I'd rather do than manage Pitchfork Ranch. Nothing," this is as strong an expression of identification with one's work as you can get.[45]

Having a job automatically means that a person also has time off (from work). And what do you do when not working? This is what a journalist found out about actor Billy Bob Thornton. His answer could have been the answer of millions of men: "I watch a lot of sports on television."[46] He also said that he watches television with his toddler daughter and goes to hockey games with his teenage sons. To millions and millions of people, television and sports are two of the most popular leisure activities that exist—especially when both are combined with the holy trio of American sports: baseball, football, and basketball. For other people, "the spectator sports" are music, theater, and art. This is the case with actor Alec Baldwin. According to a magazine bio, "Baldwin's . . . a classical-music guy, and proud of it. It's been fundamental to how he defines himself since . . . the early eighties." Baldwin is a big fan of the New York Philharmonic Orchestra.[47]

Being a collector of everything from art to stamps is a popular leisure activity, as is shopping, especially when shopping for designed objects (from clothing and home decoration to cars and toys). We get inspiration for shopping by browsing through newspapers such as the *New York Times* and *USA Today*, and by surveying the vivid pictorials in the growing number of magazines that report on both design and style. They write about or have whole sections on everything from gardening to all forms of design and style. *Style* is the word we use when we are very systematic in combining designed objects in a certain way. When we are systematic in how we dress, we turn our clothing into a style. And when we are very systematic in how we dress over a long period of time, we turn our clothing into dress codes, such as preppy, hip-hopper, biker, or pinstriped. When we have a name for a dress code, it can become part of our identity.

Brand names—with which we may have an emotional connection—also help us define who we are. Once when fashion designer Tommy Hilfiger, who grew up in the 1950s, was interviewed about his childhood, he described what had defined his childhood this way: "Schwinn bicycles, Converse sneakers, Levi's, Mickey Mouse."[48] All these are products that are also signs and symbols. To Tommy Hilfiger they are symbols of a very typical American upbringing in the 1950s. (In the interview he added, "Nothing in our home was made outside of the United States.") In the 1950s there were few brand names to know and remember. Now there are literally thousands of brand names available to help define who we are.

The point is that all the stuff that we surround ourselves with—from cars, furniture, and kitchen utensils to sports equipment, accessories, and clothing—helps define us. If we are not aware that our shopping defines who we are, then we can be pretty sure that other people will know how different activities, brands, and products categorize us. For instance, if foreigners toured a home with American Windsor chairs, quilts in a few distinct colors, Navajo blankets, Norman Rockwell artwork, wooden shorebird decoys (an original native invention) or other folk art, and a tunnel-shaped rural mailbox, they would right away think "American" if asked to name the nationality of the person who lives there.

Finally, sexuality is also part of our identity, though sexuality is different from the other identity categories because it is based on biology *and* psychology. The biology part is about gender and about having a sexual orientation. As for gender, several factors determine what it means to be a man or a woman. There is the sex of the person, which is about being biologically male or female. Then there is gender identity, a person's perception of being a man or a woman. One's gender role is a reflection of either a feminine or a masculine identity. Finally, there is the question of body language, which involves a person having feminine or masculine body language that may not necessary match his or her gender. A man can invariably show his feminine side, for instance, as a woman can show that she has traits that are generally considered within "man territory."

Being a man or a woman is about being biologically male or female. Most adults are not in doubt about which gender they are, and they are happy about their gender identity.[49] Gender identity is perhaps the strongest and most important identity giver that a person can have, and we are defined by it from the day we are born. Sexual orientation is also about biology: you are born heterosexual, bisexual, or homosexual, according to current scientific research, which is furthermore credible because homosexuality is common among animals.[50] In this aspect of life an individual has no choice. A person can then suppress or acknowledge his or her sexual orientation according to society's norms, customs, and other standards of behavior. However, sexual identity is not just about the gender of whom you choose for your partner or partners. Behaviors such as being asexual, being celibate, being in a monogamous relationship, being promiscuous, being a "playboy," or identifying as a sado-masochist or a fetishist (being into, for instance, black leather or lace or one of scores of other fetishes) are also about sexual identity.

IDENTITY COMBOS

It is fairly easy to identify the ten identity categories, but it is not the identity categories as such that give us identity. For instance, a person can get identity from religion, but if she is a Christian she has an identity as a Christian, or an even more specific identity as, for instance, an Episcopalian or a Southern Baptist. The same goes for politics. A person may get part of his identity from politics, but generally it will be from belonging to a particular political party, like the Republican Party (if he is a Republican). To find out about an individual's identity we have to look at the concrete sources of his identity, at what we can call the *identity givers*. For ethnicity, *African-American* is an identity giver; for sexuality, *bisexual* is an identity giver. The actual identity givers that are available to us will vary from time to time. Some examples of typical identity givers in the United States in the twentieth century are highlighted in figure 2.1.

Figure 2.1. Examples of Identity Givers for Race, Ethnicity, Geography, Religion, and Politics

Racial Identity Givers:

Native — European (Caucasian) — African — Hispanic — Asian

Ethnic Identity Givers:

Anglo-Saxon — Irish — Italian — Korean — Chicano

Geographic Identity Givers:

Kansan — Virginian — New Yorker — Montanan — Californian

Religious Identity Givers:

Episcopalian — Baptist — Catholic — Jewish — Muslim — Hindu

Political Identity Givers:

Democrat — Republican — Independent

In the past, many people combined their identity in the same way through the generations, based on the identity givers in figure 2.1, among others. Six very typical combinations are highlighted in figure 2.2.

Figure 2.2. Typical American Identity Combinations in the Twentieth Century

White	Black	White
Anglo-Saxon	African-American	Irish-American
Protestant (WASP)	Baptist	Catholic
Republican	Democrat	Democrat
White	White	Hispanic
Southern	New Yorker	Mexican-American
Rural Working Class	Jewish	Catholic
(Redneck)	Democrat	Republican
Republican		

These identity combinations certainly still exist—in the millions—but there are also millions of Americans who are not represented by them.[51] Their identities have other sources, often based on new identity givers that come with changes in society. For instance, the concept of family, as mentioned earlier, underwent dramatic changes in the late twentieth century. In the middle of the twentieth century a traditional family consisted of a mom, a dad, and two children, and mom and dad were married. In 2000, only 50 percent of Americans were married, down from 78 percent in 1950.[52]

With a high divorce rate, the traditional family is not a constant, at least in many people's lives. Divorced parents who remarry create new families with children from different marriages. And while many people experience extreme happiness with their family, other people experience all kinds of abuse, neglect, and exclusion, which affect their identity.

Another dramatic difference is that a large number of people are single—some by choice. In his book *Urban Tribes*, Ethan Watters writes about the strong friendships that can exist among groups of single people. The book's subtitle is *Are Friends the New Family?* and Ethan Watters's answer is *yes*. To document this he describes some very convincing examples of people who live together based on non-sexual relationships. After living as a single person with close friends for more than a decade, he felt like belonging "to an intensely loyal community of people," perhaps not unlike belonging to a village community, except this was in urban San Francisco.[53] In his memoir, the novelist Edmund White writes about a female friend, "we have become family members and we care about each other as siblings do."[54] This is an identity that is different in name from the traditional family, but one that can be just as strong as any other family identity.

Pets play a greater role in society. In the late 1950s there were about 15 million dogs in the United States. At the beginning of the twenty-first century the number had increased to approximately 68 million.[55] Some people see their dogs as members of their families or even as partners.[56] There is no doubt that the emotional bonds between a pet and its owner can be very strong. Pets come along on vacations, and many eat very well. The pet accessories industry has boomed since the early twenty-first century.[57] Some companies have specialized in creating dog clothing that matches the style of the owner. There is an airline—Pet Airways—that specializes in transporting dogs and cats.

Just as family life changes, so do many other aspects of life. Some other dramatic changes that affect our sense of identity occur in nature, the climate, and even the landscape. So when great landscapes that people relate to are destroyed, they can feel their identity being threatened. This is why some people acted against the government programs under the presidency of George W. Bush that reduced the number of wild mustangs on the Midwest plains and that supported mining that would destroy large parts of the Appalachian Mountains.[58]

Most people probably do not consciously identify with landscapes. But most people do relate to their ethnicity. However, today, more than ever, people with the same racial background can have vastly different ethnic identities. If you are a Korean living in the United States, you can identify as Korean, American, or Korean-American. This is the case for Patrick S., who was born in Korea and lived there until he was four years old. An adult with a doctorate in philosophy, he wrote an essay called "Balancing Two Worlds." In it, he states, "I don't remember anything of the Korea I experienced before moving to the States. . . . Those memories now seem inaccessible to my thoroughly Americanized consciousness. The several times I have returned to Korea, I felt completely the foreigner, and Korea seemed for the most part unfamiliar to me."[59]

As for race, there are also changes. One example of how the racial composition of the United States has changed is documented by the Census Bureau's listing of the most common last names. In 2007 two Hispanic names—Garcia and Rodriquez—were for the first time on the top-ten list of the most common last names in the United States.[60] The changes are also reflected in the title of the autobiography *Black, White and Jewish* by writer Rebecca Walker, daughter of African-American novelist Alice Walker and a Jewish father, and in the autobiography *YellowBlack* by the poet Haki R. Madhubuti, the son of a Chinese–African-American couple.[61] The Black Native American Association is another reflection of the changing racial landscape of America. Professional golfer Tiger Woods has created his own ethnic identity by using the word *Cablinasian* to describe his

ethnicity. The word reflects that Tiger Woods is one-eighth Caucasian, one-quarter African-American, one-eighth Native American,
one-quarter Thai, and one-quarter Chinese.[62]

Aside from being one of the most multiethnic societies, the United
States is also a multireligious society. But even when people have the
same religion, they can hold highly different viewpoints. They may
share the same faith, but they can have different values. Some Christians are against abortion; others are not. A new pattern was created
when some Christians started using violence to protest abortion. In
the United States there have been several examples of extremist
Christians who have used violence to kill abortion providers.[63] Then
again, there are Christians who are against abortion and yet would
never support or condone such violence and murder.

Christians can have vastly different attitudes on many issues,
including school prayer, death penalty, gay marriage, and war. Some
Christians will at certain times advocate war, as President George W.
Bush did in Iraq in 2003. Then there are Christians who are against
war as a principle. The Quakers take their nonviolent Christian beliefs
very seriously, as did Christian peace activist James Loney, who went
on a peace-keeping mission to war-torn Iraq in 2006. There he was kid-
napped and held hostage by Iraqis for four months before being
released.[64] Obviously this creates different groupings in religious life—
not to mention numerous more pieces in the lifestyle puzzle.

Perhaps the biggest change with respect to religion is that
although there are many people who are religious, there are also
many who are not.[65] People have different reasons for becoming nonreligious. Religious hypocrisy is one of them. When some Christian
leaders preach against having affairs outside of marriage and then do
just that themselves, some people lose their respect for them and
extend these feelings toward other religious leaders as well. When
leaders in the Catholic Church seemed more interested in protecting
the child molesters among its clergy than the abused children, some
people became so appalled that they lost faith in organized religion.[66]

Politics is another area that is affected by how politicians behave.
Terms like *conservative* and *liberal* are well-known political categories. In politics, for instance, being conservative meant at one time,
quite literally, that you wanted things to stay the way they were and

not change too much from what was "God given," so to speak. To many people this would probably include nature, something that has stayed the same for millennia. However, when conservative politicians create policies that are forever changing natural landscapes all over the United States—not least when exploring for oil in national parks—it is a new pattern in politics.[67] Now being conservative can also be about instigating dramatic changes in the natural environment.

Along the same line, corruption, lying, cheating, and hypocrisy when involved with taxpayer money is affecting how people view politics and their identification with political power. Corruption is not new in politics. However, corruption on Capitol Hill in the beginning of the twenty-first century came as a shock to many people, as when Washington, DC, lobbyist Jack Abramoff was charged and convicted of bribing politicians and government officials.[68] And when politicians fight against gay rights while they themselves are gay, for instance, this kind of hypocrisy makes some people disillusioned with politicians—and, consequently, politics.[69]

Many people are experiencing changes in their job situations. Unemployment is a factor that can have consequences not only for one's financial situation but also for one's identity. Many people define themselves by and get most of their self-worth from their profession. Losing a job can be like losing one's identity. When former New York City Ballet dancer Sophie Flack at the age of twenty-five did not get her contract with the ballet company renewed, she told the *New York Times* that her dismissal "felt like receiving a diagnosis of terminal illness."[70] She had other interests and goals, but for others such a change leaves a vacuum in their identity. Like other losses of identity, this loss has to be replaced—either with a new work identity or an identity based on something else.

The job market is also changing in other ways that affect our identities: technology is constantly changing, it eradicates old jobs and creates new jobs. As a consequence, there are more different job descriptions today than ever before. There are creativity officers, chief knowledge managers, corporate masseurs, and real estate style enhancers, to name but a few of the many job titles that have recently come into existence.[71] Food stylist is another career that is available to creative people, in this case styling food for photo shoots.

A job title like food stylist is derived from the perception of food presentation and its value. After World War II, instead of being a chore, preparing food became a leisure activity for many. New food trends became part of the culinary map, perhaps best exemplified by Julia Child. After having lived in France after World War II, Julia Child wrote her first cookbook, *Mastering the Art of French Cooking*, which sold six hundred thousand copies in the 1960s in the United States alone and which also made her a popular cook on television.[72] Other Americans also got inspiration from abroad and changed their food and drinking habits. Winery owner Robert Mondavi revolutionized wine production in Northern California after having studied wine production in France.[73] Chuck Williams was inspired by the French before founding his business, Williams-Sonoma, selling kitchen utensils to match needs when preparing fine French-style dishes.[74] Howard Schultz's vision for Starbucks was born in Italian coffee shops.[75]

Like food, music is also about taste. This is reflected in the many new music genres that emerged and became popular in the twentieth century. More than twenty-five music genres that were established in the twentieth century are listed below. Many of these music genres now have subcategories, and music connoisseurs will probably be able to divide these genres into several hundred subcategories. The consequence of this growth in the number of music genres is the obvious fact that there are many choices in music. And as is typical in situations with many choices, what you choose becomes a matter of taste, simply enjoying something for the pleasure of it. Though religious and ethnic identities are also expressed by music, music is more than ever about taste.

Music Genres Established in the Twentieth Century:

- Alternative rock
- Ambient
- Blues
- Classic rock
- Country
- Electronica
- Dance
- Jazz
- Latin
- Musicals
- New age
- Pop
- Punk
- R & B

- Disco
- Funk
- Garage
- Heavy metal
- Hip-hop
- House
- Industrial
- Reggae
- Rap
- Rock
- Soul
- Trance
- Techno

Leisure and style are often linked by way of shopping. Both identity categories are also affected by many of the sociodemographic changes (that were mentioned in chapter 1), for instance, marrying later in life, the growing number of singles, and age elasticity. When single people have time to explore and experiment with their identity, a need is created for activities and products that help people feel young and attractive. This is one of the reasons that lingerie brand Victoria's Secret has become so successful. Originally the name of a sex shop in San Francisco, Victoria's Secret was bought by retail magnate Leslie Wexner and turned into a famous American undergarment brand—with inspiration from European lingerie stores.[76] Wexner wanted to sell sexy lingerie to American women, reflecting the changes in gender roles that affected both men and women in the late twentieth century. This change is reflected in what former Columbia Pictures chairman Andy Pascal told *Time* magazine in 2001: "A bad thing about old-style feminism was that you could be a brain surgeon but you couldn't be a sexy brain surgeon. Finally some women said: 'I want to be both.'"[77] With Victoria's Secret this is possible.

Going from the twentieth century into the twenty-first century, one of the major changes certainly was about gender roles. Men and women once had fairly fixed gender roles and body language, so each sex stuck to the traditional masculine and feminine behavior in order to fit in. But with the many combinations of sex, gender, gender roles, body language, sexual orientation, and sexual identity, there is enormous complexity. One aspect of this was commented on by the actor Ryan Reynolds (who is heterosexual) in an interview: "I have gay friends [who] are incredibly masculine and I have straight friends [who] are incredibly feminine."[78]

In the late twentieth century men in particular started refining their nonverbal communication through their dress and grooming. For a period of history, men who cared about how they looked and dressed often used to be called often unflattering names, and for that reason it was rare to see men using fragrances, skincare creams, and hairstyling products. Some people still like to believe that all men who groom themselves are gay. But gay men, who constitute only about 3 percent of the population,[79] cannot consume all the grooming products that are used by men.

The fact is that the majority of well-groomed and fragrance-using men are heterosexual. As this became evident, we needed a new term to acknowledge and communicate this. The term we embraced was *metrosexual*. Metrosexual is about combining gender roles, body language, and sexual orientation. A traditionalist might define a metrosexual as a feminine, heterosexual man. As for the actual meaning of metrosexual, *metro* is used because the typically well-groomed man started out as a big-city phenomenon, and *sexual* because there was a need to find a word other than *homosexual* for the growing number of men who are well groomed, style conscious, and interested in how they look. When British journalist Mike Simpson coined the term, he was describing British soccer player David Beckham—who in 2007 joined the Los Angeles Galaxy soccer club—as the archetypical metrosexual man.[80] Before joining the Los Angeles soccer club, he played with some of Europe's most famous and best soccer clubs. He is married to Victoria Beckham, a member of the former British all-girl band the Spice Girls, and he is the father of three children. He is thus yet another variation on what a family man can be like—a well-groomed, style-conscious husband and father.

All in all, the many changes in society create new sources for our identities, and all of these new identity givers can be combined in thousands of ways, along with the many traditional identity givers. Just the simplest calculation will show that this literally creates thousands and thousands of different identity mixes. To get an impression of what identity can be about today, some typical identity givers from each of the ten identity categories are highlighted in figure 2.3. Figure 2.4 illustrates combinations of identity givers for four different persons.

Figure 2.3. Examples of Identity Givers in the Ten Identity Categories

FAMILY							
Mother	Father	Daughter	Son	Grandfather	Grandmother	Grandson	Granddaughter
GEOGRAPHY							
New Jerseyite	Texan	South Carolinian	New Yorker	Angeleno	Pennsylvanian	Iowan	Missourian
HISTORY							
World War II	Korean War	Vietnam War	Assassination of John F. Kennedy	Civil rights movement	Gulf War	Hurricane Katrina	9/11
RACE/ETHNICITY							
Anglo-American	African-American	Irish-American	Cuban-American	American	Hispanic-American	Native American	Italian-American
RELIGION							
Protestant	Anglican	Catholic	Baptist	Jewish	Hindu	Muslim	Atheist
POLITICS							
Conservative	Moderate Repubican	Independent	Independent Republican	Independent Democrat	Moderate Democrat	Liberal	Apolitical
EDUCATION/WORK							
Computer programmer	Gardener	Lawyer	Farmer	Brewery worker	Government official	Flight attendant	Store manager
LEISURE							
Golf	Bruce Springsteen	Harvard Alumni Society	Skateboarding	Antiquing	Watching television	*Oprah*	New York Knicks
STYLE							
Biker	Minimalist	Surfer	Skater	Cowboy	Lumberjack	Hip-Hopper	Goth
SEXUALITY							
Heterosexual	Bisexual	Gay	Lesbian	Fetishist	Asexual	Celibate	Sadomasochist

Figure 2.4. Identity Givers for Four Individuals

Identity Categories	Woman, 32 years old	Man, 43 years old	Woman, 58 years old	Man, 76 years old
Family	Single, no children	Married, father	Divorcée, mother, grandmother	Widower, father, grandfather
Geography	Californian	Minnesotan	Oregonian	Wisconsinite
History	Iraq War	9/11	Feminist movement	Vietnam War
Race/ Ethnicity	African-American	Hispanic-American	Irish-American	Anglo-American
Religion	Baptist	Catholic	Buddhist	Episcopalian
Politics	Independent	Moderate Democrat	Liberal	Republican
Education/ Work	Dentist	Hotel receptionist	Writer, publisher	Retired stockbroker
Leisure	Surfing	Hiking	Literature, reading	Golfing
Style	Surfer	Sporty	Artsy	Pinstriped
Sexuality	Celibate	Heterosexual	Lesbian	Asexual

In the first decade of the twenty-first century some not-so-traditional mixes of identity got the attention of the media and the public. One example was former New Jersey governor Jim McGreevey, a Democrat, who in 2004 came out of the closet. A few years later he explained that "saying 'I'm a gay American' is similar to saying 'I'm an Irish-American,' a Cuban-American or an African-American. It is a sense of identity—to say that I'm gay but that I'm also American."[81] In his book, *The Confession*, he also wrote about his identity as a Christian. In other words, he is Christian, gay, and a Democrat. He is also the father of two girls.[82] He is far from the only one with this mix; there are actually many people with this identity mix, otherwise there would not be www.gaychristian.net, a Web site with thousands of users, most of whom are gay Evangelicals. Some of them may also be organized in associations like the Gay Fathers Association of Seattle.

When Congress convened in 2007, it was with first-time representative Keith Elisson, a Democrat of Minnesota, as a member.
Ellison, who is African-American and a criminal defense lawyer,
converted to Islam as a college student. He became the first Muslim
to be a member of Congress.[83] Singer Lenny Kravitz is also African-
American, but he is Jewish;[84] as is Alysa Stanton, who in 2009
became the first African-American rabbi in the United States. She
grew up in a Pentecostal home.[85] In 2005 the National Black
Republican Association was founded with Frances Rice as chair-
woman.[86] Another African-American, Michael Steele, became
chairman of the National Republican Committee in 2009.[87] Bobby
Jindal, who was elected governor of Louisiana for the Republican
Party in 2008, was born in India and raised as Hindu. As a grown-
up he became a Catholic.[88] When Barack Obama, son of a white
American mother and a black Kenyan father, became the forty-
fourth president of the United States in 2009, he also became a
symbol of the many social changes in American society happening
at the beginning of the twenty-first century.

Another real—and symbolic—change came with the confirma-
tion of Sonia Sotomayor, who is Latina, as Supreme Court justice in
2009. She became the third female Supreme Court justice. By 2010,
the United States had also had three female secretaries of state. The
Obama administration had seven female cabinet members; in 1971
there were zero.[89]

Lenny Kravitz has said about his early career in the late 1980s,
"Here [was] a black Jew, light-skinned, he [was] not doing hip-hop. I
didn't fit in."[90] That could still be true in the twenty-first century if
he were the only one with his mix of identity. Also, if there were just
a few people like him, Jim McGreevey, Keith Elisson, and Frances
Rice, this would not indicate much change in society. But when there
are millions with similar identities, society will "automatically" be
transformed—as these identities become entrenched with others as
part of everyday living.

Chapter 3

ORGANIZED LIVING
How the Pieces Fit

*W*here we live, the jobs we have, and our hobbies are important to most of us. All three elements are about identity based on geography, work, and leisure, respectively. How these three identity categories are transformed into practical everyday living varies from person to person. But we can take a closer look at how they are transformed into everyday living for Jim Harrison, the author of popular novels, including *True North, Legends of the Fall,* and *Returning to Earth.* He has written nearly thirty novels, and writing is his full-time job.

What kind of life does Jim Harrison live? Well, there may be at least a bit of his own life in his books, which are rugged and outdoorsy. This also appears to be the best way to describe Jim Harrison's way of life. A newspaper portrait of him said that during winters he lives in southern Arizona in an adobe casita with his wife and their dog, a Scottish Labrador. They spend summers in Montana. He is out in the rugged terrain in his SUV, "splashing through creeks, lurching down hills, bouncing over rock-strewn dirt roads in the country of southern Arizona."[1]

Jim Harrison does his writing in longhand, in a rented ranch house near his home. "The house itself looks like a time capsule from the early 1950s, with shriveled rattlesnake skins on the wall and rusting canned goods in the kitchen," according to the newspaper article. Jim Harrison likes the style of the house because "it has absolutely nothing to do with life in our time."[2]

The article describes him as a heavy smoker and someone who enjoys drinking (vodka and red wine) and eating (especially carefully prepared meals of game). Though he feels that "food is a part of the whole of life," he has no use for huge, restaurant-style kitchen ranges.

As he put it, "Why should I spend $7,000 for a stove when I could spend $7,000 on food?"[3] He likes to hunt but is "no longer a serious American sportsman of the blast-and-cast school." He enjoys the landscape too much, he pointed out in the portrait. The landscape is "almost savannah-like, with knobby hills, rolling ridges, and stately emory oaks [and] the Huachuca Mountains, sometimes dusted with snow."[4]

Jim Harrison's life is about his writing, cooking, and masculine outdoors pursuits in a landscape that he loves. To other people, writing, cooking, and hunting are usually hobbies and interests, but in Jim Harrison's case it is his lifestyle; this is how he has organized his life, and this is what his life revolves around 24/7. There is little doubt what the direction of his life is.

When the direction of a person's everyday life is organized in a way that progresses according to expected life cycles, we can categorize it as a fixed lifestyle. This does not mean that it does not change, only that it mostly progresses like following a one-way street where you have the opportunity to take different routes, also down one-way streets. Jim Harrison's lifestyle is an example of a fixed lifestyle. This is the kind of lifestyle that sociology's founding father, Max Weber, had in mind when he wrote about the subject. However, not all people have the same everyday life, day in and day out, year in and year out.

To some people the reality is that it is not obvious which way their life is going. They experience that their lives are more fluid. Instead of "fluid," some would say "unstructured," "messy," or "disorganized." The latter terms have an especially judgmental or negative tone to them, which *fluid* does not have. And *fluid* also has a positive tone to it, especially for the people who feel that it is a plus that they get to experience different kinds of lives throughout their life and not just pass through life's traditional phases.

Compared to Jim Harrison, the best way to characterize Pat Dollard's life is fluid. When Pat Dollard was in his twenties and thirties, he was a Hollywood agent working with major agencies representing, among others, the director Steven Soderbergh. According a 2007 *Vanity Fair* article, he was purportedly abusing alcohol and drugs for periods of time.[5] By that time he had been married four times but had also been involved in "orgies with hookers" on many occasions, also while married. He had considered himself a Hollywood liberal, but at some point this changed. He became a conservative with a mission to wage a war on "liberal Hollywood." He became a documentary filmmaker, he went to Iraq during the war twice with US Marines, and he was 100 percent pro-war. His drug taking and alcoholism was also part of his life while in Iraq. He ran of out money and was almost living like a homeless person, certainly sometimes looking like one. He also changed his clothing style—instead of wearing suits, he started to wear combat clothes. When he was forty-five years old, his buddies were twenty-something former marines, people from his Hollywood life, and conservative political pundits.

In the four years that the journalist from *Vanity Fair* closely chronicled Pat Dollard's endeavors, it would also be rather difficult to put the former Hollywood agent's life into one formula. One year he had one kind of life; a year or two later he had a completely different kind of life.

That people can change their lifestyle during their lifetime is not new, though until before World War II it happened rarely, unless people were afflicted by unemployment, sickness, natural disasters, or war. Whether people were rich or poor, man or woman, most of their lives did not change dramatically during their lifetime. People were certainly socially mobile in the twentieth century, but that had little to do with changing their way of life dramatically several times as an adult. Having a fluid life with many variations and changes is a more recent occurrence. It does not have to be as dramatic or as extreme as in the case of Pat Dollard. But in the twenty-first century people's lives are sometimes more fluid than what has been typical in the past history of humankind.

The fluidity in present-day lifestyles is a consequence of the fact that identity is not nearly as fixed today as it used to be. People can change almost all aspects of their identity, even gender. For instance, people change their religion more frequently than before. Historically it had been rare for people to change their religious identities. But according to the 2001 Religious Identification Survey, nearly 20 percent of all Americans at that time had changed religion at some point in their lives.[6]

People can also change their sense of place, and many do. According to the United States Census Bureau's Current Population

Survey, only a quarter of American teenagers expect to live in their hometowns as adults.[7] With more and more people not living in the same community all their lives, people do not have to adopt the lifestyle in the community where they grew up. They can make their own choices and create the life they want somewhere else.

ORGANIZING LIFE

If a person likes to read comic books, go to church, or shop for clothing once in a while, this does not necessarily make any of these activities a lifestyle. Each of these activities may give an individual identity, but all identity is not necessarily transformed into a lifestyle. This has to do with an important behavioral occurrence: identity can be transformed into human behavior in many ways. For instance, identity can also be expressed as a hobby, an infrequent activity, knowledge, curiosity, or concern. Rodeo can be an infrequent activity or a job. A cowboy may participate for fun in a rodeo once in a while, or it may be his full-time job if he is a professional rodeo rider. The fact is that there are quite a few ways for humans to transform identity into behavior. For instance, identity can be transformed into:

- Making a living
- An occasional activity
- A frequent activity
- A hobby
- Knowledge
- An observation
- An appreciation
- A respect
- A concern
- An interest
- A memory
- A curiosity
- An awareness
- A lifestyle

All these terms can be called organizing principles. A dress code is also an organizing principle with respect to style (as was mentioned in chapter 2). Organizing principles can play a part, big or small, in how we as individuals organize our lives. Lifestyle is the organizing principle—and the term we use—when we want to indicate that an identity is really dominating a person's life. This quote from a Web site about Savannah, Georgia, makes the distinction between a hobby and a lifestyle succinctly: "Savannah is filled with all kinds of auto racing fans. For many people in Savannah and the surrounding area, auto racing is more than just a hobby; it's a way of life. Some fans travel with their favorite racers each week to see how their racers perform week in and week out. And it's not uncommon to see bumper stickers on many of their cars and trucks around town touting the driver's favorite racers."[8]

Like the person who wrote the quote, most people are well aware that when using the term *lifestyle* we are referring to what dominates and organizes a person's everyday life, 24/7. To a sociologist, lifestyle is a very strong manifestation of identity.

It is essential to be aware that *24/7* does not literally mean 24/7. Many people have jobs that will prevent them from letting a lifestyle dominate 24/7. And if a person is 100 percent into something—be it rodeo riding, politics, or something else—though he can't be into "his thing" at work, that does not preclude it from being a lifestyle.

Reading comic books, going to church, and shopping can in fact each be lifestyles if the activity dominates one's life. This would be the case with, for instance, a graphic artist who regularly attends Comic-Cons, a nun living in a convent, and a shopaholic. In the case of Jim Harrison, his lifestyle is about writing, hunting, and cooking his favorite dishes using game he has hunted. Part of his identity is also his past as a part-time Hollywood screenwriter and the times he was hanging out with directors Orson Welles and John Huston and actor Jack Nicholson. But this part of his identity appears to be about memories. It is not what he lives and breathes. It is not his current lifestyle.

We cannot equate identity with lifestyle; if we could, the two things would be the same. Identity is what is inside our heads. Lifestyle is about how this part of human nature is transformed into how we actually live our lives—the practical organizing of our lives. People often say they have a certain lifestyle, but in fact lifestyle is much more about something you do. So to sum it up in academic terms: identity is a psychological phenomenon whereas lifestyle is a sociological phenomenon. Our identity is who we feel we are. Our lifestyle is how we practice who we are.

Lifestyle can be about one, some, or all ten of the identity categories described in chapter 2. If a person has one strong identity dominating his life, this will often be his lifestyle. If a person gets her identity from many sources, it can be trickier to define her lifestyle. But we can exemplify the intricacies of present-day lifestyles by taking a closer look at the identities of the four individuals profiled in figure 3.1 (this figure is identical to figure 2.4 in chapter 2). We know what their identities are, but just from the description of their identities we cannot know what their lifestyle is. To learn about their lifestyle we have to find out how they transform their identity into everyday life. This can be done by asking them about their individual organizing principles or by observing them. By doing so we can create a lifestyle profile.

The thirty-two-year-old woman in figure 3.1 gets her identity from ten distinct identity givers, but they are not equally important to her. Her identification with California is not strong. She could easily live in another state—as long as she can surf. She is part of the peace movement and goes to different rallies—though she would not let this interfere with her surfing. She is very happy with her work as a dentist, especially because it gives her time and money to pursue her all-encompassing passion: surfing. As much as possible, her life revolves around surfing. Surfing is her lifestyle, it is what dominates her life. She would like to go surfing every day, but that is not always possible. When it is not, she will be reading surfing magazines and chatting with surfer friends on the Internet. The destinations of her vacations will almost always be determined by the possibility to surf and meet other surfers. Figure 3.2 sums up her lifestyle profile.

Figure 3.1. Identity Givers for Four Individuals

Identity Categories	Woman, 32 years old	Man, 43 years old	Woman, 58 years old	Man, 76 years old
Family	Single, no children	Married, father	Divorcée, mother, grandmother	Widower, father, grandfather
Geography	Californian	Minnesotan	Oregonian	Wisconsinite
History	Iraq War	9/11	Feminist movement	Vietnam War
Race/ Ethnicity	African-American	Hispanic-American	Irish-American	Anglo-American
Religion	Baptist	Catholic	Buddhist	Episcopalian
Politics	Independent	Moderate Democrat	Liberal	Republican
Education/ Work	Dentist	Hotel receptionist	Writer, publisher	Retired stockbroker
Leisure	Surfing	Hiking	Literature, reading	Golfing
Style	Surfer	Sporty	Artsy	Pinstriped
Sexuality	Celibate	Heterosexual	Lesbian	Asexual

Figure 3.2. Lifestyle Profile No. 1

Identity Giver	Organizing Principle
Single, no children	Observation
Californian	Observation
Iraq War	Memory
African-American	Awareness
Baptist	Occasional activity
Independent	Appreciation
Dentist	Making a living
Surfing	Lifestyle
Surfer	Dress code
Celibate	Awareness

The organizing principles reflect that you can be just barely conscious of an aspect of your life (observation) or quite conscious (awareness) or very conscious and feel very positive about it (appreciation). Organizing principles can be about all kinds of behavior, with lifestyle being the organizing principle that affects all aspects of your life.

Though there are patterns in how we combine organizing principles, there are many variations. The forty-three-year-old man in figure 3.1 not only has a different identity from the thirty-two-year-old woman, but he also has different organizing principles. Being married and a father is the most important thing to him. He moved to Minnesota because of his wife, who is from there, but Minnesota is not a big part of his identity. He could live in many different places, as long as he is with his family. He is Catholic but not churchgoing. Moving to Minnesota has made him appreciate his Hispanic ethnicity more than when he lived in Los Angeles. Being a hotel receptionist is mostly about making a living. Hiking, trekking, and being outdoors are his hobbies. His organizing principles and complete lifestyle profile are described in figure 3.3.

Figure 3.3. Lifestyle Profile No. 2

Identity Giver	Organizing Principle
Married, father	Lifestyle
Minnesotan	Observation
9/11	Memory
Hispanic-American	Appreciation
Catholic	Awareness
Moderate Democrat	Awareness
Hotel receptionist	Making a living
Hiking	Hobby
Sporty	Dress code
Heterosexual	Biological need

The fifty-eight-year-old woman in figure 3.1 is a mother and a grandmother. Her only daughter lives in Paris, along with her two grandchildren. This means that they get together only about once a year. She has for many years organized her life around two great passions: reading and writing. She has worked in publishing for a couple of decades, and she has written three books herself that also have been published by her own small press. She has no other really great passions in her life. What has mattered in her life is that she finally realized that she is a lesbian, and at the age of forty-five she came out to her family, friends, and co-workers. Now most of her social life revolves around her lesbian friends. Her reading is focused on lesbian literature, and the three books she has written all have a lesbian theme. When she goes on vacation, it matters to her to be around other lesbians, so she goes to resort towns with many lesbians or on an Olivia cruise, the cruise line that caters to lesbians. Being a lesbian and a novelist have simply become her lifestyle. This is also clear from figure 3.4.

Figure 3.4. Lifestyle Profile No. 3

Identity Giver	Organizing Principle
Divorcée, mother, grandmother	Appreciation
Oregonian	Appreciation
Feminist movement	Memory
Irish-American	Knowledge
Buddhist	Awareness
Liberal	Frequent activity
Writer, publisher	Lifestyle
Literature, reading	Lifestyle
Artsy	Dress code
Lesbian	Lifestyle

The seventy-six-year-old man in figure 3.1 considers himself a patriot and he likes to show it: Stars and Stripes are everywhere in his life. Inside the house, outside on the front lawn, he proudly displays a flag and he wears a pin with the flag on his jacket. He is an avid reader of American history. Having fought in Vietnam, he is aware that he has played a part in history. He is a member of the Republican Party and considers himself a conservative. His view of the world is observed through a conservative lens. He is an Episcopalian and goes to church every Sunday. He is not a born-again Christian—he has always been a Christian. He has taken on different fundraising tasks at his church and in support of local politicians. He has five children. They live in different places and have very different lifestyles from him and each other, so he decided he could not organize his life around their lives. He is always happy to be with his children and grandchildren, but it is only an occasional activity. This is reflected in his lifestyle profile in figure 3.5.

Figure 3.5. Lifestyle Profile No. 4

Identity Giver	Organizing Principle
Widower, father, grandfather	Appreciation
Wisconsinite	Observation
Vietnam War	Memory
Anglo-American	Awareness
Episcopalian	Lifestyle
Republican	Lifestyle
Retired stockbroker	Memory
Golfing	Hobby
Pinstriped	Dress code
Asexual	Awareness

LIVING AND BREATHING AN IDENTITY

Working is not just about making a living. Jobs are about identity, but not everybody turns his job into a lifestyle. While being a cashier, a window cleaner, or a valet are useful jobs, they rarely become lifestyles. If a job in itself does not give much of a sense of identity, the job is not likely to influence the person 24/7. However, many jobs do influence a person's identity in an all-consuming way. These are jobs people "live and breathe." This is the case with many performing artists (such as singers and actors) and other creative artists (like writers). Their work often becomes such an integral part of their life that their entire life will revolve around their work. If a person is a chauffeur and also likes car driving in his spare time, driving can be a lifestyle. Nursing can be a job, but it can also be a vocation. When this is the case, the person could decide to travel to poor areas around the world and devote herself to nursing, living close to patients in need of care. Then nursing is a lifestyle.

Some professions are more likely to become lifestyles because a person is on-call outside of normal working hours or when working is not just a nine-to-five job. This can be the case, for instance, of fishermen or tour guides. Many small-business owners have to organize their lives around their business, sometimes because they want to, and other times because they cannot afford not to. Jennifer Louie, whose father, James, emigrated from China to the United States in 1980, said in an interview about her parents, "In their first ten years here, they never took a single day off from work. Not one day. I am not exaggerating. . . . They simply had never left the kitchen of their restaurant."[9] Not doing much else than working means that the job is a lifestyle.

If a job does not become a lifestyle, then there are plenty of other identity categories that can be the source of a person's lifestyle. In a book about new patterns in consumption, the authors introduce Jake, a thirty-four-year-old construction worker from Chicago with a regular construction-worker income and a great passion for golf. He buys the best in golf equipment. Golf in this case clearly is his lifestyle because "during the eight-month golf season in Chicago, Jake works the 6 a.m. shift so he can be on the course by 2 p.m.; he plays eighteen holes nearly every weekday after work and . . . twice on Saturday and twice more on Sunday."[10] When a sport dominates a person's life, it has evolved from being a hobby to being a lifestyle.

Like work, without a doubt religion is the big organizer of many people's lives. But actually we have gone from a society in which religion played a big part in almost *all* people's lives to a society with religion dominating only the majority. Another point is that religion can organize people's lives in many different ways. This is what Max Weber originally pointed out in his studies of seventeenth-century Protestants and Catholics in western Europe, as noted earlier.

Catholics and Protestants have different theological teachings but are quite alike with respect to some rituals (praying), norms (sex within marriage only), and traditions (celebrating Christmas). But the actual lifestyles within Christianity can vary enormously. A present-day Christian lifestyle can be like the one once practiced by Rich Merritt, who wrote about his upbringing as a Christian fundamentalist in South Carolina in his memoir. He writes, "[my life] revolved around my immediate family and religion. To say it plainly, our religious faith was the center of the family. . . . Placed on [the coffee] table, rather symbolically, were a family photo album and a large white Bible. Every night before we went to bed, we'd gather around that coffee table with my dad, reading the Bible, and then we would all pray. Our family devotions lasted from twenty minutes to an hour each night."[11] They were members of the Pentecostal Church. And young Rich went to a Christian school, high school, and college, where the Christian faith also played a big role during weekdays. About his teenage years he wrote, "Each year religion became more and more central to my life. I never missed my daily devotional period—a personal time of quiet prayer, Bible reading, and meditation." Religion affected his behavior—no smoking, no drinking—as well as his views on many subjects.

Other religions can have completely different ways of organizing people's lives with respect to rituals, norms, and traditions. Traditionalist Muslims have to pray five times a day, turning toward the holy city of Mecca; they do not eat pork; and they celebrate Ramadan, one month of fasting every day between sunrise and sunset. Jews have other traditions and rituals, as do Hindus and Buddhists. How strictly organized a religious lifestyle is varies, but when religion is one's lifestyle, this normally means that it is very strictly organized with little room for other aspects of a person's identity. This then affects the norms and the rituals that the person lives by.

The Amish make up a community with some very strict norms and rituals. Presently there are about one hundred fifty thousand Amish in the United States.[12] Many live in Dutch County, west of Philadelphia, in Pennsylvania. Their preferred means of transportation are horse-drawn carriages and sledges when there is snow. Though they can be passengers in cars, they are not allowed to drive others' cars themselves. They are vehemently against the use of electricity. There are no telephones on their farms. In reality, Amish life has not changed very much since the first Amish migrated to America in 1714.[13]

The static Amish way of life is possible because of the ritual practice of shunning, which means exclusion from the Amish community. The threat of complete exclusion from the Amish community is a reality if someone who is part of the Amish community wants to do things differently. For instance, if an Amish man dons modern clothes, cuts off his beard, behaves in a manner considered vain, or acts in any way that is not strictly Amish, it is a duty to report this to the elders. The elders can then decide to shun him for not following the Amish way of life. The practice of shunning is an effective tool for the Amish to keep the flock loyal to the norms and rituals of the Amish way of life. The Amish have institutionalized exclusion, but it is something that is practiced—more informally—in all kinds of groups. When a person breaks the written or unwritten rules of a group, he always runs risk of being excluded from the group. This keeps everyone in line with respect to his or her behavior.[14]

FLAUNTING THE FLAG

As a result of the very unique history of the United States, the image of the jigsaw puzzle that we are laying out is going to be colorful. For the past several hundred years people have created American symbols, traditions, and rituals based on the unique geography and history of the United States that reflect an American way of life. But there are hundreds and hundreds of other symbols, traditions, and rituals that represent specialized lifestyles around the country.

People all over the country celebrate different ethnic festivities and rituals and dress in certain national costumes at certain occasions. Irish-Americans celebrate St. Patrick's Day (St. Patrick being a patron saint of Ireland) by wearing the colors of the Irish flag and participating in a parade. However, this does not constitute an ethnic lifestyle. An occasional celebration of your roots is not an ethnic lifestyle. Indeed, witness scores of parade goers at any St. Pat's parade who are with and without Irish heritage, yet both handily celebrate with pints of Guinness and bottles of Jameson. On the other hand, someone who lives in China-town in New York or San Francisco, who is Chinese by birth, who speaks mostly Chinese, and who prefers to eat Chinese food will have an ethnic Chinese lifestyle.

In large cities people have many different lifestyles. One could have a bohemian lifestyle. The term *bohemian* originally referred to a geographical place, Bohemia, in what is the present-day Czech Republic. Nowadays *bohemian* refers to a lifestyle completely devoid of geographical meaning. Historically this lifestyle is about artists and intellectuals who populated private homes, bars, and cafés in New York, Paris, and Rome. It is about a way of life that is the opposite of a pious, Christian, small-city way of life. A bohemian lifestyle is about feeling free of other people's moral judgments and enjoying life and risks, sometimes on a very small income.

Human life is also about sexuality. Having sex is first of all about biology. But if a person is highly promiscuous—that is, having the need to have sex all the time with different people—and this really dominates a person's life, then promiscuity can be said to be a lifestyle. Sexuality can also be about belonging to a sexual minority. If a person lives in a predominately gay neighborhood, goes to only gay cafés and restaurants, and goes on holiday with a gay travel company to a destination where he will be around only other gay people, then a gay identity is transformed into a gay lifestyle. But if a gay man or a lesbian couple live in a predominantly heterosexual neighborhood and only occasionally go to a gay café or bar, this is a leisure activity—just like when a heterosexual person or couple will go to a café or bar. Not that going to bars and cafés cannot be a lifestyle. (In France going to cafés for lunch and after work for a drink has been a part of a French lifestyle for decades.)

In the same vein, if a person has many healthful habits, you can say that the person has a healthful lifestyle. The same goes for a person who has only unhealthful habits. Nowadays you can hear people say that smoking is a lifestyle if it dominates a person's life. If a person will choose only restaurants, airlines, and friends who allow smoking, then smoking certainly becomes a matter of lifestyle. The same is the case with drinking alcohol. Drinking alcohol can be about appreciation, or it can be a hobby. Rarely will it be a lifestyle. But if a person is an alcoholic, alcohol may run the person's life to the extent of being a lifestyle. When Augusten Burroughs, the memoirist, was an alcoholic, alcohol was certainly running his life 24/7. In his memoir, *Dry*, he writes about being drunk most of the time, even when at work.[15]

To many enthusiastic athletes, sport is a lifestyle—it is what their lives revolve around. They constantly concentrate on exercise and diet. This is what Sam Fussel did when he was a bodybuilder. In his memoir he describes a lifestyle that was devoted solely to bodybuilding. In order to gain weight, Sam Fussel was as ritualistic about his eating habits as any religious practice. He recounted, "For breakfast, six poached eggs, six pieces of whole wheat toast, a whole grain cereal mix, a can of tuna. For my first lunch (around ten thirty), a pound of ground hamburger, a monstrous baked potato, a fistful of broccoli, a small salad. For my second lunch (two thirty), two whopping chicken breasts, spinach pasta, two slices of whole wheat bread. And dinner (eight thirty), dinner topped it all. Another pound of hamburger or steak, a super-size of tuna, another potato, more bread." Between eating there was heavy exercising at the gym according to a strict regimen, four hours a day, six days a week. There was intake of food supplements and regular visits to the tanning salon. His aim was to look like a "condom filled with walnuts," the aesthetic ideal of many bodybuilders.[16]

Yet it may be surprising that Sam Fussel had finished his education and majored in English literature at Oxford University before he began working out in his midtwenties, eventually becoming a competitive bodybuilder back home in the United States. The bodybuilder lifestyle dominated his life for four years. But just as he changed and his life revolved around bodybuilding, he changed back. This is an example of fluid living.

Family is an important lifestyle to most people, but it is also a lifestyle that changes as you grow older. When a person leaves home, her lifestyle may not be about family. But when she starts living with another person, married or not, and has children, then family becomes a lifestyle. Then one's life revolves around being part of a family. For some people, family is the only thing that dominates their lives. They have no other superseding interests. But many other people do have other identities, and sometimes these—which can be anything from the Catholic Church to tennis—will be part of the person's lifestyle.

People can let many different aspects of their identity become their lifestyle. In chapter 1 we were introduced to some of the first books that used the word *lifestyle* in their title or subtitle. Books like *Open Marriage: A New Lifestyle for Couples*; *Water Squatters: The Houseboat Lifestyle*; and *It's Your Life: Create a Christian Lifestyle* were more or less how-to books about how to transform one's identity into practical everyday living. These writers certainly were aware of what lifestyle is about!

Most lifestyles are not limited to just a few individuals. In fact, many people have the exact same lifestyle, and often they prefer to cluster together in the same villages or neighborhoods.

This again is the story behind the many diverse neighborhoods around the country, which I mentioned at the beginning of this chapter. This is also one reason why a guidebook about the East Village neighborhood in Manhattan stated, "The East Village—particularly everything east of First Avenue—is for some as exotic and intimidating as the Congo" (more on the diversity of neighborhoods in chapter 7).[17] We cluster together with people who are like ourselves because it makes sense on many levels: it is easier to find a spouse or partners and to make new friends. There is the obvious fact that you have something in common and something to talk about—a psychological explanation may be that we use other people as mirrors: we look at other people like we look at ourselves in a mirror and when we are with people who are like us or look like us, this mirror gives us acceptance without asking questions. "Mirroring" is wonderfully comforting to most people no matter their individual personalities.

Mirroring also leaves us with a need to communicate who we are when we are among other people. The obvious communication tool—language—is not the best tool in all situations because we have to get physically close before we can talk. But there is another tool: nonverbal communication. For ages signs or symbols have served as nonverbal communication tools. In ancient Greek, the word *symbol* literally meant "a recognizable sign."[18] In Roman times, the Latin word *signum* was the easily identifiable sign held high on a shaft that the Roman soldiers gathered around in battles.[19] Symbols more or less serve the same purpose today—something to gather around.

The difference between a sign and a symbol was pointed out in chapter 1, using the Stars and Stripes to illustrate the difference: to someone who has never seen the red, white, and blue rectangular flag before, the flag is a sign (a visual expression), but to Americans and many other people all over the world this flag is symbol (an emotional expression). This emotional relationship can be positive—or negative—but feelings are involved. This was certainly the case during one Mardi Gras in New Orleans when a twenty-something man had painted a variation of the Stars and Stripes on his face. A colorful celebration like Mardi Gras is an obvious opportunity to use a little face paint, but when he was photographed for *National Geographic Magazine*, he said to the photographer, "My name doesn't matter, I'm just an American. I love my flag, and I'm very proud of it."[20] Even if he had not explained this, many people would have concluded that he is a proud American just by looking at his painted face. This "silent language" is possible because the Stars and Stripes is such a strong symbol.

The Stars and Stripes is a symbol with some very specific symbolic parts that may engender even more positive feelings among those who know how to "read" the flag. The thirteen red and white stripes represent the original thirteen colonies. The fifty white stars represent the fifty states that are now the United States (a star has been added every time a new state has become part of the United States; the most recent to become a state was Hawaii in 1959).[21]

The fifty individual state flags use other symbols—at least they are symbols to those who know the stories behind the flags. To others, the flags are just signs. Colors can also be symbolic. In many cultures white symbolizes purity and peace. Black is the color of death and mourning. Purple is a color that is considered regal and represents pride and justice. When President George Washington created the first US military medal in 1782, it was a heart-shaped badge on purple cloth. The award was discontinued then revived in 1932 and named the Purple Heart. It has since been awarded to soldiers wounded or killed in battle, symbolizing exceptional bravery.[22]

Like colors, clothing and accessories can also be both signs and symbols. In the case of author Jim Harrison, his clothes are practical, outdoorsy, and rugged. By wearing the clothes that he does, he has classified himself. He may not consciously define himself through his clothes, but other people are likely to classify him based on the clothes that he wears. Whether or not he knows or cares, the fact is his clothing style speaks volumes whenever he is around other people.

Chapter 4

STYLISH COMMUNICATION
An Image Emerges

*I*ntroductions are an ingrained part of American sociability. People introduce people who do not know each other, and people introduce themselves if there are no others to do so. This ritual of introducing other people is not part of all cultures across the globe. The ritual of making introductions is as American as apple pie. It is certainly not a ritual practiced by the British. English anthropologist Kate Fox has pointed out that a greeting like "'Hi, I'm Bill from Iowa,' particularly if accompanied by an outreached hand and beaming smile, makes the English wince and cringe." As she explains, "the English do not want to know your name, or tell you theirs, until a much greater degree of intimacy has been established—like maybe when you marry their daughter."[1]

The United States is a populous country with a highly mobile population, and this has taught many that you may never get the chance to meet a particular person again if you do not get yourself introduced at the first chance. In the same vein, rituals that stress politeness have been cultivated. American English is full of polite phrases that make it easy to socialize, even among strangers—from the "Pleased to meet you" to the "Nice talking to you."

With the many immigrants from non-English-speaking parts of the world and the introduction of sometimes difficult-to-pronounce last names, a solution was found to that as well: before this also became popular in other countries, Americans started using first names. When Mr. Shalikashvili or Ms. Brzezinski was too tricky to pronounce, most people just said Bill and Anne instead. It is not just our verbal communication skills that have been adapted and refined as society has changed; we have also refined our nonverbal communication. Nonverbal communication includes facial mimicking, body language, and what we wear. The latter is especially under our control and, therefore, clothing is an important tool used to communicate with *many* people at the *same* time. At some point in history clothing may have just been about keeping us warm. But for a long part of human history clothing has also been about sending signals about who a person is—mostly reflecting gender, work, and income. For hundreds of years clothing was an excellent way to convey wealth and power. Wealthy people could afford to wear better clothing, and powerful people wanted to make sure that their clothing also communicated their status.

Today, clothing is not effective in giving us surefire clues about a person's income. In the twentieth century people who were very wealthy and had been so for generations had a long tradition of dressing down and avoiding anything flashy or flamboyant lest they risk being considered nouveau riche. But in a period of time when many self-made, super-wealthy people made their mark, there were those who wanted to let the world know that they were rich—and therefore dressed in a flashy and flamboyant style. The bottom line is that we rarely can deduce from a person's clothing if she has a regular income or is mega-rich. Just by looking at how they dress, there is no way to know that Bill Gates and hundreds of other company founders are billionaires.

For a part of the twentieth century, age was also reflected in how people dressed. The most common pattern was that people would dress more conservatively as they aged. People who were in their twenties dressed differently from people in their seventies. In the 1950s granddaddies did not wear black leather jackets; in the 1960s few people over the age of forty were hippies; and in the 1970s women over the age of fifty did not wear disco-style clothing. Today, a growing group of both aging men and aging women do not follow that pattern.

From the earliest times, the specialization between men and women with respect to how labor was organized also resulted in differentiated clothing for the two sexes. Men were out hunting, and women were closer to the living area gathering fruits and berries and watching over the children. Skirts had been the original clothing for both sexes for thousands of years, but when men started riding horses, trousers became the most functional clothing for them.[2] Consequently, trousers became a symbol of manliness. Skirts were for women. From that point on, unique dress codes for men and for women evolved.

But no matter how we look at it, clothes are not just about function. In their book *Intergroup Relations*, social psychologists Marilyn Brewer and Norman Miller write that "many of our day-to-day choices about what to wear . . . are influenced by a desire to symbolize or represent our important group memberships."[3] In other words, clothes help us in communicating with and navigating among other people, privately and in public.

Most people are aware of how one specific type of clothing—uniforms—is used to communicate, and few uniforms communicate as much as military uniforms. If a military officer wears his dress uniform with insignia, badges, patches, ribbons, and medals, you can take one look at him and know everything about him. That is, if you know how to decode the uniform. One example of a military officer is US Army General David Petraeus. In one photo he had four silver stars on each shoulder, the Ranger tab on his upper left sleeve, a colorful mini-placard with ten rows of ribbons (signifying multiple awards), yellow combat service stripes on his lower right sleeve plus a number of badges, for instance, for being a master parachutist.[4] To other military personnel his clothes and his distinctions speak for him. But it is not just uniforms that hold such strong codes. Everyday clothing does, too.

Especially when clothing becomes a dress code, what we wear speaks for us. We do not get the chance to have personal conversations with all the people we meet, certainly not when out in public. But often our clothing communicates to the people we come across, whether or not we know them.

Dress codes are just as effective nonverbal communication tools as any uniform (indeed, a dress code could be termed a uniform). When a group of people is very systematic in how they dress by using fixed combinations of apparel and accessories of specific colors, patterns, and fabrics over a long period of time, they turn their clothing into dress codes. By wearing dress codes that do not change too often (or not at all), people make their clothes much more effective in communicating because people can recognize and identify each other. For all practical purposes a dress code that does not change very often is a uniform (two characteristics of uniforms are that they are fixed and stable). One example of a dress code that illustrates this is the Amish dress code.

The Amish have not changed their way of life or their dress code since they came to the United States from Europe in 1714 (as mentioned in chapter 3). They still wear the same frocks their ancestors wore in the 1700s: monochrome handmade clothing without zippers, buttons (they use only hooks and eyes), belts, lapels, neckties, gloves, and pockets. The clothing style is plain and most of the clothing is black, though other colors are used for bonnets and children's clothing. The men have long Abe Lincoln beards, that is, without the usual moustache (omitted because the soldiers back in Europe they came to America to escape from had stylized moustaches).[5] The men wear wide-brimmed felt hats, and the women keep their heads covered with bonnets.[6] No matter where they are, their style certainly makes them easily identifiable to themselves but also to people who are not Amish. The different elements in the Amish dress code are shown in figure 4.1.

Figure 4.1. The Amish Dress Code

Designs
Calf-length plain-cut dresses (women)
Capes (women)
Vests (men)
Suspenders (men)

Colors
Black
White
Blue

Patterns
Solid colors only

Accessories
Straight-pins to hold clothes together
Wide-brimmed straw summer hats (men)
Black felt winter hats (men)
Bonnets (women)

The Amish dress code is one of the longest-existing dress codes still in use today. But it is not the most universally recognizable dress code. That distinction goes to a truly original American dress code—that of the cowboy. Even though the cowboy dress code has existed for a shorter time than the Amish dress code, it represents such strong symbolism that it overshadows almost all other dress codes in terms of its projected image. It is iconic—as strong as a symbol can get.

On the symbolic level the cowboy dress code represents everything from great functional clothing to farmhand, country boy, loner, American, masculine, and horseman—all depending on who the observer is and where he lives. This symbolism exists because cowboys typically have comprised these images and qualities.

Nobody sat down and decided that there should be a cowboy dress code. It came about and has stayed the same because cowboys have an especially strong need for functional clothing. Cowboys do their job outdoors, most of the time on horseback. Historically they have been far away from access to medical assistance and without easy access to buy new clothes. This is reflected in the protective qualities of the clothes they wear.

The creation of the cowboy dress code took place during the same period that the job function as horseback-riding ranch hand evolved in the United States in the 1870s. It was in the late 1860s that the great cattle adventure on the Great Plains began. In 1867 twenty-nine-year-old Chicago cattle merchant Joseph McCoy started having his herds of longhorn cattle drifted from Texas to the newly opened railroad station in Abilene, Kansas. He hired men riding horses who could make sure that the cattle would get safely to their destination.[7]

The horse riders were called herders, and there was nothing glamorous or idealized about them. For instance, in 1875 author Laura Winthrop Johnson reported herders (that is, cowboys) as being "rough men with shaggy hair and wild staring eyes, in butternut trousers stuffed into great rough boots."[8] The hero worship and glamorization came later: first, in 1882, when a fictional biography of herder Buck Taylor became a success,[9] and then in 1883, when Buffalo Bill started touring with his Wild West shows featuring lassoing cowboys, fierce-looking Native Americans, and Annie Oakley (of *Annie Get Your Gun* fame).[10] Then in 1887 the cowboys lost their drifting jobs after a massive snowstorm hit the Great Plains and destroyed most of the cattle.[11] That could have been the end of the cowboy. But with the publication of Owen Wister's novel *The Virginian* in 1902, the cowboy myths—and the realities—again started getting the attention of a wider public.[12]

Owen Wister, who wrote the book after a memorable stay at a ranch in Wyoming, started America's twentieth-century fascination with the cowboy. When the book was turned into a movie, the Western movie genre—a truly American genre—was born. Movie producers realized that the Wild West was a treasure trove for stories about rugged, outdoor masculinity, and the cowboy became a vivid—and is still a vibrant—part of American culture.

The story of the cowboy dress code as such has one famous link to the California Gold Rush, which began in 1848 when a Scottish carpenter who was building a saw mill in the mountains east of Sacramento, California, found gold in the America River.[13] The rush commenced and Northern California became the favored destination for thousands of "Easterners." Because of the gold rush, the population in California rose from ten thousand to two thundred fifty thousand in the six years from 1846 to 1852.[14]

When the California Gold Rush ended in the 1850s, some of the out-of-work gold diggers got employment as herders, and they kept wearing the denim trousers that a young tradesman named Levi Strauss had introduced to them in 1853 while they were futilely digging for fortune. For cowboys spending a lot of time on horseback, blue jeans were and are perfect because they are durable and tight. The first was essential because there were no chances to buy new trousers when on the prairie, and the tightness gave the cowboy good maneuverability atop his horse.[15]

The most iconic part of the cowboy dress code—the cowboy hat—was invented by a Philadelphia hat maker by the name of John B. Stetson, a contemporary of Levi Strauss. While he was traveling from the East Coast to Missouri to join in the gold rush at Pike's Peak he made a felt hat to protect himself from the extremes of the weather. The result was a wide-brimmed hat with the brims turned up. This unique shape made it possible to protect both the neck and the face against the burning sun. The upturned brim also served as a kind of umbrella so that the wearer would not get wet all over when it rained. In the winter, the cowboy could press the brim down over his ears to protect them from the cold, and in the summer the high top allowed air in to cool his scalp. The high top also came in handy because it could be used as a water bucket.[16]

Cowboy boots are another defining element of the cowboy dress code. The history of the boots goes back to the same time as the origin of blue jeans, though from a different place: Coffeyville, Kansas. Cowboy boots are highly functional: They are tall in order to protect the lower leg from thorny bushes when riding. They are tight in order to give a good connection with the stirrups. They are pointed in order to easily get into the stirrup, and they have high heels in order to stay put in the stirrup. The underslung heel prevents the cowboy from being stuck in the stirrup should he be thrown off his horse.[17] When cowboys in Texas began wearing leather chaps in about 1870, cowboy boots became shorter because the chaps would offer protection. Chaps were practical because they offered protection not only from thorny bushes but also from horse bites.[18]

Cowboys also wore shirts in toned-down colors with a red bandanna around the neck. The bandana had an important function for the working cowboy: It was folded into a triangle and tied round the neck with a knot. The knot was typically placed in the back so that the cowboy could quickly pull it up over his nose as protection against dust. At the same time, the bandana was worn loose so that it could easily be turned around to give protection when the sun was burning the neck.[19] The elements in the cowboy dress code are summarized in figure 4.2.

Figure 4.2. The Cowboy Dress Code

Designs
Blue jeans
Brown leather chaps
Plaid shirt
Cowboy boots
Cowboy hat

Colors
Earth tones, especially brown, black, and blue

Patterns
Plaids

Decorative Details
Big buckle on belt

ON THE ROAD

The biker lifestyle is also an American original, and like the cowboy lifestyle it is associated with strong symbolism. The motorcycle is to bikers what the horse is to cowboys, and almost any biker you talk to will describe the freedom the motorcycle has come to represent. These quotes from three bikers in *The Biker Code* say it all.

James "Spike" Basso: "We're America's symbol of freedom."

Thomas "Road Kill" Anderson: "I ride alone. It's a feeling of freedom, noise, wind and speed."

Carlos "Marlboro" Rivera: "I feel free like an eagle flying on the heights."

All three men are bikers and wear black leather jackets.[20] To some people a black leather jacket may be just a black leather jacket, a piece of clothing. To them the black leather jacket is a visual expression, a sign. To other people the very same black leather jacket can mean *rebel, freedom, macho, sexy,* and/or *motorcycle duds.* To them the black leather jacket is an emotional expression, a symbol. This symbol again can be positive, negative, or neutral, depending upon one's taste, knowledge, experience, associations, and attitudes. A black leather jacket (or, for that matter, a Lycra bikini or cotton underwear) does not have a moral attitude. This is the symbolic meaning that we establish based on our experiences with people who wear black leather jackets—either through personal experience or through movies and television.

The symbolic qualities of the black leather jacket are closely linked to the biker lifestyle that emerged after World War II. It began when a group of former GIs and combat pilots began touring California on Harley-Davidson motorcycles. They were soldiers who felt restless after having been discharged and who had difficulty fitting into civilian society after the war. That was especially true for some of the fighter pilots who had been used to getting huge adrenalin kicks during combat.

The term *Hell's Angels* had been bouncing around the US Air Force personnel during World War I, and during World War II there were squadrons that had adopted the name. Back in civilian life after World War II, some of the former Air Force pilots formed a motorcycle club and continued using the name.[21] The first Hells Angels Motorcycle Club (sans apostrophe) was founded in 1948 in San Bernardino, Southern California. The members of this club and all the Hells Angels clubs that followed dressed in a similar style, with an emphasis on wearing black Schott leather jackets. (The leather jackets came from the same company that had supplied Air Force pilots with their leather bomber jackets.)[22]

During the next few decades, Hells Angels Motorcycle Clubs were founded in other states and, by the 1960s, in Europe as well. The members were typically men, and they generally joined the clubs in their late teens or early twenties. The biker lifestyle that grew out of the Hells Angels still thrives in many countries, inside and outside of motorcycle clubs.

The bikers' way of dressing was adjusted to life on the highways.

It was practical and casual: blue jeans, a white undershirt, and a leather jacket. Levi's became the bikers' preferred brand of jeans. In many cases the bikers identified with the cowboys as the free spirits of the prairie and adopted part of the cowboys' dress code, not only the blue jeans, but also the chaps—black leather chaps, as opposed to cowboys who wore brown.

The bikers were among the first to use graphics on their jackets to individualize their clothing. In his autobiography, *Hell's Angel*, biker Ralph "Sonny" Barger wrote, "I organized a small street corner club in 1954 when I was still at [high school and thirteen years old]. We wore our jackets with the collars up and had 'Earth Angels' embroidered on the back. The Earth Angels never did anything special. We didn't stand for anything. It was just something to belong to . . . it was all about belonging to a group of people just like you."[23]

Like the cowboy dress code, the biker dress code has not changed for decades. First, because the leather jacket and leather trousers have a protective function. Second, it also has to do with effectiveness. To be effective as nonverbal communication, clothing also has to be unique and distinct. The bikers realized this early on. The biker dress code is summarized in figure 4.3. The communicative part of the biker dress code has been further underlined by insignia on the back of the leather jacket, stating which motorcycle club the wearer belongs to.

The Hells Angels have for a long time been considered a gang privy to organized crime, violence, and drug dealing. While the black leather dress code is still popular among a huge number of non–Hells Angels bikers, others have taken on another dress code consisting of a fitted leather racing suit in color combinations of, for instance, green/white or red/white. The reason is threefold: (1) The fitted leather racing suit offers optimal protection, (2) It is a way to create distance from the Hells Angels dress code that has come to represent unlawfulness to many people, and (3) It signifies speed, which is what many bikers like about biking.

Figure 4.3. The Biker Dress Code

Designs
Pilots' bomber leather jacket
Blue jeans
Black leather chaps
T-shirt
Leather vest
Engineer's boots
Military leather cap

Colors
Black, blue
White (T-shirt)

Patterns
Monochrome colors

Accessories
Bandanas

Decorative Details
Jacket decorations
Insignia on back of the leather jacket
Chains

RIDING THE WAVES

Surfing is a another post–World War II California lifestyle that became a global, thriving pastime. Historically, surfing started in Hawaii, where the native people called it *heénalu*, which directly translated means "wave gliding." When the English captain James Cook came to Hawaii in 1778, he noted in his diary that heénalu was "a most supreme pleasure." Later—when Christian missionaries came to the islands—surfing was stamped as a heathen pastime and more or less banned.[24]

But, by way of California, surfing became much more than a pastime. It became a lifestyle that also evolved with its own dress code. The California version of surfing began when the writer Jack London, who lived in San Francisco, came to Hawaii in 1907 with his friends Alexander Hume Ford and George Freeth. All three became avid surfers. Upon returning from their trip they formed the world's first official surfing association, the Outrigger Canoe and Surfboard Club. Jack London later depicted his adventures in his novel *The Cruise of the Snark*. Upon his return from Hawaii, George Freeth mounted surfing demonstrations in Redondo Beach near Los Angeles.[25] Over the following decades the sport became more and more popular along the California coast. One important figure in this process was Hawaiian Duke Kahanamoku. Born in 1890, he went on to be both a surfer and an Olympic swimmer, winning gold and silver medals at the Olympics in 1912, 1920, and 1924. Between the Olympics and after retiring from the Olympics in 1924, he traveled in the United States and to Australia to give swimming and surfing exhibitions, thus popularizing the sport. His surfing exhibition in Sydney, Australia, in 1914 is considered a significant moment in the development of surfing in Australia because trendsetters there realized that Australia had ideal conditions for this new, exciting sport.[26]

Duke Kahanamoku and the other surfers used surfboards made of wood. But when Southern Californian surfer Hobie Alter developed a light, plastic surfboard in the late 1950s, surfing became even more popular.[27] The first group to wholly embrace surfing as a lifestyle were rootless young people who lived near the beaches—the 1950s beach bums. Their laid-back style became known and popularized through a number of movies with titles like *Beach Party* (1963), *Ride the Wild Surf* (1964), and *Beach Blanket Bingo* (1965). At the same time, bands like the Chantays, the Ventures, the Astronauts, Dick Dale & the Del-Tones, and most famously, the Beach Boys, introduced a new music style—surf music.[28] Later, surfing became a competitive sport.

The 1950s surfers developed their own dress code, with Hawaiian shirts and Bermuda shorts.[29] The Hawaiian shirt is not part of the present-day surfer dress code that now consists of T-shirts with prints, surf trunks, and flip-flops (the latter are inspired by the zori sandals worn by Japanese immigrants who labored in Hawaii's cane fields in the late 1800s). Popular accessories are wrap-around sunglasses and leather or hemp short necklaces, bracelets and/or anklets.

Some of the original surfwear brands are Quiksilver, Rip Curl, Billabong, and O'Neill, but now they have broad appeal and as a consequence the surfer style is worn by millions of people who are not surfers. Actual surfers often wear full-body surfer suits when riding waves. The surfer dress code is summarized in figure 4.4.

Figure 4.4. The Surfer Dress Code

Designs
T-shirt
Surf trunks

Colors
Varied but often colorful

Patterns
Graphic prints

Accessories
Sandals, flip-flops
Wrap-around sunglasses
Leather or hemp short necklaces, bracelets, and/or anklets

ELVIS, FOUNDING FATHER

Heavy metal rock is a music genre that has existed since the 1960s. But the roots go further back—to the earliest rock'n'rollers. The heavy metal rockers were also aware that to be truly effective, nonverbal communication has to be distinct. For many popular singers and musicians, it is crucial that their combination of clothing, other designed objects, and colors makes them easily distinguishable.

In the 1950s leisure came to play a bigger part in young people's lives, and their preferred leisure activity was often music. Singing cowboys like Roy Rogers and Bob Wills had appealed to young people in the 1940s,[30] but in the 1950s it was the biker look that appealed to many young people. And it was the black leather/macho biker look that appealed to the musicians who were creating the new music that became popular during the 1950s, fusing country, blues, and R & B into something new, loud, and with a back beat.

In 1954 then truck driver Elvis Presley sang a few songs in a Memphis, Tennessee, studio and ended up being a pioneer, a founding father of a new music genre. The performers and fans—at least the ones dressing like the performers—became known as rock'n'rollers. Rock'n'roll became hugely popular with many different performers, and black leather for the most part became an integrated part of the dress code. However, the rock'n'rollers were not bikers; their lifestyle revolved around music, not riding motorcycles. Also being into music and playing on a stage necessitated musicians to dress lighter than bikers. The rock'n'rollers consequently discarded the heavy engineer's boots for pointed shoes. With tighter leather jackets and shoes, Elvis Presley and the other rock'n'roll performers could hip-swivel and raise the hackles of concerned parents much more easily than if weighed down in engineer's boots and leather chaps.

The genre evolved and branched out into glam rock, hard rock, and heavy metal, among other subgenres. The original sound, that of Elvis, Chuck Berry, and even the early Beatles, became known as classic rock. This diversifying reflected the fact that young people became more individualized and wanted to show it, in their music tastes and in their clothing styles. In the 1960s and the 1970s the heavy metal rockers (also known as head bangers) came out of the biker and hippie lifestyles, and as a consequence took inspiration from both of these lifestyles when creating their unique dress code. The black leather pants came from the bikers and the long hair came from the hippies, creating a mix of the macho biker and the flamboyant hippie, as seen with bands such as Led Zeppelin, Black Sabbath, and Judas Priest. The heavy metal rocker dress code is summarized in figure 4.5.

Figure 4.5. The Heavy Metal Rocker Dress Code

Designs
Long black leather jacket
Black T-shirt with print
Leather pants
Snakeskin boots
Snakeskin, spiked cowboy boots

Color
Black

Patterns
Psychedelic
Leopard prints

Accessories
Fringe
Chains
Big-buckled belts

Symbols
Cross
Music band logos

Hairstyle
Elbow-length hair

BIG CITY STYLE

Since the beginning of the twentieth century, sociologists have been studying how new lifestyles and new styles emerge. One of the first theories about how something new becomes popular is known as the "trickle-down" principle, the assumption that in a society with a social hierarchy, new style innovations start with the upper class and then trickle down to the middle and working classes. American social critic Thorstein Veblen was a proponent of this theory in the early 1900s. He described how wealthy people were the first to adopt new styles. The working class—the majority of people—could not afford to buy these clothes, but they looked up to wealthy people and aspired to adopt their style innovations. In pre–World War II society, that was the way many changes in style and taste came about for the very obvious reason that wealthy people were the only ones who could afford to buy new, innovative clothes.[31]

Now we know that there is also another process, the "bubbling-up" process. This process reflects that new lifestyles and trends can emerge from outcasts, poor people, and underground subcultures.[32] The cowboys, the bikers, and the hippies are all examples of the bubbling-up process—as are the hip-hoppers.

The roots of hip-hop go back to the 1970s, to poor African-American boys and men in large cities.[33] At that time, many US cities had neighborhoods that were characterized by decay. This was particularly the case in the African-American neighborhoods of New York City. Violence and crime were rampant, and inevitably many gang members were jailed. The men who were doing time influenced other young people in their community in terms of their way of dressing. For instance, in jail you are not allowed to wear a belt—for safety reasons. This inspired friends and family of the jailed men to also wear trousers without a belt, with the trousers often hanging low on the hips. Another early style was the backward baseball cap, inspired by Muslims who turned their baseball caps around in order to get their forehead to the ground when praying.[34]

Musically, it was a DJ from Jamaica with the moniker DJ Kool Herc who played a pivotal role in the emerging hip-hop culture. In the mid-1970s he started organizing street parties in the South Bronx. The Jamaican DJ noticed that the dancing teenagers especially liked certain musical passages. Therefore, he introduced the "merry-go-round": he put two copies of the same record on two parallel turntables playing at the same time, and thus he could prolong the most popular music rhythm breaks and riffs.[35]

Another Bronx DJ called Grandmaster Flash is credited with

inventing scratching, another hip-hop musical invention. Scratching is the technique of audibly rotating a disk back and forth while the turntable is running. It led to the creation of a whole new staccato sound, which in turn inspired a whole new way of dancing, with acrobatic and staccato movements—a dancing style that we know today as break dancing. Break dancing was done in the streets, and soon a ritualized form of break dancing competitions emerged. (One of the most spectacular steps in break dancing is head spinning—standing on your head and spinning.) The break dancers' clothing was inspired by their physical activities: they wore functional activewear and sneakers.[36]

When DJ Kool Herc was busy being a DJ, he needed another person—a sort of toastmaster—who could urge dancers and party guests to get down. The Jamaican toasters, who had incited the audience when reggae music was first invented in Jamaica, inspired him. With the introduction of toasters, yet another musical style emerged: rap music. Rapping (speaking in verse with music) also turned into a competition and a way to show off your skills at improvising with words.

Until 1979, rapping was exclusively a live musical genre. It was not until then that Sylvia Robinson, an independent record company owner, put three rappers together in a studio and recorded them. The Sugarhill Gang released the first rap record. The group's single "Rapper's Delight" was a big hit, which helped sell more than two million copies worldwide in the next few years.[37]

The term *hip-hop* was coined by Afrika Bambaataa, the founder of the Universal Zulu Nation, now the world's oldest and largest grassroots hip-hop organization.[38] The word was coined to describe a whole lifestyle, including music, clothing, and language, as well as events and gatherings. Together with activewear training suits, luxury-brand clothing became an important ingredient in the hip-hop style. At the same time, the hip-hoppers did not deny their roots. Many African-Americans have traditionally worn gold jewelry and bright colors. This style is about looking sharper and richer, regardless of whether you actually are. So hip-hop style became a mix of activewear, luxury brands, and oversized gold jewelry.

As hip-hoppers aspired to look like rich people, they took a keen interest in the preppy clothes that were fashionable in the 1980s. This had a huge influence on a relatively new brand called Tommy Hilfiger, a brand with a style somewhat similar to that of Ralph Lauren, but less expensive. As the African-American hip-hoppers became more and more visible, becoming the idols of Caucasian middle-class teenagers, Tommy Hilfiger became one of the popular brands of the 1990s, both among hip-hoppers and among young people outside the African-American neighborhoods.[39]

The original hip-hop dress code has been expanded to the extent that most hip-hoppers now dress in a variation of the original dress code. As some people involved with hip-hop music have become rich, they have also changed their way of dressing to reflect their new wealth and status as music moguls. The hip-hop dress code is summarized in figure 4.6.

Figure 4.6. The Hip-Hopper Dress Code

Designs
Low-hanging, baggy pants
Loose, white T-shirt
Hooded sports top (hoodie)

Colors
Bright colors
Monochrome colors

Accessories
Oversized gold jewelry
Oversized pendants shaped as $
White, big-tongued sneakers
Colorful baseball caps

Decorative Details
Fake or real diamonds

"REGULAR FOLK"

Having a dress code is not exclusive to some select individuals and groups. Actually, it is interesting to observe that with all the choices we have in clothing items, colors, fabrics, accessories, and brands, most people choose to wear the same clothing items, accessories, and colors in the same mix again and again, often for their entire lives. In her memoir of growing up in a New England family, Lee Montgomery describes how her father—"a classic Yankee"—always wore Lands' End polo shirts when relaxing and blue- and white-striped Brooks Brothers button-down shirts when going formal.[40] In his book of portraits, *What Should I Do with My Life?* author Po Bronson portrayed Don Linn, a businessman with an MBA from Mississippi. When Bronson first met Don Linn in the early 1990s, he was purportedly wearing the same style as when he met him ten years later: pleated khakis, pink polo shirts, deck shoes.[41]

The fact is that a big part of the population likes to combine specific elements into easily recognizable dress codes. The only difference from the well-known and most iconic dress codes is that the dress codes of "regular folk" do not always have as well known a name as that of, say, the cowboys or hip-hoppers. But this does not mean that the vast majority of the population does not use dress codes in their nonverbal communication. Because they do.

The actual number of present-day dress codes available is debatable. First of all, not all clothing items are symbols. It takes time for something to become a symbol, and today a lot of clothing is not used long enough to become symbolic. But if we go by dress codes that have been around for at least twenty years without having changed, there probably are fewer than a hundred present-day dress codes. Some of the most prevalent present-day dress codes—thirty-two in all—are highlighted and named in figure 4.7. The names are descriptive of the style and do *not* indicate any job preferences, other preferences, or actual jobs held by the people wearing the dress code.

Figure 4.7. Thirty-Two Dress Codes

It is primarily the men's version of the dress codes that is described. In some cases specific elements in the women's version are described after that. How these dress codes were identified is documented in the appendix.

DRESS CODE	ELEMENTS
Cowboy *Unisex*	Cowboy hat, blue jeans, Western shirt, bandana, buckskin jacket with or without fringe, brown leather chaps, cowboy boots
Lumberjack *Men*	Red-and-black checkered flannel shirt, suspenders, turned-up blue jeans, fleece jacket, chukka boots or hiking boots, trapper hat
Hillbilly *Men*	Denim overalls, white wifebeater, John Deere mesh cap, boots
Biker *Men, Women*	*Men*: Perfecto leather jacket, leather vest, white T-shirt, blue jeans, black leather chaps, engineer's boots, bandana around the head *Women*: Leggings
Heavy Metal Rocker *Unisex*	Long black leather jacket, black T-shirt with print, leather pants, snakeskin boots
Pimp/Hooker *Men, Women*	*Men*: White suit, colorful shirt, white loafers, snap-brim hat *Women*: Miniskirt, décolleté top, fishnet stockings, feather boa, plateau shoes/boots
Hip-Hopper *Men*	Baggy blue jeans, oversized T-shirt, logoed clothing, chunky gold jewelry, necklace pendants, diamond-encrusted rings, baseball cap or beanie, white sneakers
Glamourist *Men, Women*	*Men*: Bright colors, leopard prints, shirt frills, ruffles, rhinestones, gold jewelry, antiquity symbols *Women*: Stiletto heels
Clubber *Unisex*	Tight pants, tank top, cropped top, Lycra, Lurex, shiny fabrics, sarong (when at the beach)
Goth *Unisex*	Black clothes, long coat, flouncy shirt, velvet, satin, lace, silver jewelry, black nail polish, long black boots *Women*: Flowing robes, black fishnet stockings
Grunge *Unisex*	Army surplus clothing, loose T-shirt with print, heavy black boots, oversized knitted cap

Hobo *Men*	Ragged, tattered clothing; hat or cap; drab colors
Hippie *Unisex*	Handmade look, caftan, patches on clothing, fringe on clothing, oversized sweater, tie-dye patterns, macramé bag, Love and Peace symbols, Teva sandals
Rastafarian *Men, Women*	*Men*: Black, green, yellow, and red crochet wool hat; cotton batik shirt; leather sandals; African jewelry *Women*: Head wraps, turbans
Dandy *Men*	Mixes of colors and patterns like paisley, stripes, and plaids and purple, orange, and red; fabrics like brocade, velour, and velvet; vest, hat (beret), and scarf
Artsy *Men, Women*	*Men*: Black vest, "granddad" undershirt, scarf, sixpence, Birkenstock sandals *Women*: Very loose-fitted dresses, layer-upon-layer, over-sized knits, extra-long scarves, turquoise jewelry, oversized jewelry, Mary Jane shoes
Romantic *Men, Women*	*Men*: Red or pastel colored trousers, cardigan, bow tie, neck scarf, Argyle patterns, pink, straw hat or fedora, loafers with tassels *Women*: Pleated skirt, twinset, Chelsea collar, floral prints, pastels, rose colors, hat, pearl earrings, pearl necklaces, ballerina shoes
Tweedy *Men, Women*	*Men*: Tweed jacket, jodhpurs, sixpence, oilskin jacket *Women*: Quilted jacket, kilt, tartans
Victorian *Men, Women*	*Men*: Bibs and braces, collarless shirt, monochrome colors, straw hat, pudding-bowl haircut, Abe Lincoln beard *Women*: Long-sleeved "prairie dress" with hems between ankle and midcalf, long stockings, monochrome colors, bonnet, shawl
Golfer *Men*	Checked-patterned trousers, diamond-patterned Argyle, golf-style shoes
Sporty *Men, Women*	*Men*: Varsity jacket, chinos/khaki, tattersall-patterned shirt, cable knits, turtleneck, deck shoes *Women*: Pantsuit, blouson
Surfer *Unisex*	Loose-fitted T-shirt with print; colorful Bermuda shorts; flip-flops; wrap-around sunglasses; leather or hemp short necklace, bracelet, and/or anklet

Skateboarder *Unisex*	Baggy pants; oversized, layered, colored T-shirt; skate-board shoes
Athletic *Unisex*	Track suit or hoodie sweatshirt, nylon, fitted T-shirt, sweat-pants, sneakers
Trucker *Men*	Blue jeans, suspenders, unbuttoned plaid shirt, loose T-shirt, work boots, trucker cap
Minimalist *Unisex*	Jackets without collars, turtleneck sweater, understated clothes, no decoration, black, beige (summer)
Amish *Men, Women*	*Men*: Vest, suspenders, straight-pins to hold clothes together; wide-brimmed straw summer hat; black felt winter hat; black, white, blue; solid colors only *Women*: Calf-length plain-cut dress, cape, hair pulled back into a bun and covered under a bonnet
Three-Piece Suit *Men, Women*	*Men*: Three-piece suit, light blue shirt, ascot, pocket watch, pocket square, suspenders, cuff links, wingtip shoes, trench coat, crocodile-skin accessories, decorative cane *Women*: Hat
Pinstriped *Men, Women*	*Men*: Black or dark gray pinstriped, single-breasted suit; discreet tie; white shirt; black shoes *Women*: Chanel-style tweed or bouclé suit, pumps
Corporate *Men, Women*	*Men*: Dark double-breasted suit, white Oxford dress shirt, blue- or claret-colored tie, Oxford shoes *Women*: Suits for women, monochrome colors
Collegiate *Men*	Dark blue blazer, monogrammed shirt, stripes, heraldic insignia, grey trousers
Preppy *Men, Women*	*Men*: Navy blue wool blazer or blouson, button or polo shirt, beige chinos/khakis, penny loafers *Women*: Shirt in pastel colors, cardigan, full skirt

DRESS CODE COMMUNICATION

When we go to work, shopping, on a vacation, to a restaurant, to church, to the movies, to a sports game, to a picnic, or to a school reunion, we venture outside of our homes and—depending on where we live—there will be crowds or small groups of people to mix with. Dress codes help us define ourselves and classify other people, and this again makes it easier for us to navigate when mingling and socializing, especially when we are among people who are representative of different lifestyles. When we see someone who has the same dress code that we have, we infer that this other person may also have the same taste in home decoration, cars, movies, and books that we do— maybe even the same political views and religion. Often this will be the case, though there are also many exceptions.

Dress codes affect the social relations that people have in other ways, too. Even people who do not know or care about style of any kind know how to use the terms *ugly*, *bad taste*, or *weird*, which are all the words we need to communicate that we do not want to relate to someone. Most people know what colors, patterns, and furniture they like—and dislike. The writer Edmund White described in his autobiography that his father disapproved of men's jewelry, colored shirts, button-down collars, bold designs, sports clothes, and white socks.[42] And many men and women are just like him: they have personal rules of style.

In many areas we use the word *taste* to describe what we like. *Taste* is the obvious word to use when we talk about what we eat and drink, what we like to read, the movies we want to watch, and the music we like. For instance, we say, "My taste in food" (not "My style in food"). Taste is about what we can see and read (art, movies, and literature), what we can taste (food and drink), what we can smell (fragrance), what we can hear (music, language), and what we can feel (dance and travel). We typically use the word *style*, however, to describe what we like in strictly visual product categories; this goes for clothing, home decoration, cars—products with aesthetic elements, products that are not solely functional. So while *style* and *taste* are synonyms, they also have distinct uses.

The synonymous qualities of *taste* and *style* are worth noting because more and more classification in the twenty-first century is about taste and style—it is about what gives us pleasure and what appeals to us aesthetically. It is about dressing in a certain style and identifying with the style, feeling that this particular style "is really me." Like, for instance, among the ladies who lunch at the ninth-floor eatery at the Manhattan department store Barney's in New York. Some of this group of women wear clothes designed by Tory

Burch. "Her clothes have become our uniform," one socially prominent woman told *Vanity Fair*. On any random day in 2007, more than 10 percent of the lunching ladies at Barney's wore clothing designed by Tory Burch. As the magazine concluded, just by wearing a Tory Burch design, women "can be members of the Tory Burch Beach and Country Club—no reference letters required."[43] Another woman told her journalist husband that when wearing Lululemon yoga clothing, "I really do feel that I'm part of a secret club." Another woman about to move from New York City to Westchester, New York, was told by a local, "It's fine if you like Lululemon because that's all women wear up here."[44] Clothing can create bonds and, therefore, clothing brand names have become part of our vocabulary (more on this in the following chapters).

Like cowboys, bikers, hip-hoppers, the Amish, and many others, the women who wear Tory Burch and Lululemon clothing also communicate with their clothes. The question is, what do the women who wear Tory Burch clothing communicate? If a group of people like the style of a designer—the cut, the patterns, the fabrics, and the colors that the designer uses—they can certainly be said to "belong" to a fan club of the designer. The dress code of the fan club is, of course, the clothes of that designer and other designers with similar flare. To the extent that the Tory Burch fans base their identity on belonging to a fan club (or, as *Vanity Fair* humorously put it, being part of the imaginary Tory Burch Beach and Country Club), the Tory Burch style is a designer dress code.

As with all designer dress codes, the exact style of the Tory Burch dress code will change as the designer changes her designs. Though there are many people who will say that they are fans of a certain fashion designer and wear his or her designs, the fact remains that the style of many fashion designers changes from year to year. This makes designer clothing difficult to classify (and decode) for people not interested in fashion. However, people keenly interested in fashion will know how to distinguish between designer styles; they can easily classify the latest fashion and label a person as, for instance, a trendsetter or a fashionista. Fashion styles can be dress codes, though it may seem contradictory that a style that changes all the time can be a dress code. But in order to make the nonverbal communication of the fashion trends effective, fashion magazines are there to inform and elaborate on what's in and what has got to go (among other reasons). Glossy pictorial spreads update the fashion conscious about what is the new trendsetter style, which enables them to better recognize each other. (It is worth noting that people who stick to well-established dress codes do not have a need for magazines to tell them about their style because their dress code is the same from year to year and they know what clothes to look for when shopping.)

EQUALITY IN STYLE

Once upon a time, when men and women had more distinct, fixed roles in American society, it made sense that there were vast differences in how they dressed. But as gender roles have changed, men and women have achieved greater equality. This was bound to lead to changes in the way we communicate—also through clothing. For instance, where it was once somewhat shocking for a woman to wear pants, nowadays it's commonplace. Men and women can better communicate nonverbally through their clothing when they have the option of wearing the same style. Both can wear preppy clothes, for example. It will, therefore, make sense that the growing equality between men and women manifests itself in creating the possibility for the two sexes to dress even more similarly. One example of this change is that jewelry is being worn more and more by men.

For a long time in the twentieth century, jewelry was something worn almost exclusively by women. If men wore jewelry, they were considered effeminate. Whatever people may think, today a growing number of men are wearing jewelry, and not just finger rings. In men's jewelry there are all kinds of styles available. For instance, there is jewelry from Jacob Arabar, who has specialized in creating expensive, glamorous jewelry for men. Arabar's customers tend to be megarich male hip-hoppers who preen themselves in a way that is how some women strive to perfect their appearance.[45] Their style may be different from the majority of men, but they have the same motives of other men: they want to attract women, and they employ the same style as the women they want to attract. As hip-hop style is available for both men and women, the two sexes have the chance to let each other know that they like the same style, in an intimate setting or from across the street.

Los Angeles Galaxy soccer player David Beckham is known for paying a lot of attention to his style. In his autobiography, *My World*, he tells about this important aspect of his life: "[My wife] Victoria and I love shopping for outfits on a Saturday, then getting ready later, going out and having a great night. Sometimes we [get] in the same gear on purpose, but other times we do it without knowing what the other one is going to wear. We just end up in similar clothes."[46] Just from casual observation it seems to be rare to see couples who have completely opposite styles.

Today's dress codes hold considerable variation for both women and men. They can be simple and practical, or colorful and decorative. But, as we shall see, our present-day dress codes cannot compete with the splendor of past Native American dress codes, though this does not mean that there are no longer tribes in North America. Because there are.

Chapter 5

TO BE OR NOT TO BE A TRIBE
Putting the Pieces in Order

*W*earing a hat to church has been customary for women for centuries. For African-American women, wearing a hat to church is an ingrained part of who they are. "I think that adorning the head is a retention of African traditions. . . . Hats are part of us," Dolores Smith told the author of the book *Crowns*, a pictorial exploring extravagant headdress styles for church. Dorothy Graham-Wheeler is quoted in the book as saying, "I don't want to go to church without my hat. They won't look at me."[1]

Hats, caps, and other types of adornments (on the head or other parts of the body) play a significant role in how we define ourselves and classify other people. Along with clothing, these adornments represent an important aspect of present-day life in the United States—just as adornments did in the 1600s when the first European settlers encountered the Native Americans.

The names of the Apache, Cheyenne, and Sioux—along with many others of the best-known Native American tribes—conjure different images to a variety of people. To many, it is probably the tribes' ways of dressing that first springs to mind. The Native American tribes back in the 1600s certainly knew how to use clothes, adornments, and other designed and natural objects to create their own unique styles. For instance, the Blackfoot had long hair while the Osage shaved their heads. The Sioux used eagle feathers in their headdress as a symbol of Thunderbird, the Eagle God. Corresponding to different climates, some tribes wore very little clothing while others were fully clothed. Back in history the Native Americans were quite systematic in how they combined different clothing and natural objects (such as feathers) into a style. And they rarely changed their style. If it changed too much, nobody would stand a chance of knowing who was friend and who was foe in case there was a clash between two tribes.[2]

Like the Native Americans of past centuries who dominated North America, today we also wear different, unique clothes and adornments that are just as varied. Every time a group of people has needed to express that they were different from others, they have created their own dress code, even though it may sometimes just be about changing or refining an existing dress code (as pointed out in chapter 4).

The Native Americans certainly did not communicate just through their clothing. They used song, dance, smoke signals, and, of course, their own languages (there were hundreds of linguistically distinct tribes).[3] Some were able to understand each other, but certainly not all. For all tribes, however, clothing served as a nonverbal communication tool—just like clothes do today. Actually, there are an abundance of similarities between then and now. If we look at the nonverbal communication tools that were available to the Native Americans and compare them with present-day nonverbal communication tools, only very few of the elements that were used by the Native Americans in the 1600s are not still in use today. Feathers still adorn some church hats. (Though not to the same extent as in the early 1900s when feathers were so popular as an adornment for women's hats that in 1903 alone, five million birds were killed to supply the demand.)[4] The number of adornments available to a Native American in the 1600s and the number available to a present-day American is about the same. This is shown in figure 5.1.

The different objects highlighted in figure 5.1 come in many different shapes and colors. In other words, we have a choice to make when we dress and decorate ourselves. By making this choice we reveal our taste—and sometimes a lot more. Clothing and all kinds of decoration that we use can be revealing lifestyle markers. How much is revealed depends upon how strong the symbolism of the lifestyle marker is.

Figure 5.1. Elements in Nonverbal Communication, Then and Now

	Native Americans in the 1600s	Present-day Americans
Head/Hair	Hairstyles Hair bands Hair adornments Head adornments Earrings Colored hair	Hairstyles Hair bands Hats Earrings Colored hair
Face	Face paint Masks	Makeup Piercings Glasses Sunglasses
Body	Clothing Body paint	Clothing Tattoos
Feet	Moccasins Boots Ankle bracelets	Shoes Boots Socks Ankle bracelets
Accessories	Jewelry	Jewelry Watches Bags Gloves
Symbols	Feathers Religious symbols	Branded clothing Religious symbols Membership and other 　symbols
Miscellaneous	Tomahawks Bows and arrows	Knives Mobile phones MP3 players

A wedding ring is one of the most universal lifestyle markers—telling the world that your life is organized in a marriage. Some of the groups mentioned in previous chapters have distinct ways of telling the world of their marital status. For instance, among the Amish unmarried women wear white aprons; wives wear black or dark colors. An Amish man with a beard shows that he is married.[5] Among the Hare Krishna an orange *dhoti* indicates celibacy, and a white one indicates marriage.

People also can tell the world that they are parents by putting a "Baby on Board" sticker on their car or lug around any of the multitude of baby accoutrements that are available in baby stores today. Mothers in particular may wear (childish) jewelry that their children have made, thereby signaling their motherhood. LA Galaxy soccer star David Beckham has tattooed the names of his three sons on different parts of his body, and more and more parents are also having the names of their children tattooed on their bodies.[6]

Tattoos were originally introduced into Western society by sailors who had learned about the technique in the South Pacific in the 1700s, but other groups, most notably bikers and heavy metal rockers, started using this originally nonconformist symbol after World War II.[7] Today so many people have tattoos that tattoos in themselves do not symbolize anything other than a preference for tattoos, but a person's individual tattoo can have specific meaning to an individual or group. Exactly as jewelry designer Anna Sheffield expressed when she was asked about her tattoos by a journalist, "Back in the day, when I was thinking about who I wanted to be in life, I thought, *Okay, no matter what, the tattoos will always remind me of the person I am now.*"[8]

Symbols that express aspects of geographical location are also popular. For decades New York's Big Apple was one such symbol (originally it was a symbol of New York State) that has adorned millions of T-shirts, coffee mugs, and bumper stickers—now in competition with the I ♥ New York T's. In Kansas, the Jayhawk is a popular state symbol that adorns clothing and other items that can function as mementos. In Texas, the Texas flag—as is the case with the flags of the other forty-nine states—is not just displayed at public buildings and private residences; it also adorns T-shirts, cups, magnets, and many other items. For residents these symbols express their identity, and for a tourist they can be a souvenir to remember a memorable holiday but also to tell the world and oneself that, for instance, "I have been to the Big Apple," "I identify with New York," or "I am a world traveler."

Lifestyle markers exist in all religions. Perhaps best known are the Christian cross and the Jewish Star of David. Catholics wear pendants showing images of religious figures, for instance, Saint Christopher, the patron saint of travelers. In several religions praying beads are used as lifestyle markers. Observant Jews wear yarmulkes. Hasidic Jews, easily identifiable because of their earlocks, also wear clothing according to how observant of their religion they are. If very observant, they wear clothing that has not changed for centuries: a large-rimmed beaver hat, long overcoat worn as a jacket, and slipper-like shoes with white knee socks.[9]

In politics, you can use the logo of the Republican Party or the Democratic Party (respectively, the elephant and the donkey) to signal political—and more directly, your social and economic—values and views. When the logos are put on badges, buttons, tiepins, T-shirts, magnets, and so on, they also function as lifestyle markers. Many other symbols that have political significance, such as the peace symbol (popularized by hippies in the 1960s), can be lifestyle markers. Many interest groups and professional organizations have their own symbols.

Signet rings are typical lifestyle markers for some men. Some wear college fraternity rings. Members of Masonic and other lodges have their own rings that can be worn to signal membership.

For many sports fans, sports merchandise plays an enormous role in creating and maintaining sports club identity. In some sports, fans will change their clothing when they go to games and dress completely in the colors of their favorite team, wearing hats and many other designed objects that they would not normally wear. Some paint their faces with the colors of their team.

More and more magazines, radio stations, and arts institutions sell T-shirts with their logos on them. For the institution it is about marketing, but for the persons who wear them they are lifestyle markers.

Communities of people with certain sexual fetishes may create their own symbols. Piercings were originally one such fetish and symbol among sadomasochists. From this sexual minority, nose rings and pierced eyebrows, lips, and navels became symbols of moderate youthful rebellion—seeming daring to peers and shocking to parents. In the beginning of the twenty-first century, body piercings became mainstream and lost their rebellious aura.[10]

In the 1960s wearing an earring in the right ear was a symbol that gay men used to communicate their sexuality, though today this is no longer the case.[11] When the gay movement came into prominence in the 1970s, lesbians and gay men started using symbols that could be worn on clothing. First it was the pink triangle, which had been used to single out homosexuals in Nazi concentration camps; it later came to symbolize the oppression of gay men.[12] Created in the late 1970s, the rainbow flag with six different colors symbolizing the diversity in the gay community has gained wide use, not only as a flag but also as pins, stickers, and bath towels. Some fly rainbow flags outside their homes.

On St. Patrick's Day people of Irish descent use the green, orange, and white colors of the Irish flag on hats, pins, or batons (as mentioned in chapter 3), though today in many big cities, people of all backgrounds wear green to the parades. Yellow ribbons have been a symbol associated with those waiting for the return of a loved one, either in prison or at war, at least since the 1800s. Originally it was family members who tied a yellow ribbon to a tree or another outside object to show that a loved one was missed.[13] The ribbon is now used in other colors as well. The red ribbon was created in 1991 by a New York group called Visual AIDS and has become a worldwide known symbol for the fight against AIDS. The pink ribbon has become of symbol of support for victims of breast cancer.

Well-known corporate logos can also be lifestyle markers. Many people relate to symbols such as Nike's Swoosh logo and the brand's in-your-face "Just Do It" slogan. Few logos are as well known around the world as the Swoosh, but there are scores of logos that have similar qualities in individual lifestyle groups. For instance, the polo player logo of Ralph Lauren has a strong appeal to people who like clothing that is understated. Among hip-hoppers the Jumpman logo has a certain niche.

The alphabet of nonverbal symbols is continuously expanding. If our identity changes, so too does the way we express our identity through the use of lifestyle markers. In the twenty-first century companies and their designers are also creating whole new categories of lifestyle markers—from cell phones to MP3 players—that can communicate consumer tastes and style preferences (more on this in the following chapters).

THE TRIBAL SPIRIT

Like the Native Americans several centuries back, today we have a whole range of objects available to express our identity and create unique dress codes. But does that make us tribal? To answer that question we first have to define what a tribe is. Many people have some idea what a tribe is, maybe based on their knowledge of tribes from history books, or from different kinds of media—Hollywood movies, perhaps. Though when we think of tribes today, many people may also first and foremost conjure images of people living on Native American reservations (or maybe of people living in Africa, South America, or Asia).

One peculiar point is that we seem to associate terms like *tribe* and *tribal* only with people living far away from the vast asphalt jungles and bustling city centers. We grant that Native Americans are tribal, and when we see people using colorful clothing in "primitive" societies in Asia, Africa, and South America, we think, *They are tribal.* But when we see different dress codes on the streets of Manhattan, at Miami's South Beach, or around the Appalachian Mountains, we prefer to use the more sophisticated term *subculture.* Sometimes we even specify a certain characteristic of the subculture, as in youth culture or biker culture or a more-or-less stereotypical category such as *hillbilly.* But we do not use the word *tribe.*

The Romans coined the word *tribe* and gave it the meaning of division of people into groups. The Romans' division of people was not about territories as such because all the tribes were in Roman territory and lived among each other. But in present-day lingo we have often defined tribes as a group of people living within a certain territory. However, it is a misconception that tribes are mostly about territory. Also, in so-called "primitive" societies, there are tribes that are not about territory or ethnicity at all. For instance, in the Pushtunwali tribe in Afghanistan there is no such thing as a Pushtun territory or ethnicity. A Pushtun is simply someone who speaks the language Pushtu. *Pushtunwali* literally means to "do Pushtu." If you can speak the language, you are a member of the tribe.[14]

If tribes were only characterized by territory, many tribes, both past and present, would not be tribes. Many Native American tribes were nomadic, such as the Apache, the Sioux, and the Shoshone.[15] Today there are also many tribes in Africa, Asia, and South America that are nomadic: the Tuaregs in the Sahara Desert of Northern Africa and the Kayapo in the Amazon Delta in South America.[16] In Africa, different tribes mix in the same geographical areas, at least in towns of a certain size. They mix in the same way as people do in the United States, and though some tribes may feel strongly about borders—just as we do about our communities (not least the gated ones)—they do not automatically start tribal wars when members of different tribes pass through each other's territories.[17]

Some tribes were—and are—territorial. When this is the case, the defining characteristic of the tribe in question is based on geography and history. But the general principle is that tribal behavior is based on a way of life. This means that the tribal behavior can come from any of the ten identity categories that lifestyle can be based on. However, tribal behavior is always based on at least one identity category *combined* with a distinct dress code. The reason for the combination of a way of life *and* a dress code is simple: since a tribe can be based on any identity category, the need to communicate differences to many people at the same time makes dress codes an extremely important aspect of tribal societies. If people did not dress in the same way, the tribes themselves would have great difficulty in recognizing members of their own tribe—contributing all kinds of misunderstandings as a consequence. A tribe must systematically dress in the same way to be called a tribe.

Tribal behavior is a reality all over the world, in the past and present. Today we seem to dislike the word *tribe* when we look at present-day society, probably for several reasons: it reminds us of the conflicts on the prairies with Native Americans that many would like to forget or ignore. Another reason is that we think that we organize our lives very differently from the Native Americans in the 1600s, as well as the present-day "primitive" societies. We like to believe that we are much more "advanced" socially. One excuse is also that for many years we had very little knowledge about tribal societies on other continents, and what little knowledge most people had was from Hollywood movies. These reasons may have made some sense in the twentieth century. But now that we know much more about our way of life *and* the lifestyles of other societies, we have to realize that we are just as tribal in present-day United States as the Native Americans were centuries back. We do what other tribes do—we also cluster together with people who share the same way of life and have unique dress codes that reflect the way of life.

Tribal behavior is certainly not a new phenomenon, neither in North America nor in Europe. Tribes have existed in Europe for many millennia. If we go back just two thousand years, there were tribes like the Cantii, the Parisii, and the Atrebates in what today is known as Great Britain.[18] If we go back five hundred years in what today is North America, there were tribes like the Lakota, the Cherokee, and the Comanche.[19] What we have to realize is that whether people live in the South American jungle, the Sahara Desert in Africa, rural Europe, or urban America, they are tribal and can be members of a tribe. The operative word is *can* because today we are not all members of a tribe.

TO BE OR NOT TO BE A TRIBE

There are tribes all over the world, and we also have to acknowledge that there are non–Native American tribes in the United States. While some of these tribes have existed for centuries, there are also tribes that have emerged during the twentieth century, and new tribes can emerge in the future.

To spot a present-day tribe we have to identify groups of people who share the same way of life *and* have the same dress code. It is not difficult to find people who qualify. We can go to the neighboring towns of Colorado City and Eldorado across the Arizona-Texas border. Here, young and old women alike dress in an old-fashioned, almost Victorian style. The women and girls usually wear homemade long-sleeved "prairie dresses," with hems between ankle and midcalf, along with long stockings underneath. The women do not cut their hair short and they wear a coif to cover it. They do not wear makeup and are not allowed to wear pants or any skirt above the knees. Men wear plain clothing, usually a long-sleeved shirt and full-length pants. Here and elsewhere in the neighboring states, there are people like the inhabitants of Colorado City and Eldorado who belong to the fundamentalist Church of Jesus Christ of Latter-day Saints, a polygamous religious sect (related to the Mormon Church, which, however, disavows any connection and no longer permits polygamy). They all have the same dress code, and, therefore, they are a tribe.

Many present-day tribes are organized around certain religious beliefs. This is also the case with the Rastafarians. Rastafarianism goes back to ancient Ethiopia and precolonial Jamaica. It is a mix of African traditions and Hebrew teachings with some Hispanic influence. The lion is an important symbol, representing virility, courage, and wisdom. The Rastafarian dreadlock hairdo and unkempt beard together represent the mane of a lion. Like lions in nature, the searing Rastafarian look is intended to spur dread in outside communities. The colors of the Ethiopian flag—red, yellow, and green—are always part of the Rastafarian attire, symbolizing a commitment to Africa. A ship motif badge is a significant symbol to the Rastafarians, representing the hope of returning to Africa.[20]

If you are a Catholic nun, you have a 24/7 job, so being a nun is a lifestyle. When nuns have their own unique dress code that they wear most of the day, often a black or grey dress with a bonnet, they are also members of a tribe. When monks all don the same dress code—the cassock—they are also a tribe. Not all nuns or monks belong to the same tribe. Variations in their religious life and the way they dress may indicate a specific tribe. The Hare Krishnas—a sect founded in 1965 by an immigrant—have their easily identifiable dress code: dhotis (a cloth wrapped around the waist), kurtas (long shirts), and saris. They are also a tribe.

Being a tribe is not just about religion. There are many nonreligious tribes, including cowboys who work as ranch hands or rodeo riders who typically live in the Southwest, listen to country and Western music, and share a unique dress code. The bikers who have a passion for motorcycles and typically listen to heavy metal music also have a tribal uniform: the black leather jacket, blue jeans, and engineer's boots. Rap music is an integral part of being a hip-hopper, and hip-hoppers have their own unique dress code. So do the Goths, who wear black clothing and black makeup and dye their hair black. Their way of life revolves around so-called death rock and horror movies. They also have an appetite for Gothic literature (themes such as horror, ghosts, haunted houses, darkness, death, decay, and madness, often from the Victorian area). Nudists prefer to live as much of their life in the nude, whether they go to the beach, play cards, enjoy a meal, or are on vacation. Their dress code is nudity. For both practical and legal reasons they cannot be nude all the time, but they live up to the definition of a tribe.

There is no doubt that dress codes are the strongest communicator when they are combined with a certain way of life, for instance, a religious way of life (the Amish, Hasidic Jews, and Hare Krishnas) or a geographical way of life (cowboys). Not all dress codes are necessarily tribal looks, but if we take a closer look at the dress codes that were identified in chapter 4, we'd find that most of these are tribal looks. Figure 5.2 lists the thirty-two dress codes from figure 4.7 and indicates if the dress code is tribal.

If a common dress code is lacking, we cannot call a group of people with the same way of life a tribe. For instance, there is a group of people in Florida who live in an old-fashioned town with pre-1940s architecture in traditional Southeastern style with welcoming front porches. The look and feel they prefer is that of a close-knit community with a traditional family focus. This particular community is called Celebration, a town founded by the Walt Disney Company in 1996. It is a gated community with around ten thousand inhabitants.[21] People have moved from all over the United States to be part of Celebration. But the inhabitants dress in different ways. When inhabitants go into the streets of Celebration, other people cannot determine from the way they dress whether they belong there or are visitors. When the citizens of Celebration go to other places, they will not be able to identify each other. They simply dress too differently—they do not have same dress code. Thus the "Celebrationists" are not a tribe.

Figure 5.2. Tribal Looks Based on Dress Codes

DRESS CODE	TRIBAL LOOK
Cowboy	Yes. Cowboys are a tribe, based on work and/or music.
Lumberjack	Yes. Lumberjacks are a tribe, based on work and geography.
Hillbilly	Yes, when based on geography and work.
Biker	Yes. Bikers are a tribe, based on motorcycle driving.
Heavy Metal Rocker	Yes. Heavy metal rockers are a tribe, based on heavy metal music.
Pimp/Hooker	For women, yes, when based on work (prostitution).
Hip-Hopper	Yes. Hip-hoppers are a tribe, based on music.
Glamorist	Rarely.
Clubber	Yes. Clubbers are a tribe, based on the leisure activity of clubbing.
Goth	Yes, it is the tribal look of Goths.
Grunge	Yes, when based on music.
Hobo	Rarely.
Hippie	Yes, when based on political values.
Rastafarian	Yes, based on Rastafarianism.
Dandy	Yes, when based on work (artist; creative professions).
Artsy	Yes, when based on work (artist; creative professions).
Romantic	Rarely.
Tweedy	Can be the tribal look of some (conservative) scholars.
Victorian	Yes, when based on religion.
Golfer	Yes, when based on golfing.
Sporty	Rarely.
Surfer	Yes, when based on surfing.
Skateboarder	Yes, when based on skateboarding.
Athletic	Rarely.
Trucker	Yes, when based on work (manual labor).
Minimalist	Yes, when based on work (creative industries).
Amish	Yes, based on religion.
Three-Piece Suit	Can be the tribal look of some (conservative) scholars and businessmen.
Pinstriped	Dress code for many working in finance but rarely a tribal look.
Corporate	Rarely.
Collegiate	Rarely.
Preppy	Rarely.

Sharing the same dress code is what most clearly distinguishes a tribe from a group. While groups play a vital role in most people's lives, they are different from tribes. What is important is that there are many different *kinds* of groups that can play a role in people's lives. Most people are not aware of the distinctions between these different kinds of groups, but from a sociological point of view we can distinguish between groups and social categories: all humans belong to social categories based on, for instance, nationality, race, ethnicity, gender, age, or sexual identity.

Belonging to a social category is not based on interaction between people. Californians, West Virginians, New Yorkers, and Chicagoans are social categories. Californians, West Virginians, New Yorkers, Chicagoans, and people with many other regional and local identities are too different to be anything like tribes. They neither have the same way of life nor the same dress code. The Conchs, the inhabitants of the Florida Keys, are not a tribe for the same reason. They, too, are a social category.

The rich also constitute a social category. You can be wealthy like rapper Jay-Z, pro basketball player Shaquille O'Neal, and Microsoft founder Bill Gates. These three men all have different backgrounds and were not born rich. Because wealthy people are not alike, they do not all organize their lives in the same way. Also, they do not dress differently from other people. Bill Gates, one of the richest men in the United States, dresses the same way as millions of other people who shop in stores like the Gap or Brooks Brothers. Therefore, rich people are a social category, not a tribe.

Likewise, gay men are not a tribe. All gay men do not think of their sexuality as their lifestyle, and there is certainly no uniform way of dressing for all gay men. Therefore, gay men are a social category.

Most people also belong to groups that are characterized by some kind of interaction between the members. How much interaction will vary, depending on the kind of group—for example, whether it is a formal or informal group. In formal groups often there are certain rules of admission, which is not the case with informal groups (an informal group may be people who get together for a barbeque and then disperse after the meal). For instance, doctors, lawyers, or similar professional groups are formal groups because they are often bound together by some kind of organization that offers membership. Their profession gives them a lot of identity and may be a lifestyle to some but not to all. For some their profession is "just a job." When not working doctors and lawyers, for example, dress too differently to be a tribe.

Sometimes the words *tribe* and *clan* are used as synonyms. But a clan is very different from a tribe. Clans are made up of extended family relations based on blood: typically the members of a clan have had a common forefather in the past, hundreds of years ago or more recently. In principle they can be very different in all other respects. Any family with a strong sense of shared history and solidarity can be called a clan, but obviously this has nothing to do with dress codes. Members of a clan can dress completely differently from each other.

It is the sharing of the same way of life *and* the same dress code that defines members of a tribe. There are many associations that may sound like tribes but they are not because this one aspect—a common dress code—is lacking. This goes for associations like the African-American Filmmakers Association, the Association for Women Geoscientists, the Organization of Black Designers, and the Hispanic Dental Association.

Even when a certain dress code plays a huge part in an association's existence, this does not necessarily make the members a tribe. Passionate fans of sports teams adorn themselves in the colors of their team—whether it be basketball teams like the Chicago Bulls, the New York Knicks, or the Indiana Pacers; or football teams like the Dallas Cowboys, the New England Patriots, or the Washington Redskins—but they only do this for a short while when watching a game. Therefore, this "costume" dress code is not what they wear 24/7. Their dress code is undoubtedly highly differentiated outside of the stadium. Only if there are people who wear the clothing of their favorite sports team 24/7 are they a tribe. However, this is a rarity.

One important aspect about being part of a tribe is that it does not require that all members of the tribe be clones of each other. In his classic study of tribes, anthropologist Morton Fried found numerous examples of tribes in which the members of a tribe did not even speak in the same way or practice the exact same rituals. Based on his research, Fried concluded that tribes in general are less rigidly organized than would be expected by many people.[22] Present-day tribes in Africa, Asia, and South America are no more rigid in their way of life than the present-day tribes in North America. And while clustering is a typical characteristic of many tribes, there is also mobility among tribes. Tribal members may move for all kinds of reasons—love, work, family relations, illness—just like everybody else. The only difference may be that nowadays we use the term *mobile* instead of *nomadic*, the latter being a word we like to reserve for more "primitive" societies.

Many people in the United States are just as nomadic as people in Asia, Africa, or South America. About 16 percent of Americans move each year,[23] and in the twentieth century there were several nomadic movements within the United States. After World War II white Appalachians took the "hillbilly highway" to boom cities, such as Cleveland and Detroit.[24] Southern African-Americans moved north, many to Chicago, in the 1950s. Senior citizens went to Florida, Southern California, and Arizona for retirement in the last decades of the twentieth century. At the turn of the twenty-first century, well-to-do people in creative industries moved away from big cities and headed to Austin, Texas; Portland, Oregon; Aspen and Denver, Colorado; and other cities that are known for a high quality of life and creative vibes but that are not as expensive as New York City or Los Angeles.

TRIBAL LIFE

Organizing one's life around one identity, 24/7, is the definition of a lifestyle. By adding a dress code and being just as systematic about the way you dress as you are about your identity is how we define a tribal life. But tribal life is often more complex than the formula

way of life + dress code = tribal life

would indicate. Tribal life encompasses all the elements that "glue" people's lives together, whether they are a tribe in North America or on any other continent.

Tribes create their own symbols, slang, meeting places, rituals, and traditions, which make them distinct. Music is often a particularly salient aspect of tribal life. Just as clothing is an important way to transform identity into everyday living and create a way of identifying like-minded people, so is music. This is what was notable about the hippies of the 1960s.

The origins of the hippies can be traced back to the mid-1950s, when a small group of young writers and artists settled in San Francisco, the California coastal town of Carmel, and the nearby Big Sur area. They were known as the Beats. (Many of the Beats originally resided in Greenwich Village in New York City.)

Several writers had been living in Carmel and Big Sur since the beginning of the twentieth century. Among them was Henry Miller, who had settled in Big Sur in 1947. It was his 1941 book *The Colossus of Maroussi* that many of the Beats regarded as their founding text. Among the original Beats were the writers Jack Kerouac and William S. Burroughs, the poet Allen Ginsberg, and the freewheeling free spirit Neal Cassady. The Beats had a preference for working-class heroes, jazz, and Eastern spiritualism.[25] It was a friend of Allen Ginsberg, Herbert Huncke, who first used the word "beat" to describe how he felt disconnected from society.[26] Jack Kerouac liked the word's suggestive tone of alienation, physical weariness, and the beatific. While writing in 1948, he used the word in his novel *On the Road*, which became one of the most innovative books of the 1950s with its breathless, ecstatic style.

What had started in the 1950s as a small group of artists settling in the Bay Area had a considerable influence on the development of the hippie lifestyle and the youth revolution that grew in San Francisco. "The mutation from Beat to hippie meant a switch . . . from a small group of writers and artists and jazz musicians to a mass youth movement. . . . The questioning of authority, the drugs, the experimental lifestyle, the leaning toward Eastern philosophy, all were carryover from the Beats," according to Ted Morgan in *Literary Outlaw: The Life and Times of William S. Burroughs*.[27]

The hippies had a completely different mix of identities than previous generations. In America in the 1960s there was a new political consciousness among young people—not least based on a strong opposition to the Vietnam War. Many young people were also influenced by Eastern religions, and some moved in together in communes. Their music taste was psychedelic and/or inspired by Eastern music, especially Indian. The hippies needed to communicate in a visual manner that they were different from "the establishment," and the most effective way to do that was—and is—through clothing and through music.

In the 1960s hippies started wearing military garments in a nonuniform way and mixing fatigues with other kinds of clothing—to "demilitarize" the army uniform. As aviator sunglasses were part of the military look, the hippies also started wearing them, as did singer-songwriter Bob Dylan (who was an inspiration to the hippies).[28] Blue jeans were also a part of the dress code, but the hippies made several adjustments to the design to make sure that they would not be confused with any of the other groups that also wore blue jeans. Their preference was for bell bottom jeans. Like many other youth subcultures, hippies transformed their identity into a way of life with a very effective dress code (including long hair for men) and distinct music.

Though the hippies are long gone (except, perhaps, for a few scattered communes), they were the epitome of a twentieth-century tribal culture. Their lifestyle was so all-encompassing that there is no doubt that they were a tribe—an observation that is also manifested in the naming of the tribute musical *Hair*, with its full title *Hair: The American Tribal Love-Rock Musical*.

Almost all tribes are "glued" together by music. For instance, to bikers the song "Born to Be Wild" is like a biker national anthem. The song was recorded by the US band Steppenwolf and played over the titles of the 1967 movie *Easy Rider*, a road movie classic. In many cases all it takes to belong to a tribe is listening to the music and dressing accordingly—which is not so different from the credo of the Pushtunwali tribe in Afghanistan who believe that if you can speak the language, you are a member of the tribe.

Tribes may have their own language, but often they have only their own codes that outsiders simply cannot understand. While it may be easy to identify a tribe by its dress code, identification by language or a tribe's jargon is another story. In many cases a dictionary can get the definitions right, but in other cases cracking the code is not that easy. When Bart Handford was in his twenties he started working at the White House, in a minor administrative position. He had not graduated from college at the time. In an interview he said, "From the moment I came to Washington, I've been surrounded by the smartest people from the best schools, and they seem to know something I don't, like they have all been taught a secret language."[29] This is not an uncommon feeling because codes—and the many symbols and rituals that connect people—serve two purposes: to invite some people in and to keep other people out. Who is invited in and who is kept out will vary from tribe to tribe or group to group. But in general, there is one thing that most typically will lead to being accepted: knowing the rules.

This is the experience of society hostess Denise Hale, who has learned personally what it takes to get accepted in some highly different social sets. Now an American citizen, she was born in Serbia with the given name Danica Radosavljevic. She married a wealthy Italian businessman when she was seventeen. After a divorce she married film director and "Hollywood royal" Vincente Minnelli. After yet another divorce she married San Francisco department store owner Prentis Cobb Hale. In an interview she said what no sociologist could express more succinctly: "If you know the rules, you belong; if you don't know them, you don't."[30]

The rules are about behavior, especially knowing how to behave among other people in the group or tribe. There are thick volumes on social etiquette, and as the many magazine and newspaper columns of the Dear Abby variety indicate, manners is a popular subject. But while there are some general rules about politeness, the reality is that events like christenings, weddings, and funerals are not governed by any universal social rules. And the rituals within different religious groups/tribes certainly are highly varied. As for nonreligious rituals among, say, bikers, surfers, hip-hoppers, golfers, and so on, their rules and rituals certainly vary. If you want to belong to a particular tribe or lifestyle group, you have to learn the rituals and other behaviors of that tribe or lifestyle group.

The rules also include knowing the names of persons, idols, places, histories, events, shared experiences, song and movie titles, as well as the names of bands and specific musicians who have become common reference points for the lifestyle group or tribe. Names of social venues (bars, restaurants, hotels, and clubs) and cultural venues (theaters, opera houses, museums) are also sometimes used to make it easier to discuss many aspects of different lifestyles and tribal life. Each group or tribe has different names for its gathering places. Figure 5.3 lists some tribes with examples of their tribal vocabulary.

Figure 5.3. Examples of Tribal Preferences, Lore, and Language[31]

Tribe Vocabulary	Cowboys	Bikers	Hip-Hoppers
Idols/Icons	The latest rodeo champ	Hell's Angels (the fighter pilots)	DJ Kool Herc
Place	Nashville, Tennessee	San Bernardino, California	South Bronx, New York
Music	Country music	"Born to Be Wild"	Rap
Movie	*High Noon*	*Easy Rider*	*White Men Can't Jump*
Gathering Place	Rodeo arena	Bike rally	Hip-hop club
Magazine	*Western Horseman*	*HOG Tales*	*The Source*
Colloquialisms	Dude	Coupon (traffic ticket)	Yo!

Returning to religious groups, they also have their own unique vernacular. In Judaism, Reform Jews usually say *temple*, Conservative Jews refer to *synagogue*, and Orthodox Jews to *shul*.[32] Besides being places of worship, synagogues, churches, mosques, and shrines are in fact also meeting places for members (but only if the attendants have the same dress code can members of a church, synagogue, or mosque be called a tribe).

Tribal meeting places are often outdoors, but they can take on many different shapes and forms:

- The Cowboys' Reunion Rodeo is an annual rodeo in Las Vegas where cowboys and country and Western fans meet to watch the traditional rodeo shows. Year-round there are similar rodeos all over the Southwest.
- The biker tribe has two huge annual gatherings: Daytona Beach Bike Week and Sturgis Motorcycle Rally. Each of these events draws about half a million attendees each year. Sturgis, South Dakota, a small township of six thousand people, is the annual host to the world's largest meeting of bikers. About five hundred thousand bikers gather there in August, where they can swap stories and purchase every type of clothing, accessory, gear, and equipment that a biker could want. There are also cruises named Hogs on the High Seas for bikers.
- Skateboarding is a sport with its own world cup, Globe World Cup Skateboarding. Throughout the year there are skateboarding competitions all over the world. Professionals, amateurs, and fans gather and the dress code typical of skateboarders dominates the scene.
- Nevada is host to Burning Man, an annual arts festival and temporary community based on radical self-expression in the Black Rock Desert. This gathering originally attracted people with a few dress codes including hippie, grunge, surfer, and skateboarder, but it is now visited by people with other dress codes as well.
- Any concert with a hip-hop artist attracts a gathering of hip-hoppers. However, there are also gatherings that are not just musical, such as the Hip-hop Summit Action Network, which is a grass-roots organization aiming to promote hip-hop through rallies, seminars, and other events in the United States.
- Nudists have the option to go on all-nude cruises (with nude diving and excursions to private islands), nudist beaches, and nudist holiday camps. Gunnison Beach, New Jersey, near Sandy Hook, is one famous nudist beach, but there are other

nudist beaches across the country. In the South of France there is an all-nude town. Each summer more than five thousand people from all over the world converge on Cap d'Agde, and they do all their socializing, eat all their meals, and go to the shops, banks, night clubs, and beach in the nude.

TRIBAL AMERICA

Apart from all the varying lifestyle markers and tribal symbols, the United States as a nation also has symbols, rituals, and traditions that are uniquely American. Not only is there the Stars and Stripes, but each of the fifty states also has its own flag, symbolizing the uniqueness of each state. The magnificent Bald Eagle of Maine is a common symbol, which was introduced by the Continental Congress in 1782 to symbolize the strength and independence of the new republic.[33] It is a powerful representation of independence, much more than just a bird.

The Fourth of July is a celebration of independence for all Americans—with school bands, volunteer fire departments, local businesses, politicians, dance troops, and veterans all waving flags. Although other countries celebrate their independence day similarly, few countries celebrate the end of the harvesting season the way Americans do. No matter what tribe or group you belong to, it is likely you take part in Thanksgiving.

Besides national symbols and national holidays many Americans also share some core values, such as individual achievement, hard work, and goal-oriented behavior. These and other American values are shared across lifestyles and tribes. In other words, a society consisting of many different tribes certainly does not equal a totally divided society.

Since the American Revolution the United States has, to a large extent, been a fairly horizontally organized society (as mentioned in chapter 2). This is still very much the case. However, this does not mean that there are no hierarchies, because there are. For example, in society at large African-Americans have been treated in a cruelly unequal way. Among all the different tribes and lifestyle groups, there exist all kinds of hierarchies. But despite the existence of many different lifestyles and tribes, the tradition of the United States continues to be that of a horizontally organized society. There are groups and social categories (men!) that dominate in political life. But if we focus on the tribes, there does not appear to be one tribe that dominates the whole country.

When the first European settlers arrived in North America, there were between three hundred and four hundred different native tribes spread all over the continent. Now with more than 300 million people living in the United States—compared to an estimated 18 million around the time when the first European settlers arrived—it would make sense for there to be many more tribes in present-day America.[34] But in all probability there are about the same number. First, the tribes are bigger today; second, most present-day Americans do not belong to a tribe. The majority of people live lifestyles that are different from belonging to a tribe. They have a well-established lifestyle and are part of a lifestyle group.

COWBOYS ARE NOT ALWAYS COWBOYS

The difference between a way of life and belonging to a tribe may not always be obvious, but the difference reflects the variety of ways we can organize our lives today. To demonstrate, we can use the cowboys.

If you want to make a living being a cowboy, there is no better place than the American Southwest. This is where being a cowboy is a way of life based on geography, work, and leisure. Yet the cowboy dress code as such does not have the same geographical limitations. There are people in other parts of the world who like the cowboy dress code and dress as a cowboy. Many may never have been on a ranch, or even on a horse for that matter. To them, dressing as a cowboy does not reflect a way of life. They may work in many different kinds of businesses, but enamored with the cowboy dress code, they will wear it when working and during their off-hours. This is the "dress code only" phenomenon.

The cowboy dress code may also just be a hobby or an interest, and dressing in the cowboy dress code is then only an occasional activity. These people will wear cowboy clothes and accessories once in a while, typically when going to a Western bar that can be found in many cities across the United States. For example, one guidebook wrote of a New York City country and Western club as a "midtown saloon for urban cowboys and cowgirls. There is no mechanical bull . . . but all the other ersatz dude ranch trappings are intact: rawhide and palomino banquettes, stage coach wheels, lassos, spurs, cacti, comely waitresses, and huge bouncers in ten-gallon-hats."[35] Outside of the club the patrons may wear a different kind of clothing. The occasional use of certain clothing items or a certain style is no indication of a lifestyle, and just owning certain clothes does not reflect a way of life or tribal affiliation.

Cowboys working as ranch hands and wearing the cowboy dress code are a tribe. Fans of country and Western music can also be a tribe. This is the case when their lives revolve around country music and they share the same dress code: Stetson hat, cowboy boots, blue jeans, and a shirt (more or less the same for men and women). The cowboy tribe has lots of similarities with the country music tribe, and they can easily be mixed up, but they get their identity from two different sources, work and music, respectively. The cowboy tribe will typically enjoy country music and also get a sense of identity from it. As this example illustrates, different tribes can have the same dress code—this may be confusing but it is a fact.

In a Western bar in Texas, or for that matter, anywhere in the United States, we can meet people who dress like cowboys but when they leave the bar, they have very different lives. Their lives can be categorized in one of three ways:

- *Way of life* is when a man works as a ranch hand and lives in the Southwestern United States. The cowboy dress code is his work uniform. When he is not working as a cowboy he dresses in a different way.
- *Dress code only* is when a person combines a number of designed objects in a fixed way, as in the cowboy dress code, but has no relation to the original way of life related to the dress code.

- *Tribe* is when a man works as a ranch hand, lives in the South-western United States, *and* adheres to the cowboy dress code 24/7; or it is when a man is a huge fan of country and Western music and adheres to the cowboy dress code 24/7.

People from all three categories may also travel to the National Rodeo Finals, where the best rodeo competitors meet to compete in such events as roping calves and wrestling steers. It is also here that the differences in lifestyle really show. Take Will Lowe, Tom McFarland, and Royce Ford. There is no doubt to which category these three rodeo riders belong. They have day jobs at ranches in Texas but are also often on the road competing in rodeos across the country. In an interview Tom McFarland said, "There [are] a lot of ways to make better money in the world, but I can't think of a better way to live. We have a blast all year long." The three cowboys are traveling partners on the rodeo circuit and are known as the Wolfpack. While competing in rodeos they have traveled a distance that corresponds to going around Earth three times. As Royce Ford said in the same interview, "We've ate, slept, and breathed rodeo. We're always talking about bucking horses."[36] The Wolfpack guys also always dress like cowboys. They combine a specific way of life and the cowboy dress code. Without a doubt they belong to the cowboy tribe.

FROM DRESS TO STYLE

How does a certain way of life and a certain dress code end up being combined and becoming a tribal look? In many cases the way of life and the dress code have evolved simultaneously. This was the case with the cowboys—it was a question of adopting a functional style that was often created by chance (nobody sat down and decided that this is how a cowboy should look, as mentioned in chapter 4). As for the bikers, their dress code evolved from the military past with a focus also on what was functional—and a need to look different from other tribes. Tribal dress codes are generally not planned or decided upon in any other way than by what is adapted by most people with a certain way of life.

As for the cowboy style, there is more to it than just Western-style clothing. The dress code is complemented by Western décor. According to *Cowboy Chic*, a book about Western home décor, present-day rugged, ranch-style furniture includes rustic wicker chairs, Navajo rugs, bleached cattle skulls, and three-dimensional cast-bronze pieces of cowboy life. Walls are made of logs and the river-rock stone fireplace is oversized. Brown and other earth tones dominate.[37] A cowboy may decorate his home in this style, but it is not a prerequisite for being a cowboy. Cowboys working as cowboys in the Southwest can—and do—decorate their homes in different ways. Cowboys for whom being a ranch hand is a way of life do not necessarily want to decorate their homes in the Western style. The style often seems to have more appeal to people who are not cowboys—people who like this particular aesthetic or are nostalgic.

Some people do identify with their home décor style to the extent that it becomes part of their identity. As with the other nine identity categories, style can also become a way of life. This happens when the person is surrounded in his home by a particular style that is a constant: she will buy products in the same style again and again. In other words, when a person wants to have the same style in clothing *and* home decoration, then that style becomes a style of living. With that we are back to chapter 1, where we were introduced to the two different ways of defining *lifestyle*: (1) Way of life, and (2) Style of living. We can be highly organized and systematic about both our life and our style. When we talk about *way of life* we mean organizing one's life systematically based on one or more of the ten identity categories. When we talk about *style of living*, we are referring to the same distinct style in home decoration and clothing. The two definitions are about the same principle of organizing something but simply have different scopes, as illustrated in figure 5.4.

In the twenty-first century a whole range of styles of living are available to us. This need to have the same style in home decoration and in clothing has some interesting consequences. A style of living not only helps make us distinct but also enables us to communicate our taste. This identification with style seems to be an important aspect of tribal life in the twenty-first century.

Figure 5.4. Scope in *Way of Life* and *Style of Living*

Way of Life {
Family
Geography
History
Race/Ethnicity
Religion
Politics
Education/Work
Leisure
Style } **Style of Living**
Sexuality
}

Chapter 6

DEVOTED TO A STYLE
Pattern Recognition

Surfing is the epitome of a youthful California lifestyle. It's a sport that has been profiled and glamorized in movies and music. The sport also has its own magazines and clothing brands, like Hang Ten, Body Glove, and Billabong. Surfers have their own dress code—loose-fitted T-shirts with floral or tropical print, colorful Bermuda shorts, flip-flops, wrap-around sunglasses, hemp necklaces, and so on. Surfing can certainly be a way of life. But can surfing also be a style of living? As a matter of fact, *yes*.

The definition of *style of living* is that the same style exists in clothing and home décor. By the 1960s the clothing part of surfing was more or less established (as mentioned in chapter 4). In the 1990s the home décor part became a reality with companies like Floorboardz Surfboard Rugs, a company that sells rugs for your living room and mats for hallways shaped like surfboards, and Boardtowels, a company that sells towels shaped like surfboards. From the Floorboardz Web site: "Express yourself and your passion for surfing with our . . . Floorboardz Surfboard Rugs. [It] is the coolest way to show your love for the classic art of surfing."

Very few people want to decorate their homes with surfboards, whether real or surfboard-shaped carpets, tables, or lamps. But some people do, otherwise Floorboardz, Boardtowels, and similar companies would not have business. Thus it is a reality that surfing can be a style of living. This may be inconsequential because of the minuscule interest in surfing-style interiors. But if other dress codes of other groups also spill into home decoration, we may be on to an important new pattern in tribal behavior in the twenty-first century. But before we can decide if there is a new pattern in how we humans embrace style, we have to find out if there are groups other than surfers who have taken up identical styles in clothing and in interior design.

Conveniently, there are numerous books on home decoration that can help us identify styles that exist in interior design. Some examples of titles of books on interior design are listed in figure 6.1. Though only a partial list of interior design books, this list alone demonstrates that there is a wide range of interior styles.

Figure 6.1. Interior Design Books[1]

- *In the Romantic Style*
- *Victorian Style*
- *Romantic Country Style*
- *Bohemian Style*
- *More Is More: An Antidote to Minimalism*
- *Divinely Decadent*
- *Glamour at Home*
- *Modern Glamour*
- *Cowboy Chic: Western Style Comes Home*
- *Santa Fe Style*
- *Natural Interiors*
- *Eco Deco*
- *The Small Adobe House*
- *Small Apartments*
- *Minimalist Interiors*
- *White Home: Pure Simplicity for Tranquil Interiors*
- *Adirondack Style*
- *Sailing Style: Nautical Inspirations for the Home*
- *New England Style*
- *Shaker: Life, Work, and Art*
- *Simple Country Style*
- *Mary Emmerling's American Country Classics*
- *Classic Interior Design*
- *Retro Style: The '50s Look for Today's Home*
- *Retro Home*
- *Modernism Reborn*

We know bookstores and libraries carry scores of hefty interior design books, and by focusing on the titles listed in figure 6.1, it would appear there are infinite distinct interior styles. But a little analysis will show that all these styles can be categorized into nine main style categories. (How the nine categories were chosen and how they relate to each other is explained in the appendix.) The nine categories are presented in figure 6.2 with the title of a book that represents the archetypical style.

Figure 6.2. Books on Nine Distinct Styles

GLAMOROUS	RAW	ORGANIC
Glamour at Home	*Cowboy Chic: Western Style Comes Home*	*Natural Interiors*
BOHEMIAN	TRENDY	PRACTICAL
Bohemian Style	*Retro Style: That '50s Look for Today's Home*	*Small Apartments*
ROMANTIC	CLASSIC	SIMPLE
In the Romantic Style	*Classic Interior Design*	*Minimalist Interiors*

The books listed in figure 6.1 are about private homes not only in the United States but also in Europe and Australia. But are they representative of interior styles in the United States? One way to answer that question is to narrow the documentation to interiors in the United States. The documentation is easily accessible in the shape of other books—on hotel interior design. In bookstores there are book series like *Hip Hotels* and *StyleCity* guiding us to hotels based on their interior design. Just by focusing on the hotels located in the United States, it is apparent that we can choose between hotels that have very different interior designs. This is illustrated in figure 6.3, which is a partial list of hotels, all located in the United States, with descriptions of their interior style.

Figure 6.3. Hotels and Descriptions of Their Interior Design[2]

HOTEL	LOCATION	STYLE
Ace	Seattle, Washington	Naked brick walls indoors, partly decorated with untreated wood
Avalon	Los Angeles, California	Retro-style 1950s-inspired interior
Beach House	Kennebunkport, Maine	Cape Cod–style, white furniture inside and outside, wooden walls painted white
Cibolo Creek Ranch	Shafter, Texas	Raw walls and ceilings, Santa Fe–inspired style
Chelsea	New York City, New York	Bohemian kitsch with many mixes of styles and colors
Estrella	Palm Springs, California	Glamorous style with old Roman-inspired furniture, atypical furniture shapes
Hix Island House	Vieques, Puerto Rico	Organic style with concrete walls and discolored effects on some walls
Home Ranch	Steamboat, Colorado	Cowboy ranch style
Hudson	New York City, New York	Trendy hotel decorated by Philippe Starck
Inn of the Anasazi	Santa Fe, New Mexico	Santa Fe style
Kennedy School	Portland, Oregon	Purple walls, quirky bohemian style with fun elements
Korakia	Palm Springs, California	Western style with many raw decorative elements

Loft 523	New Orleans, Louisiana	Naked brick walls, untreated wood, organic style
Lowell	New York City, New York	Classic style with antiques and trimmings
Maison 140	Los Angeles, California	Glamorous style, lots of decorative elements, black walls, patterned wallpaper and furniture, zebra skins on floor
Mercer	New York City, New York	Trendy hotel with few discreet colors
Mondrian	Los Angeles, California	Trendy hotel decorated by Philippe Starck
Orbit In	Palm Springs, California	1950s-style, in the graphic tradition of that period
Pelican	Miami Beach, Florida	Psychedelic and bohemian style, owned by Diesel, the fashion brand
Rancho de la Osa	Tucson, Arizona	Western style
Shaker Inn	Enfield, New Hampshire	Shaker style
XV Beacon	Boston, Massachusetts	Glamorous style with many prints and gold decorations

A closer look at the descriptions of the hotel interior reveals that more or less the exact same descriptive style terms that were used in the book titles also describe the hotel interiors of just a few hotels located in the United States. The nine main interior style categories identified in figure 6.2 exist in the United States, too. While there are many different interior design styles—and many subcategories to the nine main interior style categories—the point is that there are also systematic patterns in how we decorate our homes. Just as with dress codes, the world of interior design is no more chaotic than other aspects of human life. Complex, yes, but not in any way chaotic. We could in principle choose to mix all the thousands of different furniture and home decoration objects in countless different ways, but we do not. We limit ourselves. In the twenty-first century there are more options than ever, but the number of interior design styles *can* be estimated, just like we can estimate the number of dress codes available.

THE STYLE TRIBES

Just as some people are religious, political, musical, sporty, and so on, some are keenly interested in interior design. Some may like a style to the extent that it becomes a part of who they are, a part of their identity. When a person will define himself as a minimalist, as being into the romantic style or the glamorous style or any of the nine main interior style categories, his home and/or his clothing is likely to reflect this. *If* he has the same style in both his home décor and his clothing, we have a combination of a way of life (a certain style) and a dress code, which is the definition of a *tribe*—in this case, a *style tribe*. In the real world this means, for instance, that people who decorate their home in the raw Western style and wear the cowboy dress code belong to a style tribe.

Style tribes add a further layer of complexity to the tribal phenomenon. The style tribe of people who like Western style is different from the cowboy tribe, whose identity is based on work. It is also different from the country and Western music tribe that identifies with country and Western music and wears the cowboy dress code. All three tribes have the same dress code but the source of their identity is different: style, work, and music, respectively. This underlines once more why it can be tricky to decode other people's lifestyle in the twenty-first century.

To identify and name other style tribes, we have to find out the extent to which people who have the same taste in interior design also have the same dress code. It would make sense that people who like a certain style in interior design would also like the same style in clothing and accessories. The alternative view, that people would like one style in interior design and the complete opposite style in their clothing, would make less sense: it would weaken our nonverbal communication with such confusing and mixed signals—something that is not very typical in human life.

Identifying with the decor in one's home is a significant part of many people's identity. But their design choices can be that of a singular interest and based on some choices they made when they had to buy furniture and home decoration objects. They are not necessarily part of a tribe. Only when their dress code matches their interior design are they part of a style tribe.

To find out if there are dress codes that match the nine main style categories (and people combine the same style in home décor and clothing), we can start out by sorting the thirty-two dress codes that were highlighted in figure 4.7. Some of the dress codes from chapter 4 are more alike than others, with some being very alike. They are all listed in figure 6.4, now organized according to how alike they are (refer to p. 136). (How this was done is explained in the appendix.)

If we start with the four squares in the upper left corner we have a cluster consisting of the hip-hopper dress code, the glamourist dress code, the pimp/hooker dress code, and the clubber dress code. They are alike in a shared affinity for strong colors, patterns, and gold jewelry. The four squares to the right of these are the heavy metal rocker, the biker, the cowboy, and the lumberjack dress codes. They are alike in a shared use of leather, monochrome colors, and heavy boots.

If we continue and take four squares at a time around the middle of figure 6.4, there are eight highly distinct clusters in all. This leaves us with one square—the one in the middle—that just says *fashion*. The thirty-two dress codes that are named around the middle square are not the only dress codes that exist, but they represent some archetypical dress codes, dress codes that could be said to be the originators of derivative versions. There are also all the "fashion designer fan clubs" that represent clothing styles that change on a regular basis. In figure 6.4, they will be placed in the middle. Because fashion designer styles change so frequently, there are no specific dress codes named in the middle. They are bundled together under the umbrella "fashion." With the inclusion of fashion, figure 6.4 consists of nine style clusters.

Figure 6.4. The Jigsaw Puzzle of Dress Codes

Hip-Hopper	Clubber	Heavy Metal Rocker	Biker	Grunge	Surfer
Glamourist	Pimp/ Hooker	Cowboy	Lumber-jack	Skate-boarder	Hippie
Rastafarian	Goth	Fashion		Trucker	Hobo
Dandy	Artsy			Athletic	Hillbilly
Golfer	Romantic	Pinstriped	Corporate	Sporty	Amish
Victorian	Tweedy	Three-Piece Suit	Collegiate	Preppy	Minimalist

There are many mixes of dress codes, especially among the dress codes that are placed next to each other. Mixes of opposite dress codes are rare. This is not to say that all people adhere to just one dress code. Some people like several different styles, and they will wear one dress code one day and a different dress code the next day. This style mixing is called *style surfing*. Although it is not common for people to choose to wear completely opposite dress codes, it certainly is part of the complex way of dressing in the twenty-first century. Of course, if someone is a style surfer, by definition she cannot be a member of a style tribe.

Figure 6.4 is arranged to resemble a jigsaw puzzle. But when all the pieces are together, it also represents a map of sorts, or a simple flowchart. It is the kind of map that we use to navigate when mingling and socializing to find those who are most likely to be like ourselves. The farther away a dress code is from another dress code in the map, the less likely it is that people with these two dress codes will be drawn to each other. In private and public places people will—consciously or unconsciously—be aware of differences in clothing style, and they will often be attracted or repelled by others, depending on what they are wearing. People who have one kind of style prefer to socialize with people who share their taste. It is a rather unrealistic scenario that Amish people would hang out with bikers—or that hip-hoppers would share the same social venues as cowboys.

A person may very well define her style as Goth or collegiate, but the majority of people often are not so specific when they define the style they like. But they will belong to—or identify with—one of the main style categories shown in figure 6.2. These nine main style categories are remarkably identical to the clusters that are identified in figure 6.4. In fact, if figure 6.2 and figure 6.4 are placed on top of each other, the similarity becomes even more evident. It appears that we have identified nine distinct styles that represent matching clusters of dress codes and clusters of interior design styles. In other words, it seems we have identified nine style tribes. They are identified in figure 6.5.

Figure 6.5. Style Tribes

The GLAMOROUS Style Tribe	The RAW Style Tribe	The ORGANIC Style Tribe
The BOHEMIAN Style Tribe	The FASHION Style Tribe	The PRACTICAL Style Tribe
The ROMANTIC Style Tribe	The CLASSIC Style Tribe	The SIMPLE Style Tribe

When people who identify with one of the nine main style categories choose a dress code that matches their style in home décor, they are signifying to the world something very strong. On a personal level, knowing that one's home base is decorated in a style that is underlined by one's dress code gives a person a sense of confidence. When this person is outside of his home, he will know he is not faking his sense of style, and when others see his home, they will be reassured that the way he dresses indeed reflects who this individual is.

Belonging to a style tribe does not mean that you will not wear other styles of clothing. There are situations when people will discard their tribal clothing and wear the kind of outfit that the situation or tradition demands. For example, when going to a funeral, tradition dictates you wear subdued, formal, black clothing. When exercising, most people go for clothing that fits a particular sport (whether baseball, horseback riding, or fencing). And if one goes on vacation, trekking in the mountains, for instance, one will likely wear what that situation demands.

In some professions there are certain dress codes based on hygiene and functionality. And at some companies there may be dress code policies that people must adhere to in order to keep their jobs. When this is the case, a person has to discard her tribal dress code while working. However, your work outfit can be different from what you'd wear prefer wearing at work and also at home—even when you choose it yourself. This was the case with Elvis Presley. In 1956 he was asked about his taste in clothes. His answer: "I like real conservative clothes. Something that is not too flashy. But onstage I like 'em as flashy as you can get."[3]

Belonging to a style tribe means that a person has a strong preference for a certain style in home décor and clothing, but in fact that preference may be strong in many other product categories. One's style tribe affiliation will likely affect choices in shoes, jewelry, electronics, cell phones, cars, and toys. Also hairstyles, makeup, and preference regarding tattoos are affected by your style-tribe affiliation. Women in the left part of the style map will have a preference for sophisticated hairdos, whereas women to the right will prefer more natural hair styles. The glamour-minded may opt for dye jobs and frequent visits to the hair stylist, while the practical-minded let their hair grow out rather than frequently visiting a stylist. As for tattoos, they are more popular in the upper half of the style map with its bikers and surfers than in the lower part with its golfers and preppies. If we just focus on shoes, we can identify an archetypical pair of shoes for each of the nine style tribes, as shown in figure 6.6.

Figure 6.6. Style Tribes' Preferences for Shoe Styles*

GLAMOROUS High-heeled pumps (w) White loafers (m)	RAW Cowboy boots (u) Black engineer's boots (m)	ORGANIC Skater shoes (u)
BOHEMIAN Mary Janes (w) Desert boots (m) Birkenstocks (u)	FASHION Changes from season to season	PRACTICAL Sneakers (u)
ROMANTIC Ballerina shoes (w) Loafers with tassels (m)	CLASSIC Bridled shoes (w) Black leather wing-tip laced shoes (m)	SIMPLE Low-heeled pumps (w) Brown penny loafers (m)

*w = women; m = men; u = unisex

Belonging to a style tribe is not very different from belonging to a religious tribe. However, belonging to a style tribe may not seem a particularly strong tribal affiliation—when all it takes to belong is to decorate one's home in a certain style and wear clothes in that style. In fact, it is probably one of the weakest tribal affiliations. But on the other hand, research in social psychology—the science of how individuals behave in groups—has documented that it takes very little for a person to form a group identity. The phenomenon is called the *minimal group paradigm*.[4] Just being told that you belong to a group—without knowing the other members in that group—can influence behavior and create a preference for being with members of this group. Actually just having the same taste in music can in itself create a bond.[5] There is no reason to believe that sharing the same style in clothing and home decoration and being able to put a name on the group identity can't also create bonds.

It is also worth remembering that just as people who share the same religion, political views, or geographical identity are not always particularly close on a one-to-one level (unless they are introduced and get to know each other), those with the same style do not necessarily bond immediately.

The style tribes are by definition *monostylistic*, that is, they like the same style all the time and throughout their lives, unless, of course, they change to another style tribe. Changing one's affiliation from one style tribe to another is on principle no different than changing other tribal affiliations, for instance, religion, except that changing one's religion may cost a lot less money than changing one's entire wardrobe and home décor.

For those enamored with a particular style, there are several important advantages to becoming part of that tribe: one is that it makes shopping for clothing and accessories, home furnishings, and many other products much easier. You always know what to look for, namely, designed objects that fit in with the clothing that you are already wearing and with the home furnishings that you have in your home. When buying designed objects, your style-tribe affiliation organizes your shopping. You just focus your attention on what you like—and you can allow yourself to ignore everything else. When people are members of a style tribe, they will go to great lengths to find clothing, underwear, shoes, glasses, jewelry, hairdos, and so on, that they like. As we shall see, this was certainly the case for Pleasant T. Rowland when she went shopping for dolls for her niece.

TRIBAL DOLLS

All tribes are particular about what they buy, which includes buying toys for children in their family. If you feel strongly about your lifestyle or your tribal affiliation, you cannot have your children playing with toys that are contradictory to your lifestyle or style tribe affiliation. The toy industry was slow to realize this, but then a woman named Pleasant T. Rowland showed them the way. Her act of defiance? She did not approve of the Barbie doll as an appropriate toy to buy for her niece, and she refused to purchase one.[6]

Since its creation in 1959 Barbie had become the world's most popular and most famous doll—because of or in spite of its somewhat unrealistic body type. It was in 1959 that Polish-American Ruth Handler was visiting Switzerland and happened to see a German-manufactured sex doll.[7] Curiously, the design of this sex doll inspired her to create a new kind of toy doll for children. Production started back home in California, and Ruth Handler called her new toy doll Barbie, after her daughter.

Barbie became an institution, and when you have created an institution, there is no reason to change it. So decade after decade, long-legged and big-busted Barbie was the doll that many girls played with when growing up. Then, in the 1980s, some suddenly found Barbie's looks a bit too provocative. More conservative attitudes were gaining momentum in political and social spheres. A conservative president—Ronald Reagan—was in the White House. The 1960s had been the decade of liberal attitudes and women's liberation. In the 1970s young people challenged even more traditions and morals. Those two decades pushed the boundaries, questioning authority and long-held norms. Sexual liberation reached a new high. Then, in the early 1980s, came AIDS. Sex became deadly. The more prudish seemed to have their "I told you so" moment, and a conservative backlash found traction.

British designer Laura Ashley had worldwide success in the 1980s in fashion industry with her focus on nostalgia. And Pleasant T. Rowland wanted to buy an old-fashioned, nostalgic doll in the vein of Laura Ashley's style for her niece. When she discovered that she could not find a doll that she would feel happy about giving to her niece, she decided to take matters into her own hands: she made a copy of a historical doll as the birthday gift. It turned out to be a very popular birthday present. When she sensed that there could be a market for this kind of doll, she decided to start manufacturing nostalgic dolls herself. She borrowed some money to start her entrepreneurial venture.

This was the beginning of American Girl dolls and the company Pleasant Co. Inc., which specialized in manufacturing dolls and doll clothing reminiscent of different periods of American history. American Girl became a very successful brand, just as Pleasant T. Rowland had sensed it would. American Girl also became a major competitor to Barbie, manufactured by toy giant Mattel, Inc. Barbie and American

Girl each represented two different life*styles*: Barbie represented a glamorous style, American Girl a romantic style—romantic in the sense that it harkened back to an idealized history.

In 1998 Mattel, Inc. bought Pleasant Co. from Pleasant T. Rowland. The price was $700 million, according to the *Harvard Business Review*.[8] This was the hefty price Mattel had to pay because executives had overlooked the popularity of the new romantic life*style*. In 2004 Pleasant Co. was renamed American Girl LLC, and the company now runs a number of very successful American Girl stores. The stores sell not only dolls and doll clothing but also books and a lifestyle magazine about the dolls, their history, and their style. From 1986 to 2003 American Girl sold 7 million dolls and 82 million books.

In the late 1990s another new life*style* became popular—a life*style* represented by a number of very popular recording artists, most notably Jennifer Lopez and the girl group Destiny's Child, and hip-hop artists such as Missy Elliot, Lil' Kim, and Mary J. Blige. Girls as young as five and six were fans of Jennifer Lopez and other Latino and hip-hop artists.

In California, MGA Entertainment, a Mattel competitor, saw that the hip-hop lifestyle was what many young girls identified with. In 2001 MGA Entertainment launched the Bratz dolls, styled just like the girls' idols. The Bratz dolls became a success almost overnight, and after a few years Bratz had become a major threat to Barbie. While the sale of Bratz dolls went up in the United States, the sale of Barbies went down. In 2003 *BusinessWeek* wrote, "Little girls just don't love Barbie like they used to."[9] As Barbie represented one-third of Mattel's turnover at the time and a larger part of its profits, something had to be done. One year after the introduction of Bratz, Mattel launched a new Barbie doll concept called MyScene dolls, which many found similar to the Bratz dolls. One year after that, Mattel introduced what some saw as a copy of the Bratz dolls called Flavas.[10]

In 2000 a fourth life*style* emerged in the doll category. The Get Real Girl dolls are sporty types, wearing clothing for sport or adventure. These dolls have realistic proportions, muscle definition, and movable joints. The dolls wear clothes for basketball, surfing, snowboarding, and other kinds of sports.[11] The Get Real Girl dolls also became successful, though not to the degree of the Bratz dolls. The market now has four different toy dolls representing four different life*styles*.

MORE STYLISH BUSINESS

Life*style* differentiation in the toy industry is a significant example of how changes in society affect business. When the same changes take place in one of the major industries in America—the car industry—we are then dealing with a major shift in American business. It is not that style is new in the American car industry, because there was a focus on style from the early part of the twentieth century—though not because of Henry Ford, who started the world's first assembly line to produce cars in Detroit in the early 1900s. His company became hugely successful with the world's first mass-produced car, the Model T (the T stood for Tin Lizzie). From 1897 to 1916, more than 16 million Model Ts were manufactured. They were all alike: same model, same color, same name. It was at that time that Henry Ford was quoted as saying that the consumers could have their Ford T in any color they desired, as long as that color was black.[12]

Ford's main competitor, Alfred P. Sloan, the president of General Motors from 1923 to 1937, was aware that car buyers needed to differentiate themselves. Sloan understood that there were social changes going on at that time—and that rich people would not like to drive the same car brand as poorer people. Therefore, GM sold five car brands—Chevrolet, Pontiac, Oldsmobile, Buick, and Cadillac. Each of these was targeted at people with different incomes, Cadillac being for the wealthiest.

In the 1920s Sloan went one step further in creating differentiation by focusing on what he called "styling," or design, as we would say today. He began by introducing cars in different colors, and from 1923 onward, he also introduced different designs. In 1927 Sloan hired a designer by the name of Harley Earl to head the Art and Color Section of General Motors. This started the development of new and more-detailed General Motors cars. (It was only at this time that Henry Ford began manufacturing different types of cars.)[13]

After World War II new car categories were developed. By the end of the twentieth century the car industry had its focus on making sure that there were cars fulfilling the needs of consumers who were leading highly diversified lives. So after having introduced sedans, town cars, limousines, sport cars, and station wagons, along came four-wheel drives, MPVs, SUVs, and microcars. Function is important to most people, but function is certainly not the only mantra in consumer behavior.

In 1977 research on buying behavior revealed that values play a big part in consumption. The researchers compared two groups of car buyers: one liberal, one conservative. The two groups had vastly different approaches to buying a car. The liberals whose values were about compassion and intellectual pursuits preferred to buy products that were good for the environment. They would tend toward buying a small car with good mileage. The conservatives, whose values were about discipline, social standing, and national security, preferred to buy high-quality products with lots of extras. They would tend to buy a big and comfortable car.

There is no reason to believe that values do not still play a role when some people buy a new car and other products. More and more people—no matter what their values are—want to buy a car with good mileage (gas is not cheap). But in addition to price and environmental concerns, the car industry is increasingly focusing on style needs. As reported in a 2004 *BusinessWeek* cover story headlined "Designer Cars": "From Munich to Tokyo, smart auto designers are driving sales more than ever. Never before has design been so vital to an automaker's success—maybe even to its survival. . . . A decade-long drive to close the quality and engineering gap among car manufacturers around the world has left the companies competing increasingly on, well, looks."[14]

Given the many different car categories, we often want to categorize people based on the cars they own, though classifying people based on their vehicle is not quite as easy as it used to be. Now there are so many layers to take into account when "decoding" a car owner. Cars are, naturally, about transportation. Cars are about income, though even poor people can buy an expensive car if they use all their life savings or extend their credit, and wealthy people may choose to have three moderately priced cars instead of one expensive car. Cars are still about values, and for many there is a focus on the environment. Cars of different sizes are also popular: some prefer an SUV while others prefer a microcar.

In the 1920s the car industry gave consumers the choice of different-colored cars. Now it gives consumers cars that match the consumers' life*styles*. We have seen cars such as the Hummer and Chrysler Prowler, some very raw-looking cars. We have seen several retro-style models being introduced when retro fashion was starting to get popular in the late 1990s, the PT Cruiser from Chrysler being the most notable example. The new Beetle's very organic style matches what is preferred by the organic style tribe. For people who like glamorous sports cars, there is the Ferrari 360 Spider, which again is different from the many classic sports cars that also hold a huge appeal for some people. It seems that cars are being designed in the exact same styles as clothing and interior design products.

For consumers this all means more possibilities to choose from for each style tribe. This is also the case with many (heterosexual) men who want products to help them communicate their style and taste as effectively as possible—because they are interested in style and also because they know that it matters to women. For men focusing on style, they choose categories that are interesting to them, for instance, cars, electronics, and DIY handyman tools, when they want to express *their* style identity.

If cars are what men identify with, women often have their focus on cooking, party planning, and home decoration. It was in exactly these categories that former caterer Martha Stewart spearheaded a small revolution in 1987. By then she had written four cookbooks and her name had become synonymous with gourmet cooking and hosting tips. She was contacted by the discount supermarket chain store Kmart. Kmart wanted to brand a new series of kitchen utensils with a celebrity with whom their customers could identify. According to the book *Martha Inc.*, she was chosen because her life*style* oozed of New England WASP traditions.[15]

Martha Stewart became a brand name not only in kitchen utensils but also for a whole range of other products for the home and the garden. Later she launched her own magazine, *Martha Stewart*

Living, and became the host of her own television show. Martha Stewart ended up packaging her own life*style* and selling it successfully all over the country.

In the twenty-first century there seems to be no end to what product categories designers will latch onto and match to a certain style tribe. Yoga got mainstream popularity in the beginning of the twenty-first century with a boom in yoga videos, yoga chain stores, trademarked yoga practices, and yoga clothing. Two early popular brands of yoga clothing were Nuola, made by sportswear giant Puma AG, and Lululemon Athletica, an upscale brand founded by Chip Wilson. As Chip Wilson has explained, "We put together yoga-inspired athletic clothing for women that fit properly and injected some style into it."[16] Stylish yoga clothing would not be so noteworthy if it were not because, as John Philip, the director of the documentary *Yoga, Inc.*, has pointed out, "You don't need anything to do yoga. You don't even need shoes."[17] But consumers want stylish clothing when they play tennis and golf—and when they do yoga.

DESIGNER FUNCTIONS

Consumerism in the twenty-first century cannot do without design or designers. For instance, many of the dress codes were actually not created by designers, at least not formally trained designers in the present-day sense of the word. Design—and most important, enduring design—has been created by people from many walks of life. Today, design is expected, and industries that sell products with even a minimum style component have a staff of full-time designers, a professional class who are keenly attuned to what consumers and markets demand.

The function of a designer came into being in the mid-1800s, in France, though the originator was an Englishman, Charles Frederick Worth. He had settled in Paris in 1845 as a dressmaker. The way Worth made dresses was completely different from the way traditional tailors did. Instead of asking the client what she wanted, he decided what kind of dress his client should have. Even with his most aristocratic customers, Worth did not hesitate to dictate how the dresses he made should look. Worth created the role of the modern fashion designer. In the twentieth century, it was no longer the customers who decided what fashionable clothing should look like. That decision was—and is—made by fashion designers, and by designers in other industries. But while designers have professionalized the design process, often the inspiration of what to wear comes from the heroes, icons, and stars who the style tribes admire.

Across all the tribes we humans need someone to look up to in one way or another. We look up to political figures, religious figures, and military figures. Historically, in Europe and other parts of the world, people have also looked up to royalty—kings and queens, princes and princesses—based on a strict hierarchy between the titled nobility. It appears to me that in the United States there is also royalty based on a hierarchy. Only, in the United States, such royalty is composed of celebrities from media, music, movies, television, and sports.

Quite a few people have an obsession with celebrities, if television, magazine racks, and blogs provide any indication. Some people want to know all about them, to look like them, and to be like them. A celebrity can have a very powerful influence and respect from some people. How powerful that influence is will depend upon the celebrity's position in what I call the "celebrity hierarchy," the six status levels of celebrities:

- Icons
- Megastars
- Superstars
- Stars
- Minor celebrities
- Wannabes

Icons are worshipped for decades and are known worldwide, whereas wannabes are often forgotten after they have had their fifteen minutes of fame. In general, the higher a celebrity is in the hierarchy, the more the celebrity can affect a huge number of people.

Who gets to become a icon or a megastar is mostly about achievements. Though there is no objective way to decide who should be placed where in the celebrity hierarchy, it seems that the more times a person has been on covers of magazine (and has had similar kinds of press coverage), the higher in the celebrity hierarchy he or she is placed.

The higher up in the celebrity hierarchy a person is, the more Americans will know the person and have an emotional connection to the person (positive or negative). But each tribe and lifestyle group will also have its own celebrity hierarchy that will have relevance and importance to the group—and not necessarily to other people. Therefore, tabloid darling and hotel heiress Paris Hilton and, for example, Caroline Kennedy Schlossberg, the daughter of John F. Kennedy, are undoubtedly looked upon differently in different social sets. The first will have a high status in Los Angeles dance clubs; the latter will have high status in New England country clubs and among New York elites. Even a minor celebrity can have a huge influence on just one group or community—teenagers, for instance.

Since the recording industry and Hollywood are so important in our lives, music, movies, and television still comprise the big conveyor belt that brings new styles to the rest of the world. We admire not only the performers in music or acting but also their style, onscreen or on-stage and off. Some identify with them and some want to look like them. The best-known celebrities have become brands, and it makes a lot of sense to transform a style brand like Jennifer Lopez, Gwen Stefani, Sarah Jessica Parker, 50 Cent, and Sean "Diddy" Combs into products that can be used by fans to emulate their idols. By using the name of a well-known style icon, it does not take a lot of effort to communicate the style that the brand represents. It is built into the name from day one. This makes celebrity brands very effective as nonverbal communication of the style tribes.

Human life on Earth is still full of patterns that we can identify, name, and classify. What has really changed during the twentieth century is the growing variation in our nonverbal communication. All the signs are there, pointing to the fact that as we go further into the twenty-first century, this part of our lives will be refined even more.

Chapter 7

DESIGNED LIFE
Filling in the Blanks

Our food habits symbolize some of the changes that took place in America in the late twentieth century. For instance, in the 1970s, "people in New York, Los Angeles, San Francisco, and Chicago became increasingly familiar with the [growing] number of sushi restaurants in their cities," according to a contemporary source. Then in 2004 the first sushi bar opened in Mall of America in Minnesota, an indication that Americans from all walks of life had begun eating sushi.[1] Sushi can no longer be said to be just for elite food connoisseurs. "Today many blue-collar Americans can tell raw tuna from raw salmon by their texture on the tongue," according to a food anthropologist.[2]

American cooking has always been influenced by food from other parts of the world, just as Americans have influenced food habits in the rest of the world. Historically most food has had specific geographical origins and was eaten by people in that region. But as people migrated they took their food habits along and thus everything from pizza to sushi has become available on all continents. Ethnic and geographical boundaries no longer apply. We choose to eat the food that we do because we like it—it is to our taste.

But it wasn't only food that changed in the late 1970s. Restaurant décor did, too. Chef Jeremiah Tower (who has a degree in architecture) was one of the important food innovators in the 1970s and 1980s, with a focus on creating an American cuisine by using local produce in restaurant cooking. In his autobiography, *California Dish*, he writes about the late 1970s, "What were new . . . were the restaurants created by young Americans . . . [who were] just beginning to express their California background and lifestyle in food, attitude, and décor." Up until that point in restaurant history, nearly all upscale restaurants were based on French cooking and decorated in a stuffy, dark style. The innovative young chefs in Los Angeles at the time wanted white walls, glass shelves, beige furniture, and waiters who wore off-white instead of the traditional black clothing.[3]

A change in décor for one restaurant can mean more than just new furniture and stemwear. When one restaurant changes (this includes décor and menu) and is successful, other nearby establishments often follow. From this, whole neighborhoods can change. Many blighted neighborhoods across the nation have changed or are changing because restaurants with innovative menus have attracted patrons willing to venture and try new places. But the point is that restaurants are not just about the menu; the décor matters more than ever. As the *New York Times* wrote in a profile of one up-and-coming Brooklyn neighborhood, "Fort Greene is Brooklyn's latest culinary mecca, bewitching foodies with hip, minimalist restaurants."[4]

In the 1990s, some of the most visually dramatic changes took place in Manhattan—the wealthiest borough of New York City. Several Manhattan neighborhoods became less distinctly ethnic or of one religion compared to what they used to be. In the early 1970s, Soho, a neighborhood that was full of factories, became home to artists and art galleries and later to trendy stores and cafés. Twenty years later, the Meatpacking District was the next Manhattan neighborhood to be transformed from slaughterhouses and prostitution hubs to a neighborhood full of busy cafés, hip restaurants, and trendy boutiques.

The pattern of neighborhood change happens across the country. Consider Miami Beach, Florida, once a popular retirement town for senior citizens from all over the United States. The South Beach part of Miami Beach is dominated by scores of art deco hotels. In the 1980s it was a sleepy and somewhat derelict resort area. This changed when a group of citizens founded the Miami Design Preservation League, which aimed at restoring the unique historical area. When designer Leonard Horowitz suggested painting the hotels in bright colors, this turned South Beach into trendy SoBe and got the attention of, among others, the producers of the television show *Miami Vice*.[5] In the early 1990s people with all kinds of creative jobs moved to the South Beach area of Miami, turning it into a neighborhood popular with many people in creative industries—from fashion to cooking.

On the West Coast there are communities that are distinct in other ways. One early example of how leisure can influence an entire community is San Clemente in Southern California. Here surfing became an important leisure activity at the San Onofre Beach in the 1950s. San Clemente is still a bustling surf town—at one time the town was home to publishers of five surf magazines.[6] Bicycling, both a mode of transportation and a leisure activity and sport, has changed cities like Seattle, Portland, and Minneapolis, according to the *Bicycle Friendly America Yearbook*.[7] Close to Savannah, Georgia, Victory Lane is a community for people who are into car racing. Here homes are built around a private world-class car racetrack. Around the country similar private racetracks are popping up.[8] Golf is a lifestyle for many people, and golfing enthusiasts move to the many communities created around the links across the nation. In some places, other leisure activities—from hiking to gambling—dominate a neighborhood, community, or city.

Another example of how neighborhoods can change when people with shared identities begin dominating an area took place when sexuality became a strong source of identity for some gay men and lesbians in the 1970s and 1980s. As this identity drew more people, several large cities suddenly had neighborhoods with many gay inhabitants, such as the Castro district in San Francisco, West Hollywood in Los Angeles, New Town in Chicago, and the West Village in New York (Greenwich Village early on had attracted many artists, including gay artists.)[9]

In the twenty-first century, style, leisure, and sexuality can define neighborhoods—as can traditional identity categories like work, ethnicity, politics, and religion. These traditional identities still play an important role in many people's lives, and they still define many neighborhoods. And they will in all likelihood continue to do so. It is certainly evident that millions and millions of Americans still cluster together based on ethnicity and religion. Take Deal, a seaside resort in New Jersey. In the beginning of the twentieth century Deal attracted people with different religious backgrounds, but in the beginning of the twenty-first century 80 percent of the population of about a thousand were Sephardic Jews, many with Syrian background. During the summer season even more Sephardic Jews flock to the town, which is full of "synagogues and yeshivas, Jewish social service agencies and a main street lined with kosher delis and Syrian Jewish grocers," according to the *New York Times*.[10] We can also go to another summer resort town, Oak Bluffs, on Martha's Vineyard, an island off the Massachusetts coast. Here African-Americans cluster together every summer for vacationing and have been doing so for generations.[11]

People's work identities also continue to influence cities and neighborhoods. One example of a major change in our work identities has been documented by Professor Richard Florida, who introduced the term the *creative class*, about the growing number of people who work in the creative industries. They comprise fashion designers and engineers to marketing professionals and artists, from architects and computer specialists to journalists and chefs. Not all in the creative class are themselves creative, but their work relates to a creative process in one way or another. At the beginning of the twenty-first century, about one-third of the workforce in the United States belonged to the creative class, according to Florida. (The two other dominating classes in twenty-first-century society are the industrial working class and the service class.)

The rise of the creative class is not just about economics—it is also about style. In the twentieth century, etiquette and the "right" manners played a big role in people's social life. Therefore, there were numerous etiquette books and advice columns on social behavior.

By displaying the "right" manners relevant to one's social set, you were part of the group, and if you didn't know them, you could read up on and learn them. But with the creative class, there are some new rules with respect to what is "right" and what matters in social relations.

Because the creative class cares about style, clothing, and interior design, all three have become important in how its members define themselves and how they classify other people. That sharing the same taste is important when people socialize privately is not new. But because of the overlap of certain style tribes, it is important to know the intricacies of several styles that are appealing to one's social set. This again explains the boom in magazines and books about style, both in relation to clothing and interior design. The creative class needs guidebooks on where to stay when traveling (the "right" neighborhood, the "right" hotel) and how to decorate in a certain style, something that has to be mastered in order to be in control of the signals that the members of the creative class feel are important.

In exhibiting an abundance of styles, these books and the many magazines on style become important elements in helping members of the creative class make choices so that they can signal what they want communicated about themselves. The high number of different books and magazines on style demonstrate that the creative class is not just one coherent entity—far from it. People in the creative class have highly varied tastes—which is why there are nine style tribes (as opposed to just a few).

Though there are taste and style differentiation in almost all categories—from music to food—the selections in our tastes and style are not as predictable as they used to be. For instance, in music each of the style tribes will have certain preferences. But while many in the raw style tribe will have a preference for rock music and many in the bohemian style tribe will prefer jazz, it will certainly also be possible to meet members of these style tribes with completely different music tastes. In food the patterns are even less predictable. The raw style tribe may be less likely to eat sushi than hearty traditional American food, and it may be the other way around for the bohemian style tribe. But one's taste is so individual that really it is a matter of personal preferences when it comes down to what any person likes to eat.

BRANDED LANGUAGE

The rising influence of the creative class also affects how we talk—what we say and the words we use. Using regular language has proved not always to be enough to define, communicate, and classify a style.

Even members of the creative class have difficulty putting into words the style they like. But designer names can do the job. Ralph Lauren, Dockers, Phat Farm, and hundreds of other brand names have become part of the code that we use. Like when a journalist asked actor Hugh Dancy, "Do you speak Prada?" (His answer was "I basically speak denim.")

When people know that a brand such as Gap represents a casual, sporty style and Phat Farm represents a hip-hop style, it is much easier to just say "Gap" or "Phat Farm" when describing one's taste. Some people will know that Ralph Lauren is coded language for understated style, and that The North Face is code for a rugged, outdoorsy style. It is easier to say you like The North Face than explaining that you like functional, outdoorsy clothing in understated colors, or that you like Ralph Lauren instead of saying you like a current yet classic style.

Today there are hundreds of brand names that represent very different styles and dress codes. For people who do not know the brand names and what style they represent, it could just as well be James Bond talking in a code about a secret mission when they overhear a conversation that includes brand names. But as with codes in general, the codes of designer and brand names in clothing can also be decoded by studying the history and style of the brand. In figure 7.1, a selection of American designer and fashion brand names have been decoded.

Figure 7.1. Brand Names and Their Styles

Brand Name	Year Established	Style Classification
Body Glove	1953	Surfer
Brooks Brothers	1818	Classic
Calvin Klein	1968	Fashion, Tends to be understated
Carhartt	1889	Street
Columbia	1938	Outdoorsy
Dockers	1986	Sporty
Ecko	1993	Skateboarder

Etnies	1986	Skateboarder
FUBU	1992	Hip-Hopper
Hang Ten	1962	Surfer
Kate Spade	1993	Fashion
Kenneth Cole	1984	Fashion, Tends to be understated
L. L. Bean	1912	Outdoorsy
Marc Jacobs	1994	Fashion
Nautica	1983	Simple
O'Neill	1952	Surfer
Patagonia	1957	Outdoorsy
Pendleton	1909	Western wear
Perfecto	1915	Biker
Phat Farm	1993	Hip-Hopper
Polo Sport	1993	Simple
Ralph Lauren	1967	Simple, Classic
Schott NYC	1913	Raw
Sean John	1998	Hip-Hopper
Sebago	1946	Sporty, Maritime
Stetson	1865	Cowboy
Stüssy	1980	Street
Teva	1984	Natural, Organic
Timberland	1918	Rugged, Outdoorsy
The North Face	1966	Rugged, Outdoorsy
Wrangler	1945	Cowboy

A brand name and the advertising surrounding the brand name add a sense of identity to a product. The product itself signals a certain style. But brands also use sponsorships, spokespersons, events, and cause-related marketing to help promote the product and the brand and to underline its "personality." By doing so brands give consumers something to identify with that exceeds the actual product. This also confers distinction on people who wear the brand. This marketing technique is most successful when the brand name and/or the brand logo are a visible part of the product. For some people it is important that others can see the brand name, too. For others it is enough to know that they are wearing the brand. Advertising and other marketing tools can also be used to instill "brand values" into their products. In that way, a brand can end up representing not just a certain style but also brand values, such as being innovative, confident, tolerant, adventurous, or antiestablishment. The consumer who buys the product will do so because he likes the style of the product and/or identifies with the brand values and wants to be associated with them.

Some brands can become part of a tribe's identity. In the cowboy dress code, Stetson is esteemed. Among surfers, O'Neill, Hang Ten, and Body Glove are popular brands. In hip-hop, that used to be the case with Adidas: one of the early successful rap groups was Run-DMC. In 1983 the band released the single "It's Like That," and in 1986 Run-DMC scored a megahit with the single "My Adidas." This song more or less canonized Adidas sneakers among hip-hoppers. In the 1990s Tommy Hilfiger became a favorite brand among hip-hoppers (as mentioned in chapter 4). Among hip-hoppers brand names are an integrated part of their style preference because brand names signal affiliation with luxury and a wealthy lifestyle. Cristal has become a preferred champagne brand among hip-hoppers on that account.

However, as the Tommy Hilfiger brand became popular among hip-hoppers and catered to them through the association with famous hip-hoppers, the brand lost some appeal among the fashion tribe that had been its original target group. As *Forbes Global* magazine put it, "The same hip-hop crowd that made the clothes famous eventually helped sink the brand, after white suburban kids decided they'd had enough of the gangster look."[12] (The Tommy Hilfiger brand has since had resurgence.) Just as easily as brands can become popular among a style tribe, they can lose their appeal if they do not reflect the taste of the style tribe in question.

CODING CODES

The creative class is skilled not only in using brand names but also in inventing new words, like *fashionista* (fashion lover) and *foodie* (lover of trendy food), while adding nuance to long-existing words, like *gourmand* (food lover) and *gourmet* (food expert). These words are rather straightforward. What is more intricate is when we—all of us—use coded language based on the status of certain artists, objects, brands, and art forms (like music) in a particular tribe or lifestyle group.

Coded language is about creating taste hierarchies—we place what we like and what we don't like in hierarchies that can vary enormously from one lifestyle group or tribe to the next. A well-educated, sophisticated person will rank authors like Herman Melville and James Joyce at the top of her hierarchy, whereas authors like Judith Krantz and Danielle Steele would be at the bottom. But for a young, low-income mother, Judith Krantz and Danielle Steele might be ranked at the top and she may have no interest Herman Melville and James Joyce. When people agree on a ranking, they feel that they have something in common.

The coded language is also about associating artists, objects, brands, genres, and so on with a "loaded term" (as was mentioned in chapter 1). For instance, in art, the Metropolitan Museum of Art (the Met) can be code for "artsy," "snob," "art connoisseur," or "sublime art," and the Museum of Modern Art (MoMA) equals "cultural," "sophisticated," or "high-brow" depending on the codes in a particular group or tribe. When talking about the Met or MoMA, we imply what we think about these two museums either as something positive or as something negative, though often we do not actually express it directly. We also often use other dichotomies to put a negative or a positive spin on something. For instance, it is popular to distinguish between what is "in" (or trendy or cool or hot) and what is "out" (or mainstream or dated). In other areas or categories we use other dichotomies. In food, we can categorize food as "local" or "processed." To some, local will be preferred; others will prefer processed. We use this kind of categorization all the time to rank everything, from hotels to food. Some examples of words that are used in ranking are shown in figure 7.2.

Figure 7.2. Words That Rank

- Known — Unknown
- Cheap — Luxury
- Trendy — Mainstream
- Original — Copy
- Factory-made — Handmade
- Mass-produced — Artisan
- Sublime — Vulgar
- Local — Global
- New — Used
- Small — Large
- Modern — Old-fashioned
- Urban — Rural
- Natural — Artificial
- Understated — Conspicuous
- Pure — Mixed
- Formal — Informal
- Decorative — Functional
- Ascetic — Glamorous

By attaching words that rank to persons, brands, and objects, the style tribes and other tribes create their own coded language. These codes have a number of purposes. They create community by including some people and excluding others. Only people who master the code feel they belong. Codes are an indirect or discreet way to keep other people out of a community. Codes can also be the indirect or discreet way to classify other people, instead of classifying people in a way that could be offensive because of the precise language. We use codes instead—we disguise what we are really saying. In religion, *Episcopalian* is code for upper class; in politics, *red state* is code for a conservative state; and in work, *white-collar worker* is code for an office worker—to name a few.

With the growth of new tribes that are dedicated to leisure, style, and sexuality, new codes have emerged that mix with codes that have existed for a long time. A member of a style tribe, for example, will make a selection of words that are opposites and mix these into a new code. The different tribes and lifestyle groups attach positive values to different words. The fashion style tribe will often categorize "trendy," "original," and "unknown" as positive and "known," "old," and "mainstream" as negative. This way of ranking is typical of the fashion style tribe and does not change. But the style that the fashion style tribe favors changes from year to year. Therefore, some ranking words they use will also change. One year "old-fashioned" and "retro" are in and thus positive, and the next "natural" and "rural" are in, and then "old-fashioned" and "retro" are out.

Most style tribes and lifestyle groups do not change codes often. For the romantic style tribe, "old-fashioned" will always be positive; for the raw style tribe, "informal" is always positive; for the simple style tribe, "understated" is always positive, and so on. Even among the tribes that have many young members, like skaters and hip-hoppers, the codes do not change often, and for the same reasons as for all the other tribes—the established codes are understood and make sense.

LOGOS AND OBJECTS

Along with the wider use of coded language and brand names, the number of logos used in advertisements and on products has grown. The slow but steady use of logos exploded in the late 1970s, but actually the origin of logos on clothing goes further back in history.

Company logos go back to the beginning of the twentieth century. However, the origins of modern logos can be traced directly back to family crests. In medieval times in Europe, prominent and wealthy families established a tradition of visually distinguishing themselves and their servants by displaying family crests. Crests were used to ensure attention and loyalty—and they were useful in battle: because of the crests on the shields, soldiers and knights were able to discern between friends and foes.[13]

One of the first uses of logos in the United States was in sports clubs. Baseball clubs such as the New York Giants, the Cincinnati Reds, and the Boston Red Sox started using logos for the same reasons that the medieval knights did: club colors and logos are a meaningful way to create loyalty and distinguish between two opponents.[14]

With French tennis star René Lacoste (who invented what we now know as the polo shirt), logos crossed over to individual sports. Because sports journalists earlier in his career had nicknamed Lacoste "The Alligator," he decided to put an alligator emblem on his shirt. This was in 1933. Two years later, American tennis player Fred Perry also placed an emblem—laurels—on his polo shirt when he won the Wimbledon Men's Singles Championships. Both men later went on to sell polo shirts with their names on them, and these symbols became their respective company logos and strong symbols of a sporty style.[15]

In the early 1970s it was still rare to see logos on fashionable clothing. At that time American fashion designer Perry Ellis was one of the first to print a logo bearing his name on clothing he had designed. Up until then, company names had been only visible inside the clothing. Then, from the 1980s on, consumers wanted to have clothing that showed to themselves—and the world—the label of the clothing they were wearing. The logic for this was (and is) that the logo holds emotional signals that help emphasize the signals of the clothes themselves. It is a way of refining the signals of the clothes. For companies, it is a way getting attention and loyalty for their brand.

Many logos are the brand name of a fashion designer, and these logos hold a strong appeal, especially to young people, because they help define who they are, that is, the logos show that they belong to a style tribe. How strong this kind of appeal can be was underscored when low-hanging blue jeans became part of the hip-hop dress code. This over—or is it under?—exposure forced practitioners of the style to take more consideration in what kind and brand of underpants they wore, and the words printed on waistbands. Especially for young people who do not have a lot of money, underwear is a fairly cheap way to show your style tribe affiliation. When this sort of communication became an established part of hip-hoppers' nonverbal communication, there was even less of a reason to pull up the pants. Since pants began to hang so low, some wondered how comfortable the low-hanging trousers were. But as this was a clear-cut case of style being more important than function, there was not much to discuss—except in some communities where lawmakers decided that sagging pants posed a threat to the public, so they enacted indecency ordinances to outlaw them.[16]

Signs and symbols, branded in one way or another, are everywhere. Most organizations, especially those with large memberships, make sure that they have a logo that makes sense to their members, that can help give identity, and that can communicate that identity. The Sierra Club organizes conservationists, nature lovers, and outdoorsy people. Because the Sierra Club has been around since 1892, wearing the Sierra Club logo on a rucksack or T-shirt (which members can buy) not only helps define the wearer but also classifies her to other people.

Since the time books were first mass-produced and music became available as LPs and CDs, they have also been used to express identity. They obviously signal something about us when we read in public or exhibit our books and CDs in our home. The same goes for magazines. A copy of the *New Yorker* or *National Geographic* on the coffee table says something about the owner. In the beginning of the twenty-first century these nonverbal communication tools have changed with the introduction of online magazines, e-books, and MP3 players. Figuring out someone else's taste, without physical album covers and dust jackets, has become more covert in light of digitized media. This only creates more focus on the objects that we can see and what we talk about. The style of MP3 player and our e-book and electronic tablets matters even more. The shift from print to screen may make decoding what people are reading and listening to more difficult, but then social networking sites allow you to display what you're reading or listening to. As each tribe and lifestyle group creates its own codes, different symbols—names, objects, or logos—will have different status within those different tribes and lifestyle groups. And, of course, that status can change over time, making these codes trickier to decode. One example of this is tattoos.

Tattoos were originally a hallmark of sailors who got their tattoos as souvenirs when traveling to Polynesia, where tattooing was popular. As tattoo parlors became common in port cities, landlubbers began to get tattoos as well. At first, only men in the navy and prison inmates got tattooed. After World War II, bikers started getting tattoos. In the 1980s, tattoos became more popular among gay men.

In 1992, the newsletter *Iconoculture* from the US ad agency of the same name wrote, "Tattoos—once strictly a trademark of military service and Harley hogsters—are showing up across the socioeconomic scale."[17] In the 1990s, tattoos had become an almost mainstream phenomenon among both gays and straights, men and women. *U.S. News & World Report* stated in an article that tattooing ranked as the sixth fastest-growing retail venture of the 1990s, right behind the Internet, paging services, bagels, computers, and cellular phone service.[18] From being closely linked to one tribe, tattoos are now appealing to a cross-section of tribes, not least several of the style tribes, especially the raw and the organic style tribes. Tattoos in themselves are no longer an easy way to classify people. Now individual tattoos may hold a lot of meaning and symbolism, but more and more tattoos are a matter of taste.

Objects can also be symbols. One such object is the plastic pink flamingo. Designed by Don Featherstone, it was put into production in 1957. The idea was to place the pink flamingo "in [a] garden, lawn—to beautify [the] landscape," as its marketers instructed. The colorful and exotic plastic lawn ornament had appeal for blue-collar workers who placed it on their modest front lawns. Consequently, the plastic pink flamingo became a symbol of working-class taste. In 1972 the symbolic quality of the pink flamingo was used by gay director John Waters in his break-out movie, *Pink Flamingos*. The movie took place in Baltimore, in a trailer park, and was used to satirically symbolize working-class taste, at its most low-brow.[19]

The movie was not aimed at a blue-collar audience. On the contrary, the audience was sophisticated, urban, mostly gay. The pink flamingo would still be a symbol of small-town, modest living, but it suddenly became kitsch—"bad taste when it's best." The pink flamingo then ended up becoming a popular house-warming gift in the 1990s among sophisticated urbanites. For people knowing that the pink flamingo was a symbol of kitsch, it became permissible to give it as a gift to people who could appreciate the campy, ambiguous nature of the plastic garden ornament. Thus, by way of John Waters' movie, the pink flamingo also signaled "sophisticated," "urban," "gay," "gay-friendly," or an appreciation of twisted humor.

However, the sophisticated urbanite market was not big and as the original target group—the blue-collar workers—changed their tastes, the famous plastic ornament was doomed. In 2007 the plastic pink flamingo became extinct. The manufacturer closed its factory. However, that the blue-collar workers changed their taste should not have been a surprise to anyone who has consulted the books by the late American psychologist Abraham Maslow.

THE HIERARCHY OF NEEDS

We have lots of evidence that present-day consumers have become extremely style and design conscious. There are several explanations for this, and for the most profound ones, we must go to Abraham Maslow. One of his many contributions to understanding human behavior is the theory of the hierarchy of needs. Maslow's theory has been presented in numerous books on marketing in the following way (read from the bottom up):

5. Self-actualization Need
4. Esteem Needs
3. Belongingness and Love Needs
2. Safety Needs
1. Physiological Needs

Maslow's main idea is that humankind's needs are organized hierarchically so that the needs at the bottom of the hierarchy must be fulfilled before the person will begin to think of fulfilling the needs at the top of the hierarchy. Put in a very simple way, a person will not think of his safety needs if he is thirsty and hungry and has no roof over his head. But when he has fulfilled these needs, and the belongingness and love needs, then he will try to fulfill his esteem needs. If all other needs are met, a person can self-actualize.[20] (There is no uniform way that people self-actualize. Often it is interpreted as living and breathing one's passion.) The hierarchy of needs touches on the psychological nature of humankind and describes some of the most fundamental traits of human behavior, namely, needs and motives (often these are thought of as synonyms). Maslow wrote in 1948 about these needs, "They are not different from or opposed to human nature; they are part of human nature."[21]

If we look ahead in time, we can be sure that society will change, but some kind of hierarchy of needs will continue to exist. In this way the theory of a hierarchy of needs differs from a number of other theories, especially sociological theories. Societies can change, but the nature of humankind does not—at least not with the same speed. Therefore, in some ways the hierarchy of needs is part of human biology, which in general does not seem to change over long ranges of time (longer than millennia).

When reading Maslow's original texts it appears that he took into consideration that humankind's needs are more nuanced than the five needs mentioned above. Maslow wrote that "we should never have the desire . . . to adorn our homes, or to be well dressed if our stomachs were empty most of the time."[22] Maslow was well aware of the aesthetic side to life because in his original text he presented a more nuanced hierarchy, namely, the following seven needs:

7. Self-actualization Need
6. Aesthetic Needs
5. Cognitive Needs
4. Esteem Needs
3. Belongingness and Love Needs
2. Safety Needs
1. Physiological Needs[23]

In the most popular interpretation of the theory, there are two needs (nos. 5 and 6) that rarely have been presented as part of the hierarchy of needs. *Aesthetic* is not a very common word, and if Maslow were writing today, he might have said "the need for style and design" instead of "the aesthetic need." Maslow himself pointed out that science knew least about the aesthetic needs, and he repeated this in an essay from 1950. But humankind has at all times been preoccupied with aesthetics. Some of the earliest traces of humankind that still exist today are aesthetic traces. Cave paintings discovered in the south of France and in other locations show that the first humans spent time on what today look like artistic displays. The earliest humans did not spend all their time hunting for food.[24]

If many consumers can fulfill their needs at the top of the hierarchy, there will be some major changes in consumer behavior, according to Maslow. In *The Hierarchy of Needs* he writes, "The pursuit and gratification of the higher needs leads to greater, stronger, and truer individualism."[25] When consumers are able to fulfill needs at the top of the hierarchy, according to Maslow, not all consumers will have the *same* aesthetic needs—their style and taste will diversify. Maslow more or less predicted that there would be many different style tribes at some point in history.

LIBERATING CHANGES

From Abraham Maslow we learn what can happen when we fulfill many or most of our needs. This relates, of course, to economic growth—for society and for individual families. In the latter half of the twentieth century there were many positive changes in the financial situation of average families. In the fifty-year period from 1947 to 1997, median family income in the United States rose from $20,102 to $44,568 (adjusted for inflation).[26] (Median income refers to the 50 percent of the population between the 25 percent with the highest incomes and the 25 percent with the lowest incomes.) Income for this part of the population has more than doubled. This means that in the long run more people are able to fulfill more than just their basic needs. Of course, if we grab other pieces from the jigsaw puzzle we are laying out of the United States, it becomes obvious just how vast the differences in incomes still are. At the end of the twentieth century the richest 1 percent of American households owned 38 percent of all wealth in the United States, according to one estimate.[27] According to the United States Census Bureau, more than 12 percent of the population was "officially poor" at the beginning of the twenty-first century.[28]

The dramatic boom in interest in style also has other explanations that have to do with two groups that were "liberated" in the

1960s (according to the vernacular of that time): women and gay men. The fact that women started earning their own income or contributing to the family income has changed many consumption patterns. In a similar way the fact that gay men can identify openly as gay men has affected their consumption patterns.

During the late twentieth century the number of women with paid work outside of the home boomed. By 2010 women represented half of the workforce.[29] Women have entered many of the professions once held exclusively by men, as evidenced by such organizations as the Women Soaring Pilots Association, the Women Marines Association, the National Association of Women in Construction, and the Women Contractors Association (though the percentage of women who work in the industries related to these associations is small). In 1971 there were zero female Supreme Court justices, cabinet members, governors, and FBI agents. In 2009 there were two female Supreme Court justices, seven cabinet members, six governors, and 2,396 FBI agents.[30] In fact, in the United States at the beginning of the twenty-first century, 25 percent of women earned more money than their husbands, which is a new pattern in the employment market.[31] The high number of stay-at-home dads is indicative that at least some men are taking over the traditional female role in the household (from cleaning to taking care of the children) and thus changing the familiar family pattern (as was mentioned in chapter 1). Men are also part of new employment patterns in other respects. For instance, there is a National Association of Professional Pet Sitters, which includes many male members. That men have filled jobs where women traditionally dominated is also one of the many new patterns established in the late twentieth century, when male nurses and male kindergarten teachers became more common.

More women than men are college students and more women than men take master's degrees;[32] and while women generally do not earn the same salaries as men, in a few areas, women are actually earning more money than men. Young, college-educated women in New York and other large East Coast cities on average earn more money than their male counterparts.[33] More women are earning their own money, which gives them freedom to spend their income in any way they choose. This changes the thinking in industries that have not traditionally catered to women. One example is that Harley-Davidson has begun making smaller-sized motorcycles because women have become motorcyclists also.

The changes that have occurred with the rise in family income are linked to the fact that more and more women are also working and having careers. This has made many women independent from men so that marriage is not the only way for women to organize their lives. A woman can decide to enter into a relationship—and marriage—if and when it suits her. She can also allow herself to pay more attention to what a man can give her (other than monetary support) when choosing a spouse. This affects the balance between men and women: now men have to pay attention to their appearance in order to attract a well-educated and well-groomed female. At other times it did not matter much how a man looked, as long as he could provide for his wife and their children. And a number of wives would not risk their marriages by demanding their husbands spend more time on their appearance. Now at work places, it has become more acceptable for men to show some vanity. Actually, in some industries it is more or less expected that a man will be well-groomed and pay more than average attention to his appearance.

The fact that a husband is not the sole provider of income for a family has to a large extent also been liberating for men. For the greater part of the twentieth century the majority of men consented to hard physical work for their pay. When they came home from work, they just wanted to relax, and watching television at home was often the best way to do that. They also had the mental stress of knowing that their family was solely dependent on them for monetary support. With women working, some of the stress has been eased for men. Now men can organize their leisure time in new ways since their work is not so physically strenuous that they would only want to relax in front of the television when off from work.

Men are also becoming interested in style and design because they are aware that design holds powerful signals about who they are. Therefore, more and more single men are consciously using clothes and accessories to send signals to potential partners that their tastes are compatible (as mentioned in chapter 6). This development is related not just to the influence of women but the influence of gay men. That gay men have come out of the closet has made the world aware that many style icons were and are gay.

Homosexual men are a very mixed group of people. The extent to which gay men are underrepresented in some professions is difficult to know, but there is no doubt that they are overrepresented in one profession: clothing designers (and related professions like makeup artists and stylists). The majority of the most famous male fashion designers are gay. To name but a few openly gay designers who are also international brand names, there are: Tom Ford, Marc Jacobs, Giorgio Armani, Domenico Dolce and Stefano Gabbana, Jean Paul Gaultier, Valentino, plus the late Gianni Versace and the late Yves Saint Laurent.[34]

Some research has indicated that a key difference between men and women is that men—contrary to the common belief—are generally more visually and aesthetically minded than women, whereas women are more emotionally minded than men.[35] Support for this theory is found in the fact that men mainly focus on looks when choosing a partner, whereas women give more weight to other qualities. The Kinsey Institute for Research in Sex has also documented that men look at faces more frequently than women do when looking for what is sexually attractive in a person of the opposite sex.[36] Throughout evolution, the value males have placed on female beauty has made women pay more attention to their own looks in order to make themselves more attractive to men.

This theory can help explain why some homosexual men are preoccupied with looks and style, both their own and their partner's. In the twentieth century, it was obvious that some—although far from all—gay men were more interested in aesthetics than even the average heterosexual man was. Already in the 1940s, most wardrobe designers and the majority of set decorators in Hollywood were purportedly gay men, and they had enormous influence on the style and taste that was being seen on movie screens all over the world. A former supervising set decorator with MGM told author William Mann that the 1934 movie *When Ladies Meet* "swept the nation" with an interest in early Americana, chintz, and ruffled organdy curtains. All thanks to a gay set decorator, according to the source.[37]

The influence of gay men on general culture and style was

reported by *Time* magazine in a 1979 cover story: "Their dress tastes and speech are being adopted by many straights who would be stunned if they knew the origins of the latest fashions or fads. . . . A male homosexual model, acclaimed as one of the world's best-dressed men, cites examples of fashion takeovers. 'The first time I saw men wearing Adidas running shoes as part of casual wear was in the homosexual community on Fire Island several years ago. Now it has become a fashion staple in the straight world. . . . There is, in fact, a saying among homosexuals that straights will adopt a fashion just as avant-garde gays are turning to something new.'"[38]

In the twenty-first century, there is little doubt that more and more heterosexual men are interested in design and style. A 2001 article in the New York–based *Village Voice* magazine titled "Post-Straight: How Gay Men Are Remodeling Regular Guys," focused on the fact that more and more heterosexual men are imitating gay men in many aspects of style. The article went on to say, "This process has been evident for years in big cities, where gay men are rewriting the rules of what it takes to be a real man. Glossy magazines have noticed that straight men are increasingly looking gay, but the influence is more than a matter of working out, waxing, and wearing Prada. It involves a profound change in consciousness. . . . The gay sensibility is rubbing off on receptive straights."[39]

Surveys have indicated that homosexuals are often trendsetters.[40] One example involves brand-name vodka. In the early 1990s, Absolut was a lower-end, no-name vodka. The marketers of it initially focused on the gay community in San Francisco, kicking off their promotion with a funky ad campaign in the gay media. As a result, gay men began to drink Absolut vodka. This helped catapult it to the top-selling vodka in the United States.[41] In 2005, a survey by Witeck-Combs and Harris Interactive showed that more gay men and lesbians than heterosexuals were interested in the then relatively new and innovative hybrid cars. The difference was considerable: 51 percent of gay men and lesbians and 34 percent of heterosexuals were interested in buying a hybrid car.[42]

Many of the final pieces in the lifestyle puzzle are now falling into place. With such a huge jigsaw puzzle it is inevitable that some pieces get lost. But even with some pieces missing here and there we should be able to grasp a full picture. The question is, of course, what is the full picture of the jigsaw puzzle we have been laying out? Well, it looks like a buffet table!

Chapter 8

SOCIETY REARRANGED
The Full Picture

*O*ur lifestyles affect us in a multitude of ways—from our romantic lives to the jobs we can get. For instance, if you want to apply for a job with the CIA, you have to take the "lifestyle polygraph." This is a screening method where applicants have to answer questions about their lifestyle to land a job with a security clearance. According to one source, "A very disproportionate number of CIA employees are from Utah" because of the lifestyle polygraph test. In this case, the Mormon lifestyle that is so typical in Utah is the right lifestyle for CIA employees: Mormons do not drink alcohol and many Mormon men have international experiences because they lived abroad as missionaries in their late teens.[1]

As for the romantic part, meeting and dating someone is not made easier by people having such varied lifestyles. We humans practice what psychologists call *assortative mating*, the desire to pair up with someone who is similar to oneself. Assortative mating is one of the reasons why people cluster together in neighborhoods with people who have the same background: it makes it easier to find a spouse, and it is easier to meet new friends with shared interests.

More than ever people meet in all kinds of settings. However, two people can experience mutual attraction at the physical level but may have completely different lifestyles. This can be about differences in their music tastes, where they want to go on vacation, what kind of car they like, and a multitude of other differences, or it can be about even wider differences because of contrasting values and life goals that are also shaped by our lifestyles.

When you are in love, you may not care if the other person has a very different lifestyle. But if and when the exuberant feeling of being in love evaporates, clashes will emerge because of different lifestyles, bringing conflict to the relationship. It is common that the emotional high of being in love dissipates after a certain time, and then the couple has to be bound together by other emotions, interests, and a common lifestyle in order to stay together. Often love alone cannot keep a couple together, and only when the two have a similar lifestyle—or aspire to have a similar lifestyle—are they likely to stay together in the long run. This is not new. Writer and commentator Walter Lippmann said early on in the twentieth century that a couple has the best chances of staying together "when the lovers love many things together, and not merely each other."[2] In the twenty-first century the reality is that with an abundance of choices in all aspects of life, there is a bigger risk that a couple can end up loving separate and distinct things.

On the positive side, the Internet is bringing new possibilities for assortative mating, even when one has an uncommon lifestyle. Someone who lives in a small town may feel alone and isolated, but when the individual has the opportunity to go online, she can join hundreds or thousands of people with similar identities and interests, and suddenly her lifestyle can be nourished and affirmed. The book *One Hundred American Teenagers* is full of teenagers who connect online with other like-minded people. For example, there is Angel, the vampire-obsessed guy from New York, and Kammie, the Manga cartoon devotee from Louisiana, who both have joined online communities of like-minded people, as have many of the other teenagers mentioned in the book.[3]

Social media are also perfect for people who have more in common with people who live in other states than with the people who live next door. There are dating Web sites that cater to people with all kinds of lifestyles—based on almost everything from politics and religion to leisure activities. With Web sites like democraticsingles.com and conservativedates.com, it is possible to find a mate who shares the same values; and with hundreds of other dating sites based on other factors and characteristics, people have many opportunities to find someone like-minded.

The abundance of lifestyles also affects families when their children grow up. A family growing up with one specific lifestyle has no guarantee that the children will end up having the same lifestyle once they are adults. Many parents experienced this for the first time in the 1960s when they were visited by their hippie children. How parents and children can end up having different lifestyles can be illustrated by the experience of the late actor Henry Fonda when in 1965 he was invited to a Fourth of July party in the Malibu, California, home of his daughter, actress Jane Fonda.

Jane Fonda had invited a mix of people Old Hollywood giants like Lauren Bacall, Sidney Poitier, Gene Kelly, and several directors and moguls, among others. The hostess's contemporaries—who made up what was soon to be called New Hollywood—were represented by Natalie Wood, Warren Beatty, Dennis Hopper, Jack Nicholson, and her brother, Peter Fonda. And then there was the upcoming director Mike Nichols, and the artist Andy Warhol representing the New York underground arts scene, the latter with some of his stars in tow.

The guests clustered together in different parts of the house based on their varied lifestyles. On one side of the house there was a formal barbecue with Henry Fonda roasting a pig surrounded by his Old Hollywood colleagues. Gene Kelly was teaching the eight-year-old daughter of French director Roger Vadim, Jane Fonda's husband-to-be, how to tap dance. On the other side of the house the young and upcoming Hollywood actors and actresses were partying and listening to the Byrds, the band that had been hired by Peter Fonda for the occasion. The band played their number-one hit "Mr. Tambourine Man." Jane Fonda had set up a giant tent with a dance floor on the beach in front of the house. Illegal drugs were plentiful. At one point Henry Fonda went over to his stoned son and yelled, "Can't you get them to turn it down?" Studio head Darryl Zanuck and director George Cukor went to the other side and were dumbstruck by the sight of a barefoot hippie nursing her baby. Inside the house there was a French-style, all-night, talking-and-smoking party. Besides Roger Vadim there were two other French: actress Jean Seberg was there, and Warren Beatty had brought his French girl-friend, actress Leslie Caron.[4]

In the 1970s the youth were out dancing to disco music all night long, in the 1980s they could be into heavy metal or punk. In the household of then president Ronald Reagan, a staunch conservative Republican, his son Ron Reagan, a liberal Democrat, might stop by for a visit.[5] In other families it could be a totally different story, maybe an openly gay son or a lesbian daughter would come visiting.

Today with an even larger variety of lifestyles, family members may end up having different lifestyles or belonging to different tribes. And parents and their teenage and adult children may end up having very little in common. In some cases, this can cause conflict, though families have very different ways of dealing with differences. Psychologists would point out that for some it may create alienation because family members focus on the differences; other families will choose to focus on what is shared, for instance, kinship and family history, with fewer conflicts as a result. Again, this may not be new, but the high number of different lifestyles in existence is new. Because we meet more people from different lifestyles and tribes at work, at the gym, at the movies, and when traveling, family life for some can end up being more complex.

MINORITY LIVING

Before the European settlers arrived in North America, all individuals on the continent belonged to tribes. Tribalism was the order of the day. Though the United States is still highly tribal, most Americans do not belong to a tribe with its combination of a way of life *and* a dress code. Now most people who have the *same* way of life often have *different* dress codes. They make up different lifestyle groups rather than tribes. Among these lifestyle groups, some have a fixed lifestyle while others have a more fluid lifestyle.

In the grand historical perspective of how humans have organized our lives, it is the fluidity of lifestyles that is new in the twenty-first century. Just the word *fluid* indicates that it is something that is difficult to define and describe. But if we look at the synonyms for *fluid*, we can get an idea of what kind of life fluid living entails: variable, adaptable, changeable, flexible, mobile, shifting, unstable. These words reflect the lives of many people today, for better or for worse. Nevertheless, fluid is a way of organizing one's life that is just as organized as any lifestyle, only it is disorganized in the way it is organized (as pointed out in chapter 3).

To many people this fluidity is positive because from their point of view it gives them opportunities to experience different aspects of life in one lifetime. They can live more varied—and sometimes paradoxical—lives. People in the twenty-first century are not nearly as constrained by family, traditions, and work as those of past generations.

With society changing toward not just more fluidity but also a huge diversity of lifestyles, it is inevitable that not all people are happy with the changes. With people being more different from each other on so many other counts than race and religion, some groups in society will not like other people's lifestyles, and they will want to ban, control, or regulate them. People who have their lives organized in a certain way sometimes think that all should have their lives organized in that way. Therefore, some people oppose abortion or gay marriage or the right to own a gun—to name some of the big issues that divide people. In reality there are hundreds of different ways of life that make people pro-this or anti-that. These multiplying differences *may* increase intolerance in a society, which can lead to conflicts, especially when political and religious leaders exploit these conflicts as a way to energize their followers.

On an individual basis some people may have difficulty in defining their own identity and end up feeling rootless and confused about who they are. Because identity is so important to human beings, this is not healthy for any individual or group. Under these circumstances, a person can end up being desperate to create an identity. Often religion becomes the most readily available choice, and as the person then clings to his newfound identity, he may gravitate toward fanaticism and, in some cases, to violence.

Therefore, in the twenty-first century we can continue to expect clashes between different groups of people with different views on how to organize life. As in the twentieth century some clashes will be violent, in the physical sense, as the 2009 killing of Dr. George Tiller, who worked at an abortion clinic in Wichita, Kansas, by an antiabortion fanatic.[6] Other clashes will be verbal, as we often hear in political and religious rhetoric from people of different values and faiths. These clashes often take place in the media.

The clashes between "old" and "new" lifestyles are often exposed by the television and movie industry—for instance, as portrayed in the 1967 Spencer Tracy and Katharine Hepburn movie *Guess Who's Coming to Dinner*, in which a white daughter from a liberal East Coast family introduces her African-American boyfriend to her parents. Later, Hollywood continued dealing with clashes between different lifestyles in movies such as *Meet the Parents*, which was about the tension between an uptight Long Island father meeting his future son-in-law, a male nurse from Chicago. Changes in our lifestyles are also often reflected in television, too. In sit-coms the reality of a society consisting of many mixes of lifestyles is presented in a humorous setting, such as in *Dharma & Greg* (in-laws consisting of a wealthy, conservative couple versus a hippie couple) and in *It's All Relative* (in-laws consisting of a well-educated gay couple versus a narrow-minded, barkeeping couple).

The clashes may be fun to watch when presented with humor. Nevertheless, it appears that viewers, listeners, and readers are mostly interested in media that reflect their exact lifestyle rather than media that represent diversity. For decades most Americans watched CBS, NBC, or ABC, but interest in exploring how other people lived sagged. This is why Fox Television came up with a focused, conservative view of the world in its news programming: Fox became successful because conservative-thinking viewers wanted a channel that they could identify with and that expressed their views on other people's lifestyles. Meanwhile, MSNBC presented programming that would reaffirm the values of liberal viewers. Similarly, Christian media have also expanded with book publishing, radio channels, television, and magazines.

The twenty-first century seems to be all about lifestyle-specific media with many people losing interest in the general-interest media. As a result, traditional media such as free-to-air television and newspapers that are targeted at a broad range of people are losing market share (although they still have millions of viewers and readers). This change is noticeable in television advertising. According to a *BusinessWeek* article, "In the 1960s, an advertiser

could reach 80 percent of US women with a spot aired simultaneously on CBS, NBC, and ABC. Today, an ad would have to run on one
hundred TV channels to have a [chance] of duplicating that feat."[7]

The lifestyle-differentiated media affect many aspects of society.
This differentiation has even affected whom we consider our heroes
and idols. At one point in the twentieth century, Hollywood stars **and**
other celebrities were known by (almost) all people who cared to go
to the movies. But now we see fewer *common* celebrities, idols, and
heroes. More and more celebrities are only celebrities among a certain group of people, a lifestyle group or a tribe. Some may cross
over, maybe from a cable show, a niche sport, or a youthful music
genre, but most will remain known among only a small minority of
people.

Each tribe and lifestyle group has its own celebrities, idols, and
heroes. This is one of the reasons why more music albums are produced and more books are published than ever before. All tribes and
lifestyle groups want what is entertaining to them. In general, we do
not familiarize ourselves with the celebrities, idols, and heroes of
other tribes and lifestyle groups, unless we want to ridicule them.

THE LIFESTYLE BUFFET

Though diversity has been an important aspect of American society
in the twentieth century, after World War II many Americans focused
on creating and sustaining one dominating culture. If groups of
people were different from the dominating culture, they were categorized as minorities, something that often resulted in disadvan-
tages, if not outright discrimination and persecution. With the rise of
more and more diverse lifestyles, the balance between majority and
minority is changing. As more and more people have more individual
identity combinations, we see new minorities emerging. And as this
is happening, terms like *majority* and *minority* are making less
sense. The United States can, in fact, end up being a society consisting of only minorities of varying sizes.

Whether the United States of America will be the United Minorities of America is difficult to ascertain, but what is already observable is that the growing number of lifestyle variations is changing the social landscape. Since it is a gradual process, there is nothing really revolutionary about it, though it is certainly rearranging major aspects of American society. Families, relationships, communication, and many other aspects of society are changing. One important point is that since many of the changes in identity typically apply to the younger generations, the shift will be stronger when those who are currently young get older and gain more influence in society. When they start being the majority, their ways of life will inevitably influence the very structure of society. How will we describe this new society? We often like illustrative metaphors to describe the society that we are a part of. For decades American society was described as the "great melting pot," because the majority of the millions and millions of immigrants coming to the United States all seemed to want to adopt the American way of life.

The melting pot metaphor became popular in the beginning of the twentieth century. It began with a play called *The Melting-Pot* by the English Jewish writer Israel Zangwill.[8] The play premiered in 1908 in Washington, DC, in the presence of President Theodore Roosevelt.

The play's protagonist is a young Russian Jew, David, who flees to America from persecution in his homeland. He is in love with a Russian Orthodox aristocrat, Vera, whose father plays an active part in the persecution of Jews in Russia. But the young Russian arrives in America, becomes a famous musician, and ends up composing an American symphony. Along the way he is reunited with Vera. The play ends with a huge and very patriotic celebration on the Fourth of July. The play was an instant success that was staged all over the country, at theaters, colleges, and high schools, and at factories like the Ford Motor Company.[9]

From then on the idea of the United States as being a melting pot became well known. It was a popular metaphor, but it was not without its critics. In 1915 the social scientist Horace Kallen started advocating against the notion of the United States as a melting pot. As he saw the melting pot metaphor, assimilation would lead to excessive conformism. For Horace Kallen (who was Jewish) and his followers, the ideal would be to create a society that allowed all ethnic groups to keep their identities and unique histories. He kept advocating for the creation of a multiethnic society in the United States during his lifetime.[10]

Even with continued immigration in the twentieth century, the United States to a large extent continued to be one culture—diverse but also alike in many ways: the language, the common history, the culture. However, in the 1970s, it was more or less apparent that the United States was not really a true melting pot. Looking across all fifty states it was more like a salad bowl, metaphorically speaking, because ethnic differences became more visible as people with the same ethnic background continued to cluster together. As futurist Alvin Toffler pointed out in his book *PowerShift*, the salad bowl is "a dish in which diverse ingredients keep their identity."[11]

The metaphor of the salad bowl became popular as new immigrants kept coming to the United States, especially from Latin America and Asia. But some critics, like former presidential adviser Arthur M. Schlesinger Jr., were not happy with the concept of a multiethnic society. In his 1991 bestseller *The Disuniting of America*, he predicted what would be the negative side of a multiethnic society. In advocating against turning the United States into an official multiethnic nation, he drew a parallel to Europe, where ethnic animosity had led to all kinds of wars and catastrophes.[12]

Both Horace Kallen and Arthur M. Schlesinger Jr., and the metaphors they argued against, the melting pot and salad bowl, respectively, referred to the ethnic character of the United States. There is no question that the United States is extremely diverse in this respect, but in the twenty-first century ethnicity is only one of the differentiating parts of our identities, lifestyles, and tribes. Therefore, with respect to metaphors that include dishes, when talking metaphorically about the United Sates, one dish—the salad bowl—is simply not representative enough of today's society. Now there are so many different identities—dishes—that there is in fact a whole buffet! To a large extent we can choose for ourselves what we want from the buffet table. We do not have to make do with one salad. We can pick one dish or choose among several dishes in this lifestyle buffet and put the selection that we like on our plate, metaphorically speaking.

However, even with the lifestyle buffet, Americans share some core values. Openness to change and reinvention come to mind, as do a fascination with and acceptance of extremes, a seemingly constant need for exploration, and a strong belief that mistakes warrant second chances.[13] "Just Do It" is the slogan of a huge American brand, but it could also be the slogan of millions and millions of Americans. America is filled with self-made people. The richest people in the United States are self-made, and many have made their fortunes in their own lifetime.

This is all connected to the Great American Dream—a dream that started beckoning people in the 1600s. The earliest settlers had dreams of abundance and freedom. As the news of new land (and later the news of gold) reached these settlers, they started exploring and dreaming of limitless opportunities. The American Dream and the core American values are not about to change anytime soon. So while there are many issues and lifestyles that are dividing the United States, there is also a culture that is unique from any other in the world and there are some very important core values that unify Americans. This will not stop changes from happening, but these changes would be more dramatic without them.

LOOKING FOR IDEAS AND INNOVATIONS

Though it is not possible to predict all the changes that will come in the twenty-first century, we can predict where to look for them—the world's most powerful cultural center. At least since the Renaissance, there have been entire countries, regions, and cities that have had a strong economic and cultural influence on the rest of the world. For many centuries, the world's cultural center was in Europe. But in the mid-1800s, the cultural center shifted to the United States. According to the French political scientist Jacques Attali, the world's cultural power centers have been in the following locations since the beginning of the 1300s:

Figure 8.1. Shifting Cultural Centers[14]

Time	Cultural Center
1300–1450	Bruges
1450–1500	Venice
1500–1550	Antwerp
1550–1650	Genoa
1650–1750	Amsterdam
1750–1850	London
1850–1930	Boston
1930–1980	New York City
1980–	Los Angeles/San Francisco

Each of these cities and their surrounding regions has had an enormous influence on the rest of the world's cultural and economic development at the time shown on the chart above. This was not about military or political power, but about the ideas, innovations, and culture these places produced. The center that produces the most original and powerful new ideas and images becomes the city, region, or country that influences the rest of the world.

The growth of California's influence is basically the result of two factors: celluloid and silicon. Silicon Valley in Northern California plays a major part in the development of new information technologies. Nowhere else on the planet is there a greater concentration of companies specializing in digital technology.

In Southern California, Hollywood produces images that have widespread influence because images transcend most language barriers. The films, television shows, and other visual media that come out of Hollywood are so powerful that they serve as a de facto marketing tool with global reach. Just how powerful Hollywood is can be illustrated by how a very unlikely fashion contender—sheepskin boots from Australia—became popular at the beginning of the twenty-first century. The history of these boots shows just how literal the influence of Hollywood can be.

Ugg is both a generic term for Australian flat-heeled, pull-on sheepskin boots and a brand name in the United States and other countries. Uggs were originally created by shearers, who wrapped Merino sheepskins around their feet to keep them warm. The name is derived from the word *ugly*, and these "ugly boots" have been made in Australia for most of the twentieth century. The sheepskin boots were mostly used indoors, but some people also wore them when they went outdoors and even when they went grocery shopping. They were considered mostly working class in Australia until the beginning of the twenty-first century, when they changed status and became popular among young, fashion-conscious women.

The sheepskin boots are comfortable to wear year-round. In cold weather, they keep the feet warm, and in warm weather, the natural fibers of the fleece have a cooling effect by wicking away perspiration. In the 1970s, Australian surfers began using them to warm up their feet after surfing in cold water for hours. The surfers also found that their sheepskin boots were comfortable in winter after skiing.

American surfers who had been to Australia also started wearing the boots during the 1970s. At that time, you could buy Ugg boots only in Australia. In 1978 an Australian surfer named Brian Smith went to the United States with a few pairs of Ugg boots in his rucksack. He tried to sell them in New York, with no success, but when he went to Los Angeles, he found his market. He set up a company and started selling Ugg boots in the United States.

In the early 1990s, when surfing became more and more popular as both a professional and a recreational sport, the market for sheepskin boots grew. At the time, the television show *Baywatch* was one of the most popular American television series. One of the original members of the cast was actress Pamela Anderson, who was also one of the first celebrities to be seen wearing the sheepskin boots, both on and off the show. In the beginning of the 2000s, Ugg had become popular with college women all over the United States and with young women in Europe.

In 2003 an English newspaper listed all the celebrities who had been photographed wearing Uggs: Madonna, Gwyneth Paltrow, Sarah Jessica Parker, Kate Hudson, Cameron Diaz, Nicole Kidman, Leonardo DiCaprio, Reese Witherspoon, Jennifer Aniston, Jennifer Lopez, and Julia Roberts.[15]

Hollywood did not do all the marketing of Ugg boots, and Hollywood is not the center of up-and-coming fashion; it only plays a role in the marketing of what goes mainstream. With respect to fashion, New York is the center of the United States. It is there that most of the best-known fashion designers, such as Ralph Lauren, Calvin Klein, Donna Karan, and Marc Jacobs, to name a few, have their headquarters. As Diane von Fürstenberg, the designer and president of the Council of Fashion Designers of America, has said, "Every designer of the entire world comes to New York to get inspired."[16] Thus the influence of New York fashion does not come about because of New Yorkers traveling all over the world promoting American fashion—it is because people from all over the world travel to New York with the specific purpose of getting inspiration.

America, however, is made up of a plethora of industries—from food to health and fitness to information technologies, among others—and for inspiration in these fields, the destination is often California. Again and again, the images that come out of California and Hollywood specifically have influenced lifestyles all over the United States and the world, and in much more profound ways than boots. Several of the best-known lifestyles of the twentieth century came out of California—bikers, surfers, and hippies (as described in chapter 4).

In the twenty-first century the influence of California is not just about blue jeans, Disney, freeways, microchips, health clubs, Apple, eBay, fusion cuisine, and Google—to name just a few of the innovations that have come out of California and that have influenced how people live not just in the United States but all over the world. In the twenty-first century California is, for instance, leading the way in clean technology. Pacific Gas & Electric, a San Francisco–based utility, has 40 percent of the nation's solar roofs in its service area. California is the nation's leader in green patents, green jobs, and supply from renewable resouces.[17] In small and grand ways the technology and behavior that comes out of California in all likelihood will continue to affect how people live in the rest of the nation.

A GLOBAL PUZZLE

It is not a given that Hollywood and the rest of California will continue to be so hugely influential. As in the past, influence can change, and another continent, region, and city can take over. Also, even though the United States has been the world's cultural center in the twentieth century, it is not as if it were not susceptible to inspiration and influence from other continents. Soccer, the most popular sport in Europe and Latin America, is becoming increasingly popular in the United States. In the 1960s, French culture was all the rave. Then First Lady Jacqueline Kennedy had a preference for everything French. Avid cook Chuck Williams got inspiration from France before founding his business, Williams-Sonoma, selling kitchen utensils needed for fine dining. In the 1960s Julia Child sold six hundred thousand copies of her first cookbook, *Mastering the Art of French Cooking*. Winery owner Robert Mondavi revolutionized wine production in Northern California in the mid-1960s after having studied wine production in France. Later in the twentieth century businessman Howard Schultz got inspiration from Italian coffee shops and founded Starbucks, and fashion retail magnate Leslie Wexner got inspiration from Italian lingerie stores as he was turning Victoria's Secret into a famous American brand.[18]

While some aspects of our habits, for instance, food, can be influenced by cultures from other continents, it seems less likely that our ways of life will be dramatically influenced by them. Though the economic influence of Southeast Asia is huge and still growing, that region is not likely to be able to compete with the United States with respect to (pop) cultural influence anytime soon.

To be the world's pop cultural center, a country or a region must have access to the rest of the world through all major communication channels, in particular television and movies. So in order to be the world's pop cultural center Southeast Asia would have to create content that the rest of the world would be interested in viewing. This requires that viewers are able to identify with the content and to relate to stories told. There are no signs that China is a contender for that position, nor is India, which already has a huge movie industry but little distribution on other continents. As for Japan and other countries in Southeast Asia, the people in these countries are adopting American lifestyles rather than exporting their own.

In South Korea the concept of a weekend did not exist for most of the twentieth century. Now most people who work take the weekend off and engage in Western-style activities. In a very short time, brunch became a big hit in Seoul and other big cities.[19] In Europe, American-style brunch had the big breakthrough in the 1990s.

In Japan where Buddhism and Shintoism are the dominant religions, being wed in a Christian church has become a new ritual to many Japanese, not because they are becoming Christian but because they like the setting and the etiquette of a church wedding.[20] A similar pattern can be observed in China with respect to Christmas. In December, big cities like Shanghai are decorated with Christmas ornaments.

In India many women are abandoning their traditional clothing, the sari. As a young sari weaver told *Time* magazine, "People don't buy saris anymore. Now they buy jeans." A student at Delhi University gave this explanation for the low interest in wearing the sari: "There is a general perception that you would consider a woman in Western formal wear more empowered than her more traditional counterparts."[21]

On other continents American ways of life are also becoming popular, also with respect to religion. Take for instance the Pentecostal Church, an American religion that was founded in Los Angeles in 1906. The Pentecostal Church is one of the fastest-growing religious movements on a global scale, supplementing existing religions especially in Africa, South America, and Europe.[22]

The point here is that it is the United States that influences the rest of the world on a massive scale rather than vice versa. So it is one of history's ironies that the people around the world whose forefathers did not immigrate (voluntarily or by force) to America are now influenced by the descendants of the people who did come to America. And, in fact, many of them are dressing in what was once the epitome of American style—blue jeans. When we want to understand how American pop culture influences the rest of the world in very concrete ways, there is no better case story than that of blue jeans.

Interestingly, the heritage of blue jeans begins (once again!) in California (as was described in chapter 4). After the bust of the gold rush, the story of California extends past the get-rich-quick notoriety of that time and into one of continual innovation—from Hollywood moviemaking and new music to information technology. Sounds and images from big screens and on handheld devices have caught and held the world's attention—and the rest of the world asks, what will the Americans do next?

The story of blue jeans—as symbolic of America as the Wild West—continued in the twentieth century. Until the 1930s blue denim jeans were little known on the East coast. But this changed during the Great Depression, when many ranch owners had to find new sources of income. Therefore, they started opening up their ranches to people from the East (then often called "dudes") who wanted to enjoy the adventure of a Western ranch vacation. Many vacationers at the dude ranches took their blue jeans back to the big cities on the East coast. Thus, blue jeans went from being part of rural life to becoming an urban phenomenon, though this process slowed down during World War II. But after the war, blue denim trousers became a component of the new urban landscape.[23]

The music industry also played an important part in popularizing blue jeans in the United States. The singing cowboys of the 1940s, the most famous of whom were Roy Rogers and Bob Wills, had a lot of success during a period of industrialization and urbanization, when many people were nostalgic for the "Old West."[24] Their songs romanticized prairie life. The musical genre that Roy Rogers, Bob Wills, and the other singing cowboys created became the roots of today's country and Western music. Though the number of actual ranch workers decreased after World War II, the popularity of country and Western style grew. Blue jeans became popular among many country and Western performers and their fans.

In Europe, blue jeans were almost unknown before World War II, but as the American military presence in Europe grew at the end of the war and after it, many Europeans became familiar with blue jeans as well as many other American products. For instance, in Sweden, the first pair of blue jeans was sold in 1947.[25]

While music made blue jeans popular in the United States,

movies made blue jeans popular in countries where Hollywood had access, especially through Westerns, which became a very popular film genre after World War II. With movies such as *The Far Country* (1954) and *Rio Bravo* (1959), blue jeans became a symbol of freedom—and, in Europe, a symbol of America. In the "rebel movies" of the 1950s, such as *The Wild One* with Marlon Brando and *Giant* with James Dean, millions of people watched attractive men playing larger-than-life characters wearing blue jeans.

In the 1960s, the new youth culture, the hippies, also favored blue jeans because of their rebellious and working-class edge. In the early 1970s some gay men in New York and San Francisco favored tight and fitted blue jeans, which became part of a hypermasculine look, with accompanying tattoos and crew cuts. Also during this time, more college students were able to afford trips to Europe and other foreign places, where the locals noticed their jeans.

At the beginning of the 1970s, blue jeans were not that popular among women, and blue jeans had yet to become mainstream among men. But this changed when a large Hong Kong–based clothing manufacturing company by the name of Murjani actively sought a famous designer who would lend his or her name to a new brand of blue jeans. Up until that time, three companies more or less dominated the blue jeans market—Levi's, Lee, and Wrangler—and Murjani learned that no high-fashion designer wanted his or her name associated with blue jeans. Therefore, Murjani started asking American royals, such as the Rockefellers and Jacqueline Kennedy Onassis, if Murjani could use their name, for a big fee. The answer was *no*, until heiress Gloria Vanderbilt accepted a deal for designing them. The Vanderbilt jeans went on sale in 1976, and "the jeans exploded like [a] cork out of [a] champagne bottle. . . . Well-dressed women everywhere were wearing jeans, and Vanderbilt's brand became so popular with women that sociologists . . . began pondering the trend," according to the Calvin Klein biography *Obsession.* A couple of years later Gloria Vanderbilt Jeans had the largest share of the market.[26]

When fashion designers such as Calvin Klein and Ralph Lauren also began manufacturing blue jeans, the term *designer jeans* came into usage. Calvin Klein launched his sexy jeans for women in 1978. At the end of the 1980s blue jeans had become a mainstream phenomenon. Now blue jeans have become so widespread as apparel that they have lost the symbolic quality of being American. Instead they are part of the "style language" that is "spoken" all over the world—as are T-shirts, sneakers, and other clothing styles that are parts of wardrobes worldwide.[27] Now blue jeans do not have any particularly strong affiliation with any one lifestyle.

The story of blue jeans is also a story of globalization, and some critics have warned that globalization will make us all look more alike. That blue jeans have replaced saris in India as the preferred clothing of young Indian women could prove this point. But these critics are actually wrong. The huge diversity in style that has emerged in America as we see more globalization proves that globalization does not make us all dress more alike. To the extent that we are becoming similar across different continents, we are simultaneously becoming just as diverse across the same borders— American-style diversity is also becoming global-style diversity. In the twenty-first century no one should be surprised to see a Dane in Copenhagen dressed as a cowboy, a Chinese in Beijing dressed as a biker, or an Iranian in Teheran dressed as a hip-hopper.

In other words, the lifestyle buffet is not only an American phenomenon—it is a global one. In many ways the rest of the world is seeing the exact same changes in society as the United States is seeing—people defining themselves based on new identities and organizing their lives accordingly. English is the lingua franca of the world. For those who still do not understand English, however, there is the nonverbal language of clothing, designer names, and logos—all of which have truly become an international language. Like the nonverbal language of dress codes, symbols, and logos, this international language has become a common language. This is the result of the images being presented to us again and again in movies, television, many other kinds of media, and advertising—and first and foremost, by the stores that sell the clothing and accessories over almost all the world.

The diversity in other countries—often based on American dress codes—also affects the United States. As people adopt multiple identities not only in the United States but also in other countries, we are all able to connect more freely with people in other places because these multiple identities transcend national borders. We can more easily relate to other people on other continents when our identity is based on not just a few identity categories, like geography, history, and religion. When leisure, style, and sexuality also get to be integral parts of our identities, new affinities and affiliations come into play. When we base our identity on these new identity categories, we can feel at home in many places, not just in one state and not just in the United States. Americans are becoming more and more cosmopolitan.

This cosmopolitan world can end up affecting many aspects of life. One aspect that may change is international sporting events. Before the creation of present-day nation-states, tribes dominated every continent. Tribes are still very much a reality today, but in all likelihood tribal society at the end of the twenty-first century will be very different from those of the past and those of today. So with the new kinds of tribes, which are not first and foremost based on geography and ethnicity, maybe we will see sporting events that are not composed of different nations competing against each other. In 2097 the hockey world championships may *not* be between the United States and Canada but between two tribes—say a match between Gay Hip-Hoppers United and Rural Bikers International.

Does this sound far out? Maybe too far out in the future to take seriously? It is difficult to predict the future. But society does change. And while we often register technological changes as they happen, all the changes that take place among ourselves, among our neighbors and our countrymen, are often slower to register with us, that is, until the day we all realize that society has changed completely.

Appendix

CREATING THE STYLE MAP
A Brief Summary

T oday many people inside and outside the fashion industry think that there are no identifiable patterns in how we dress. Their thinking is that fashion is chaotic, in the sense that there are a multitude of styles that cannot be categorized. But just as the letters in the alphabet are not combined in a random and haphazard way to create language, neither are clothes. Designed objects are also combined again and again in the same way so that we have easily recognizable and identifiable dress codes that we can choose among in order to express who we are as clearly as possible.

That such dress codes exist is documented in chapter 4. But presupposing the documentation of these dress codes was the creation of the style map, which was introduced in chapter 6. The aim of the style map was to understand clothing styles in three continents: North America, Europe, and Australia/New Zealand. The aim was also to create a style map that must be exhaustive of all styles in existence, that is, the dress codes of all people in the three continents should be accounted for in the style map.

My starting point for the creation of the style map was studying fashion history. After studying the history of clothing since the earliest times, there is little doubt that most clothing has had a functional purpose because of climate considerations, comfort, and other needs. In other words, the map I wanted to create had to include "functional style." If we want to know what "functional style" could be as a style, we can look up *functional* in a dictionary. We then learn that some synonyms are *plain*, *practical*, *useful*, and *utilitarian*. Certainly not everybody is content to wear functional clothing, so, in order to find out what other styles there are, I started out by defining what the opposite of functional style could be. By looking up *functional* in *Chambers Synonyms and Antonyms*, we find *decorative* to be its opposite. Decoration is about clothing that has many elements for the sake of these elements, not function. Therefore, it was clear that there should be a *Decorative—Functional* scale in the style map.

There are a lot of traditions in clothing, but words like *traditional* and *untraditional* are not very descriptive because there are traditions in both formal and informal ways of dressing. Therefore, *traditional* and *untraditional* are not very precise or descriptive words. But from fashion history we also know that there are people who dress very formally—many men wear a formal suit with a tie and among women there is also a formal way of dressing, with a skirt and jacket or a classic dress. And there are also people who dress in a completely different way: quite informally, in blue jeans and a flannel shirt. If we look up these two words in *Chambers Synonyms and Antonyms*, we will learn that they are also antonyms. Thus there needed to be a *Formal—Informal* scale in the style map.

Some people dress in a glamorous way, with lots of bold colors, gold, rhinestones, and other shiny objects. And then there is the opposite of that; for example, we can point to the style of Christian monks. Their style is the exact opposite of glamour—they prefer an ascetic or simple way of dressing, always dressing in toned-down colors. According to *Chambers Synonyms and Antonyms*, the words *glamorous* and *ascetic* are antonyms. In the style map there should be a *Glamorous—Ascetic* scale.

In the south of France, on the Mediterranean coast, there is a town by the name of Cap d'Agde. During the summer, tens of thousands of people flock there from all over the world. The inhabitants all prefer a certain style: nude. Cap d'Agde is the world's largest organized nudist meeting place. It is an entirely self-contained nudist town with its own shops, post offices, gas station, and around thirty restaurants and bars. Everywhere employees and the inhabitants are in the nude. This is the preferred style of the inhabitants, who like a natural way of "dressing." People come here from many parts of the world; such people include members of the American Association for Nude Recreation or one of the European nudist associations that arrange many other similar nudist events.

Nudity is certainly also a style, albeit one without clothes. It is a natural, or rather, an organic style (*organic* is a synonym for *nature-like* according to *Chambers Synonyms and Antonyms*). There are variations to this organic style. For instance, just go to New Zealand and see the many people who go barefoot for much of their lives—at the supermarket and stores, and even at airports and other public places. And then, of course, there is the Fundamentalist Church of Jesus Christ of Latter-day Saints, a polygamous religious sect once related to the Mormon Church, whose female members dress with long skirts and blouses to cover the whole body and bonnets to cover their hair. So nude and covered are also variations that are available when choosing how to dress. In the style map there should be a *Covered—Nude* scale.

I carried out a study in which I created an all-inclusive graphic model that represents the different styles that we can choose from.[1] The graphic model has four scales combined in a map with four axes:

Decorative—Functional on the west–east axis,
Informal—Formal on the north–south axis,
Glamorous—Ascetic on the northwest–southeast axis, and
Covered—Nude on the southwest–northeast axis.

The combination of the four scales is illustrated in figure A.1.

Figure A.1. Style Map Scales

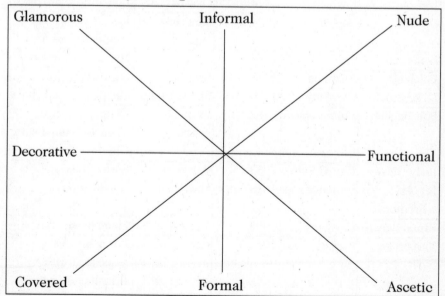

Figure A.1 does not document the existence of any styles. In order to document the existence of any style in the map, I had to prove that clothes representing different styles are actually worn. This was done by selecting some of the world's best-known clothing brands and analyzing and identifying the style that each brand represents. The result is presented in figure A.2.

Figure A.2. Designer and Brand Names in the Fashion Industry

Name	Country of Origin	Year Established	Original Product Category	Code
Aquatscutum	England	1851	Raincoats	The epitome of classic British style
Anne Klein	United States	1968	Womenswear	Mainstream style
Armani	Italy	1974	Apparel	Simple style with subdued colors
Baby Phat	United States	1998	Womenswear	Hip-Hopper style
Bally	Switzerland	1851	Shoes	Classic shoes
Banana Republic	United States	1978	Apparel	Casual style
Barbour	England	1894	Oilskin coats	Romantic style
Belstaff	England	1924	Motorbike apparel	Raw style (but also technical qualities)
Benetton	Italy	1965	Apparel	Mainstream style
Billabong	Australia	1973	Swimwear	Surfer style
Birkenstock	Germany	1774	Shoes/sandals	Organic shaped shoes
Bob Mackie	United States	1982	Evening gowns	Glamorous style, often associated with Cher
Body Glove	United States	1953	Surfwear	Surfer style
Brooks Brothers	United States	1818	Menswear	Classic style
Bruno Banani	Germany	1993	Menswear	Flamboyant style
Burberry	England	1856	Coats	For many years associated with British classic style*

Calvin Klein	United States	1968	Apparel	Understated style, often using few colors (white, beige, brown, black)
Carhartt	United States	1889	Work clothes	Street style
Caterpillar	United States	1925	Machines	Heavy boots
Chanel	France	1910	Womenswear	Classic "ladylike" style
Christian Lacroix	France	1987	Womenswear	Romantic style
Church's	England	1873	Men's shoes	Classic-style shoes
Clark's	England	1825	Shoes/boots	Associated with desert boots
Columbia	United States	1938	Activewear	Outdoorsy style
DAKS	England	1894	Menswear	Classic style
Diesel	Italy	1978	Apparel	Trendy style
Dior	France	1947	Womenswear	Dramatic style
Dockers	United States	1986	Menswear	Casual style
Dolce & Gabbana	Italy	1985	Apparel	Glamorous style
Dries van Notennon	Belgium	1985	Apparel	Style inspired by Western clothing
Doc Martens	England	1959	Shoes/boots	Functional footwear, often associated with skinhead style
Ecko	United States	1993	Skateboarding shoes	Skateboarder style
Emanuel Ungaro	France	1965	Womenswear	Romantic style
Emerica	United States	1996	Skateboarding shoes	Skateboarder style
Emilio Pucci	Italy	1949	Womenswear	Glamorous style
Energie	Italy	1983	Menswear	Trendy style
Esprit	United States	1964	Apparel	Mainstream fashion
Escada	Germany	1976	Womenswear	Classic "ladylike" style
Etnies	United States	1986	Skateboarding shoes	Skateboarder style
Etro	Italy	1968	Fabric	Bohemian style, known for paisley patterns

Evisu	Japan	1991	Blue jeans	Trendy style
Fcuk	England	1972	Apparel	Trendy style
Fred Perry	United States	1949	Sweat bands	Sporty style, sometimes used by skinheads
FUBU	United States	1992	Apparel	Hip-Hopper style
Gant	United States	1941	Apparel	Simple style
Gap	United States	1969	Apparel	Casual style
Gianni Versace	Italy	1978	Apparel	Glamorous style
Gucci	Italy	1921	Leather goods	Trendy style
Hang Ten	United States	1962	Swimwear	Surfer-style shorts
Hardy Amies	England	1946	Womenswear	Romantic style
Havaianas	Brazil	1962	Sandals (flip-flops)	Beach style
Henry Cotton's	Italy	1970s**	Womenswear, menswear	Romantic style
Holland & Holland	England	1835	Menswear	Classic British style
Iceberg	Italy	1974	Womenswear	Glamorous style
Jaeger	England	1883	Underwear	Classic style
Jean-Paul Gaultier	France	1976	Apparel	Decorative and flamboyant style
Jill Sander	Germany	1973	Apparel	Minimalist style, often black colors
John Smedley	England	1784	Apparel	Romatic style, pastel colors
Kaffe Fasset	United States	1937	Knits	Bohemian style
Kangol	England	1938	Hats, caps	Skater style
Kate Spade	United States	1993	Handbags	Fashionable style
Kenneth Cole	United States	1984	Shoes	Fashionable style
Kenzo	France	1970	Womenswear	Decorative, bohemian style
Lacoste	France	1931	Polo shirts	Sporty style
Laura Ashley	England	1953	Fabric, home decoration	Romantic style

Levi's	United States	1853	Blue jeans	Practical style
Liberty	England	1875	Fabric	Romantic style
L. L. Bean	United States	1912	Boots	Outdoorsy style
Lloyd	Germany	1920s**	Men's shoes	Classic style
Loden-Frey	Austria	1842	Coats	Romantic style
Marc Jacobs	United States	1994	Womenswear	Trendy style
Marni	Italy	1992	Womenswear	Trendy style
MaxMara	Italy	1951	Womenswear	Simple style, subdued colors
Missoni	Italy	1953	Knits	Bohemian style, many colors
Mulberry	England	1971	Home decoration	Romantic British style
Musto	England	1965	Yachting clothes	Sporty style
Nautica	United States	1983	Apparel	Simple style
Nicole Farhi	England	1983	Womenswear	Fashionable style
Nikos	Germany	1980s**	Men's underwear	Decorative details
Olaf Benz	Germany	1980s**	Men's underwear	Decorative details
O'Neill	United States	1952	Surfwear	Surfer style
Paul Smith	England	1973	Apparel	Trendy style
Patagonia	United States	1957	Activewear	Outdoorsy style
Pendleton	United States	1909	Blankets	Western wear
Perfecto	United States	1915	Leather jackets	Raw style
Phat Farm	United States	1993	Menswear	Hip-Hopper style
Philip Treacy	England	1990	Hats	Dramatic style
Philips– Van Heusen	United States	1919	Shirts	Classic style
Polo Sport	United States	1993	Apparel	Simple style
Prada	Italy	1913	Leather goods	Trendy style
Prince of Scotland	England	1815	Apparel	Romantic style
Quiksilver	Australia	1969	Surfwear	Surfer style, street style

Rado	Switzerland	1957	Watches	Geometric style
Ralph Lauren	United States	1967	Apparel	Classic style
Redskins	France	1984	Leather jackets	Raw style
Reef	United States	1984	Sandals	Surfer style
R. M. Williams	Australia	1932	Boots	Australian cowboy (jackeroo) style
Roberto Cavalli	Italy	1972	Apparel	Glamorous style
Rodier	France	1852	Womenswear	Classic style
Schott NYC	United States	1913	Raincoats	Raw style, known for the Perfecto leather jacket
Sean John	United States	1998	Menswear	Hip-Hopper style
Sebago	United States	1946	Shoes	Sporty, maritime style
Stetson	United States	1865	Cowboy hats	Cowboy style
Storm	England	1992	Watches	Flamboyant style
Stüssy	United States	1980	Streetwear	Street style
Teva	United States	1984	Sandals	Natural, organic style
Timberland	United States	1918	Boots	Originally beige-colored boots, also worn by hip-hoppers
The North Face	United States	1966	Coats	Outdoorsy style
Thierry Mugler	France	1974	Apparel	Dramatic style
Thomas Pink	England	Late 1700s**	Shirts	Glamorous shirts
Tod's	Italy	1900	Shoes	Understated style
Vans	United States	1966	Skateboarding shoes	Skateboarder style
Versus	Italy	1995	Womenswear	Glamorous style
Wrangler	United States	1945	Blue jeans	The original cowboy style
Zandra Rhodes	England	1968	Womenswear	Flowing, colorful style
Zara	Spain	1975	Apparel	Trendy style

* Brand has changed style since this survey was made in 2000. Because designer and brand names in clothing sometimes change style, it is worth noting that the designer and brand names were decoded at the beginning of the twenty-first century. The styles of the designers and brands may have represented different styles at other times and may have changed since. Often there is a time lag in the way people perceive a style brand, so even when brands have changed their style, consumer perception of the brand may not have changed.

** Existed at this time, no precise founding year made public.

Today, designers are the main creators of style, but they are only successful if there is a need for their designs. Figure A.2 represents only some of the best-known international clothing designers and brands. Many have been highly innovative and some have ended up creating their own iconic style that other designers end up copying.

If we take a closer look at the numerous designer and brand names in figure A.2, we learn that some designers and brands change their style on a regular basis while others rarely change their basic style (though they may change the products). The former are termed *trendy*; the brands that do not change so often all have very specific style names. Among American designers, Ralph Lauren, Calvin Klein, and Donna Karen do not change their styles very often. Among European designers, Giorgio Armani and Versace also have stuck to certain styles for decades. Then there are designers like the American designer Marc Jacobs and European designer brands like Gucci and Prada, whose clothing collections change style often.

So, while much of fashion changes from season to season, the point here is that consumers have the option of choosing a style that they can count on being the same for many years. This is important because it makes this kind of designer clothing much more effective as a nonverbal communication tool and, as a consequence, the designed objects can meaningfully be part of dress codes.

In figure A.2 we also have designer names like Prada and Gucci. They are fashion brands whose clothing style changes from season to season. For some brands there are maybe a couple of years or more between changes in their style; they wait until the style is more mainstream before adopting the new style. But the trendy brands have to fit into any map that includes all existing styles. This means that there should be a place for fashion that changes in the style map.

Without a place in the style map for fashion that changes, we cannot say that we have accounted for all the styles that people can wear today. However, in the middle of the style map there seems to be a center where all the styles "originate." It is like identifying the place on an atlas that is the origin of the human species (which would be somewhere in eastern Africa, according to our current knowledge). Actually, this makes some sense because then we can illustrate that all new styles that will (after some time) end up on the map are fed into the style map from the middle. So we can place the dynamic dimension—fashion that changes—in the middle of figure A.1.

In the survey, I placed all the designer and brand names from figure A.2 in figure A.1. Along with the designer and brand names I also included other style signifiers—colors, patterns, fabrics, and accessories. There are some types of clothing, colors, and so on that have been so widely accepted that they cannot be said to represent just one style, and therefore they can be difficult to decode in an unambiguous way. This goes for blue jeans, the suit, the color black, and fabrics like cotton and wool, all of which are not placed on the map. These style signifiers were not included in the survey.

Figure A.3 (refer to pp. 202–203) clearly documents that the map has designer and brand names all over. No single way of dressing is left out by the selection of designer and brand names that were included in figure A.2.

Figure A.3 highlights only style that represents clothing styles that were originally created and worn in Europe, North America, and Australia/New Zealand. In principle, the map can include any style from all three of these continents—whether historical dress style or uniforms or sports clothing—it just has to be filled out with the words and terms used to describe these styles. Several clothing elements, such as the Nehru jacket and paisley pattern, which were both originally from India, are now part of how people dress outside of India and are therefore included. To reduce the complexity, European national dresses have been excluded, as they are mostly used for festive occasions and not for everyday use.

Styles that originated outside of North America, Europe, and Australia/New Zealand but are now worn by people in these continents could easily be included on the style map, but it would make the map more complicated. However, the map can also be used to document the styles worn on other continents.

The style map gives us an overview of the landscape that we navigate when we wear clothing. There are literally thousands of different designed objects, colors, fabrics, and accessories that can be mixed in numerous ways. The style map, of course, shows only some of the choices that exist with respect to all the included individual objects. But what the style map reveals is that there are some patterns in the way all these individual objects are mixed. Overall, the style map reveals that there are some distinct clusters of styles in different parts of the map. By placing a simple grid on the map, nine different and distinct style clusters appear:

- Classic style
- Romantic style
- Bohemian style
- Glamorous style
- Raw style
- Organic style
- Practical style
- Simple style
- Fashion style

The clusters reveal that there are patterns in how we combine the different objects. With more and more people—who are more diverse than ever before—crowding the large urban landscapes, it certainly makes sense that there are more ways of combining the designed objects than these nine style clusters. Though highly distinct, these nine style clusters together do not make up a very refined nonverbal communication tool. But if we make the style map grid smaller, we can see the contours of many more style combinations. How many different archetypical clothing styles there are is open for discussion, but the discussion can begin by dividing each of the eight squares outside of the fashion theme into four smaller squares. In that way we can spot the contours of at least thirty-two different dress codes. There are more, but those that are most commonly spotted in Western societies are highlighted in chapters 4 and 6.

In a survey of interior styles that I made in the beginning of the twenty-first century, it became clear we have more or less fully integrated

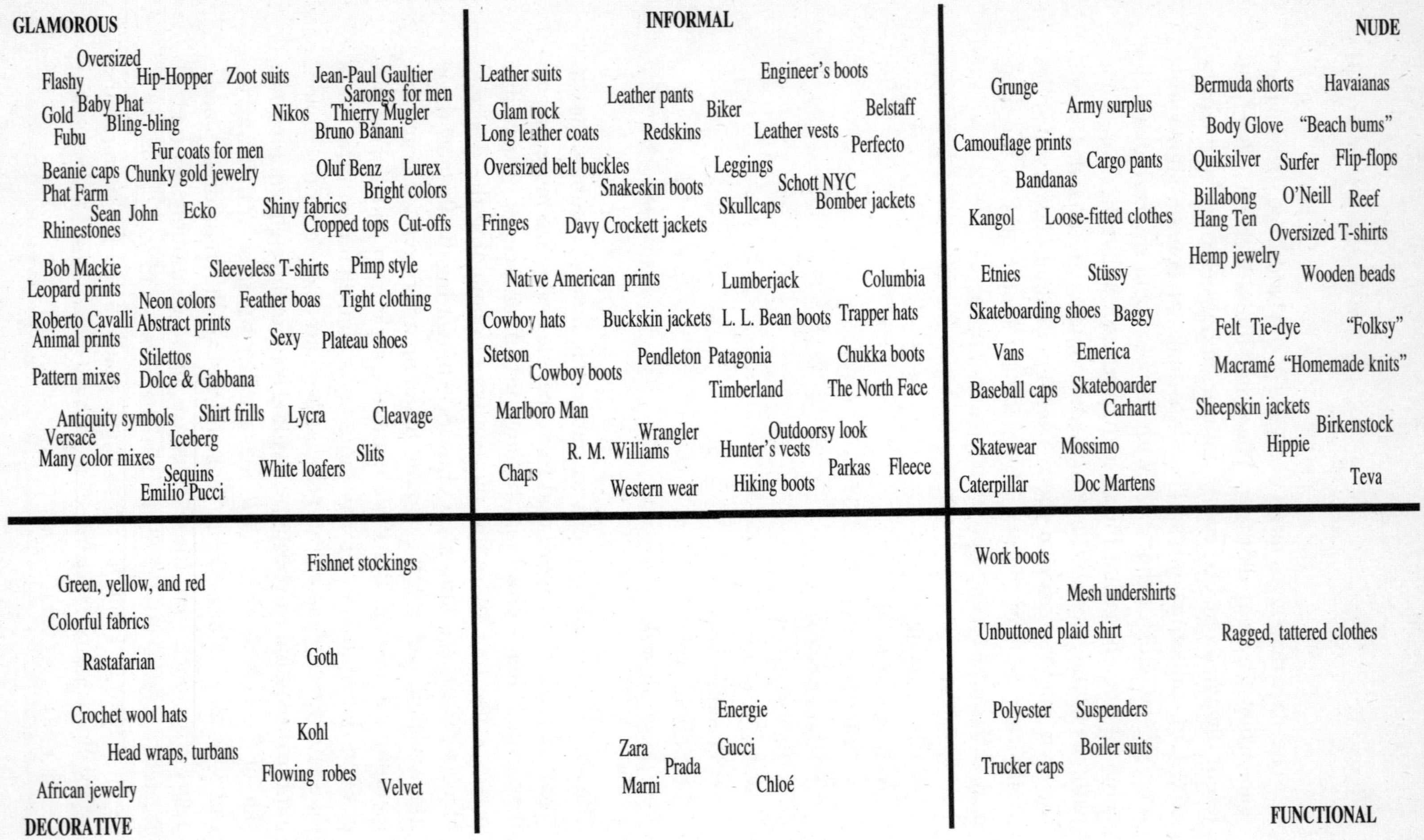

NUDE quadrant (top right):

Bermuda shorts   Havaianas
Body Glove   "Beach bums"
Quiksilver   Surfer   Flip-flops
Cargo pants
Camouflage prints   Bandanas
Billabong   Reef
O'Neill
Hang Ten   Oversized T-shirts
Hemp jewelry   Wooden beads
Felt   Tie-dye   "Folksy"
Macramé "Homemade knits"
Sheepskin jackets   Birkenstock
Hippie
Teva

Grunge   Army surplus
Loose-fitted clothes
Kangol
Etnies   Stüssy
Skateboarding shoes   Baggy
Vans   Emerica
Baseball caps   Skateboarder
Carhartt
Skatewear   Mossimo
Caterpillar   Doc Martens

Ragged, tattered clothes

FUNCTIONAL quadrant (bottom right):

Work boots
Mesh undershirts
Unbuttoned plaid shirt
Polyester   Suspenders
Boiler suits
Trucker caps

FUNCTIONAL

INFORMAL (top center / right of glamorous):

Leather suits
Engineer's boots   Belstaff
Glam rock   Biker
Leather pants   Redskins   Leather vests   Perfecto
Long leather coats   Leggings   Schott NYC
Oversized belt buckles   Snakeskin boots   Skullcaps   Bomber jackets
Fringes   Davy Crockett jackets
Native American prints   Lumberjack   Columbia
Buckskin jackets   L. L. Bean boots   Trapper hats
Cowboy hats   Pendleton   Patagonia   Chukka boots
Stetson   Timberland   The North Face
Cowboy boots   Outdoorsy look
Marlboro Man   Wrangler   Hunter's vests
R. M. Williams   Parkas   Fleece
Chaps   Western wear   Hiking boots

Energie
Zara   Prada   Gucci
Marni   Chloé

GLAMOROUS quadrant (bottom left):

Oversized
Flashy   Hip-Hopper   Zoot suits   Jean-Paul Gaultier
Gold   Baby Phat   Nikos   Sarongs for men
Bling-bling   Thierry Mugler
Fubu   Bruno Banani
Fur coats for men   Oluf Benz   Lurex
Beanie caps   Chunky gold jewelry   Bright colors
Phat Farm   Shiny fabrics   Cropped tops   Cut-offs
Sean John   Ecko
Rhinestones
Bob Mackie   Sleeveless T-shirts   Pimp style
Leopard prints   Feather boas   Tight clothing
Roberto Cavalli   Abstract prints   Sexy   Plateau shoes
Animal prints   Stilettos
Pattern mixes   Dolce & Gabbana
Antiquity symbols   Shirt frills   Lycra   Cleavage
Versace   Iceberg   Slits
Many color mixes   Sequins   White loafers
Emilio Pucci

Fishnet stockings

Green, yellow, and red
Colorful fabrics   Goth
Rastafarian
Crochet wool hats   Kohl
Head wraps, turbans   Flowing robes   Velvet
African jewelry

DECORATIVE

Hoodie
Denim overalls Hillbilly
Track suits White wifebeater John Deere mesh caps
Sweatsuits
White socks
Nylon

Dior   Marc Jacobs
Kate Spade Donna Karan
Anne Klein Banana Republic
Kenneth Cole Nautica
Paul Smith
Esprit Benetton

Amish
Monochrome
Chinos/khakis Fred Perry
Loafers Sebago Docksides
Musto Sporty
Tod's
Cable knits
Polo Sport Tattersall prints
Beige
Gant Dockers
Varsity jackets Few colors Turtleneck sweaters
MaxMara Clarks Linen
Cardigans and tie Armani
Wool blazer
Lacoste Navy blue Duffel coats Jill Sander
Polo shirts Preppy
Calvin Klein
Penny loafers Understated Minimalist

ASCETIC

Single-breasted suits Suits for women
Bally Lloyd Pantsuits
Chanel Pinstriped Corporate look
Rodier Bridled shoes
Escada Diplomat coats Dark double-breasted suits
Bouclé Crocodile-skin accessories White Oxford dress shirts
Savile Row Blue- or claret-colored tie
Lodenfrey
Philips–Van Heusen Button-down shirts Stripes
Burberry Brooks Brothers
DAKS Three-piece suits Mink coats
Pocket square Aquascutum Church Grey trousers
Decorative hankies Trench coats Crests Oxford dress shirts
Pocket watches Wingtip shoes Monogrammed Ralph Lauren
Cuff links Heraldic insignia

FORMAL

Purple Gypsy style Berets Layered clothing
Dries van Noten Missoni Embroideries
Scarves for men Kosak shirts Zandra Rhodes Oversized jewelry
Long scarves indoors Artist style Turquoise
Folklore Brocade Vest over T-shirt
Kenzo Paisley Etro Cordoroy
Nehru jackets Christian Lacroix Mary Janes
Ruffles Flamboyant Peasant style Knickers

Province prints Butterfly Henry Cotton's
Hardy Amies Cardigans for men
Mismatched colors Pearls Pastels Chelsea collars
Ballerina shoes Twinsets
Golf clothes Golden colors Straw hats
Quilted jackets John Smedley
Checkered prints Pink Derby hats
Earth tones Golf shoes Emanuel Ungaro Tasseled shoes Fedora
Plissé
Floral prints Safari jackets Jodhpurs Mulberry Tweed
Laura Ashley Bows Hunter green Kilts
Oilskin jackets Barbour Sixpence caps
Loafers with tassles Liberty
Prairie dresses Argyle pattern Tartans
Long skirts A-line skirts Holland & Holland Jaeger
Buttoned-up Pringle of Scotland

COVERED

interior design products into our nonverbal communication.[2] The survey showed that we use many of same words when we talk about interiors as when we talk about clothing. The survey focused on hotel interiors because they include all kinds of product categories—from rugs to lamps, and so on. Figure A.4 lists hotel names and descriptions of their styles. In describing the overall style we can use many of the same terms as we did when decoding the clothing styles in figure A.2.

Just like it was possible to place the clothing terms and brand names in figure A.2 in a style map, it is also possible to place terms related to home furnishings—colors, patterns, fabrics, and interior design styles—in the interior style map. With all the different names and terms placed on the style map, it was documented that the same style clusters that were identified in clothing also exist in the home decoration categories. The style map for interiors can be seen in figure A.5 (refer to pp. 208–209).

Figures A.3 and A.5 reveal that that same styles exist in clothing and in interiors; in other words, the style maps for the two categories are identical. The consequences of the two identical style maps are discussed in chapter 6.

Figure A.4. Dictionary with Names in the Hotel Industry*

NAME	LOCATION	DECODING
Ace	Seattle, Washington, United States	Naked brick walls indoors, partly decorated with non-treated wood
Atelier Sul Mare	Messina, Italy	Painted brick walls indoors, a bar decorated with graffiti, untreated wood
Avalon	Los Angeles, California United States	1950s-inspired interior
Beach House	Kennebunkport, Maine, United States	Cape Cod–style, white furniture inside and outside, wooden walls painted white
Buffalo Mountain Lodge	Banff, United States	Rustic log cabin style, lots of visible wood

Cibolo Creek Ranch	Shafter, Texas, United States	Raw walls and ceilings, Santa Fe–inspired style
Charlton House	Shepton Mallet, Somerset, England	Classic with four-poster beds and lots of trimmings
Chelsea	New York City, New York, United States	Bohemian kitsch style with many mixes of styles and colors
Copenhagen Airport Hilton	Copenhagen, Denmark	Minimalist style with a retro touch
Costes	Paris, France	Bohemian style, à la late 1800s boudoir
D'Angleterre	Copenhagen, Denmark	Romantic style with many floral prints
De Vendôme	Paris, France	Classic style with antiques and trimmings
Eden	Arosa, Switzerland	Bohemian style with quirky mixes
Eleven Cadogan Gardens	London, England	Classic style with antiques
Estrella	Palm Springs, California, United States	Glamorous style with old Roman-inspired furniture, atypical furniture shapes
Gastwerk	Hamburg, Germany	Former steelworks, naked brick walls, lots of visible iron piping
George V	Paris, France	Classic style with antiques and trimmings
Helvetia & Bristol	Firenze, Italy	Classic style with antiques
Hempel	London, England	Minimalist, mostly white and subdued colors
Hix Island House	Vieques, Puerto Rico	Organic style with concrete walls and discolored effects on some walls

Home Ranch	Steamboat, Colorado, United States	Cowboy ranch style
Hudson	New York City, New York, United States	Trendy hotel decorated by Philippe Starck
Inn of the Anasazi	Santa Fe, New Mexico, United States	Santa Fe style
Kennedy School	Portland, Oregon, United States	Purple walls, quirky bohemian style with kitschy elements
Korakia	Palm Springs, California, United States	Western style with many raw decorative elements
L'Hotel	Paris, France	Bohemian style with many quirky details and mixes of styles
La Maison Rose	Eugénie-les-Basin, France	Romantic country house style with many patterned fabrics
La Pérouse	Nantes, France	Spartan, minimalist style, only white and similar light colors
Le Lodge Park	Megève, Haute Savoie, France	Bohemian style with many quirky mixes of fabrics and bric-a-brac
Le Sénéchal	Ars de Ré, France	Naked brick walls, organic style
Loft 523	New Orleans, Louisiana, United States	Naked brick walls, untreated wood, organic style
Lowell	New York City, New York, United States	Classic style with antiques and trimmings
Maison 140	Los Angeles, California, United States	Glamorous style, lots of decorative elements, black walls and patterned wallpaper and furniture, zebra skins on floor
Mercer	New York City, New York, United States	Trendy hotel with few discrete colors
Mondrian	Los Angeles, California, United States	Trendy hotel decorated by Philippe Starck

Orbit In	Palm Springs, California United States	1950s style, in the graphic tradition of that period
Pelican	Miami Beach, Florida, United States	Psychedelic and bohemian style, owned by Diesel, the fashion brand
Pelirocco	Brighton, England	Bohemian style with many mixes of styles
Penzance Arts Club	Penzance, Cornwall, England	Bohemian style with many mixes of styles
Perivolas	Santorini, Greece	Organic pueblo shapes, furniture made by untreated wood
Rancho de la Osa	Tucson, Arizona, United States	Western style
Ripa	Rome, Italy	Almost minimalist style
Ritz-Carlton Schlosshotel	Berlin, Germany	Classic style with antiques and trimmings and old master paintings
Royal	Copenhagen, Denmark	Decorated with 1950s furniture
Sanderson	London, England	Trendy hotel decorated by Philippe Starck
Shaker Inn	Enfield, New Hampshire, United States	Shaker style
St. Martin's Lane	London, England	Trendy hotel decorated by Philippe Starck
Trianon Palace	Versailles, France	Classic style with antiques
Villa d'Este	Cernobbio, Italy	Classic style with Como antiques
Villa Gallici	Aix-en-Provence, France	Romantic style with many floral prints on fabrics
XV Beacon	Boston, Massachusetts, United States	Glamorous style with many prints and gold decorations

*Because hotels sometimes change interiors, it is worth noting that the hotel interiors were decoded at the beginning of the twenty-first century.

GLAMOROUS ———————————— INFORMAL ———————————— NUDE

NUDE (upper right region)

Straw mats
Bamboo furniture
Rush mats

Zinc   Round shapes   Graffiti
Ron Arad   Pueblo style
Eero Aarnio
Psychedelic patterns   Graphic-organic patterns
George Nelson   Frank Gehry
Sheepskin as carpets   Driftwood
Humorous design
Isamu Noguchi   Raw wood
Beanie chairs   Eco-deco

Plastic furniture   Sod house style

Naugahyde   Trashy

Slum

FUNCTIONAL

INFORMAL (upper left region)

Visible steel
Shiny metal
Concrete floors/walls
Industrial style

Log cabin style
Rustic style

Raw stone

Dwell

Marc Newson

GLAMOROUS / INFORMAL (lower left region)

Art Deco
Geometric patterns
Deco style
High-backed chair
Lucite
Zebra print
Empire
Postmodern
Pop art
Antiquity statues

Contrasting colors
Decorated walls
Angular shapes
Soft leather furniture
Oversize leather furniture

Native American patterns
Ranch
Western style
Santa Fe style

Philippe Starck

GLAMOROUS / DECORATIVE (bottom left region)

Gold (color)
Supersizes
Bold colors
Flamboyant   Glass art
Versace Home
Oversized porcelain animals
Leopard prints

Mixes of patterns   Art Nouveau
Sculptural
African art   Opulence   Brocade
Ornamental
Mix of historical styles

Boudoir

DECORATIVE

ASCETIC

COVERED

INFORMAL

Homemade carpentry

Pinewood furniture

La-Z-Boy recliner

Wall-to-wall carpeting

Amish quilts

Monochrome colors

Beige

Armani/Casa

Arne Jacobsen

Shaker

Japanese style

White/black

Mies van der Rohe   Le Corbusier   Alvar Aalto

Photo art   Deckchairs   Long Island style   Minimalist

Red, blue, and white   White-painted wooden walls

Polished wood

Two-colored stripes   White   Donald Judd

Maritime style

Adirondack style

Nantucket style

Wallpaper
Retro

Elle Deco

Martha Stewart Living

Colonial style

Parquet flooring

Mahogany furniture

Crystal chandeliers

Plantation style

Silver candlesticks

Persian carpets

Trimmings

Wing chairs

Chesterfield couches   Old masters art

Antiques

Fleur-de-lis

Sister Parish

Heraldry

Old-fashioned four-poster beds

Tiffany   Expressive art   Crafts

Purple   "Artist's studio"

Kaffe Fassett   Cavelike

Paisley   Eclectic

Pottery

Mexican style

Spanish mission style

Mediterranean style

Windsor chairs

Terracotta colors

Pastels   Rose color

Wickerwork furniture   Liberty

Stencils

Bric-a-brac

Kilims

Floral patterns   "Shabby chic"   Tartans

Laura Ashley   *Victoria*   *Town & Country*

Chintz

Ruffles

Filigree work

Bows as decoration   William Morris   Draped curtains

ACKNOWLEDGMENTS

I have used several autobiographies, memoirs, and portrait articles as sources in this book. The subjects of the books certainly were a highly varied group of people, but it was a pleasure to get to know them all. In the future study of lifestyle sociology, autobiographies, memoirs, and biographies can be highly valuable sources, so I would like to thank future writers of these genres in advance.

On a more personal level I would like to thank my agent, Ed Knappman, who is a true professional. It is a privilege to have Ed as an agent. It has also been a great privilege to work with Linda Regan, my editor at Prometheus Books. Thanks also to Nicole Lecht for creating a book cover that I found perfect the minute I saw it.

Lifestyle sociology was not a huge discipline in the twentieth century, but judging solely by the encouragement that I have gotten from students, colleagues, business associates, family, and friends, I predict that the interest in this discipline will multiply in this century. We need it to understand who we are—no matter where we live. Thanks to all who have been supportive, both before and after I started writing *The Lifestyle Puzzle*.

NOTES

These endnotes are only references. The author has not made any comments or further elaborations in the endnotes. The few sources that are not in English as a rule refer only to factual information.

INTRODUCTION: PATTERNS AND GENERALIZATIONS
1. Henrik Vejlgaard, *Anatomy of a Trend* (New York: McGraw-Hill, 2007).

CHAPTER 1: LIVING IN A MILLION WAYS
1. Correspondents of the *New York Times*, *Class Matters* (New York: Times Books, 2005), p. 2.
2. "Facts for Features," US Census Bureau, http://www.census.gov/ (accessed May 3, 2010).
3. *BusinessWeek* (USA), October 20, 2003.
4. *Time* magazine (Holland), October 26, 2009.
5. Ibid.
6. *Newsweek* (USA), May 12, 2003.
7. *Time* magazine (Holland), October 26, 2009.
8. Ibid.
9. *Newsweek* (USA), May 12, 2003.
10. *New York Times* (USA), April 19, 2005.
11. *Time* magazine (Holland), April 2, 2007.
12. *Empire* magazine (England), March 2007.
13. Jon Galluccio, Michael Galluccio, and David Groff, *An American Family* (New York: St. Martin's Press, 2001).
14. *Advocate* magazine (USA), March 28, 2006.
15. *BusinessWeek* (England), October 20, 2003.
16. 2005–2007 American Community Survey, http://www.census.gov/.
17. *New York Times* (USA), April 28, 1997.
18. Faith Popcorn and Lys Marigold, *Clicking* (London: Thorsons, 1996).
19. Henrik Vejlgaard, *Cool & Hip Marketing* (Denmark: Nyt Nordisk Forlag Arnold Busck, 2001), p. 52.

20. Walt Wolfram and Ben Ward, eds., *American Voices: How Dialects Differ from Coast to Coast* (Malden, MA: Blackwell, 2007), pp. 64, 106.

21. Erling Bjøl, *USAs Historie* (Denmark: Gyldendal, 2005), p. 162.

22. Bridget Harrison, *Tabloid Love* (England: Corgi Books, 2007), p. 369.

23. Ibid., p. 371.

24. Po Bronson, *Why Do I Love These People?* (New York: Vantage Books, 2005), p. 63.

25. Jeannette Walls, *The Glass Castle* (New York: Scribner, 2005).

26. *New York Times* (USA), September 25, 2001.

27. Daniel J. Boorstin, *The Americans: The Colonial Experience* (England: Cardinal, 1958).

28. Allan Metcalf, *How We Talk: American Regional English Today* (Boston: Houghton Mifflin, 2000), p. 62.

29. *Webster's College Dictionary* (New York: Random House, 1995), p. 834.

30. "About Connecticut," The Official State of Connecticut Website, www.ct.gov/ctportal/site/default.asp (accessed May 3, 2010).

31. *Webster's College Dictionary* (New York: Random House, 1995), p. 1543.

32. Alan Taylor, *American Colonies: The Settling of North America* (New York: Penguin, 2001), pp. 118, 136, 241.

33. Daniel J. Boorstin, *The Americans: The National Experience* (England: Cardinal, 1965), pp. 171–79.

34. David Herbert Donald, *Lincoln* (New York: Simon & Schuster, 1995).

35. Anthony Harkins, *Hillbilly: A Cultural History of an American Icon* (New York: Oxford University Press, 2005).

36. Richard A. Bartlett, *Rolling Rivers: An Encyclopedia of America's Rivers* (New York: McGraw-Hill, 1984).

37. *Webster's New World Dictionary of American Language* (Fawcett Popular Library, 1995).

38. Michael C. LeMay, *From Open Door to Dutch Door: An Analysis of U.S. Immigration Policy since 1820* (New York: Praeger, 1987).

39. Taylor, *American Colonies*, pp. 67–90.

40. *Webster's New World Dictionary of American Language*.

41. Gawani Pony Boy, *Horse, Follow Closely: Native American Horsemanship* (Irvine, CA: BowTie Press, 2006).

42. Howard Lamar, ed., *The New Encyclopedia of the American West* (New Haven, CT: Yale University Prss, 1998).

43. Boorstin, *The Americans: The National Experience*, p. 56.

44. Ibid., pp. 62–65.

45. Jeffrey Odgen Johnson, "Determining and Defining 'Wife'—The Brigham Young Households," *Dialogue: A Journal of Mormon Thought* 20, no. 3 (Fall 1987): 57–70.

46. Taylor, *American Colonies*, pp. 320–21.

47. Allen J. Scott, *On Hollywood: The Place, the Industry* (Princeton, NJ: Princeton University Press, 2005).

48. *Webster's College Dictionary*, p. 784.

49. Ron and Barb Hofmesiter, *An Alternative Lifestyle: Living & Traveling Full-Time in a Recreational Vehicle* (Livingston, TX: R & B Publications, 1955); Nena and George O'Neill, *Open Marriage: A New Lifestyle for Couples* (New York: Evans, 1972); Beverly Dubin, *Water Squatters: The Houseboat Lifestyle* (Santa Barbara: Capra, 1975); Graham Tucker, *It's Your Life: Create a Christian Lifestyle* (Toronto: Anglican Book Centre, 1977); Fritz Klein, *The Bisexual Option—Today's Most Surprising New Lifestyle* (Berkley Books, 1978); Craig R. Wilson, *Total Health Tennis: A Lifestyle Approach* (Ardmore, PA: Whitmore, 1979).

50. *New York* magazine (USA), June 8, 2009.

51. *American Heritage Dictionary of the English Language* (New York: Dell, 1976); *Webster's New World Dictionary of American Language*.

52. Max Weber, *The Protestant Ethic and the Spirit of Capitalism* (Mineola, NY: Dover, 2003).

53. *Vanity Fair* (England), July 2009.

CHAPTER 2: WE ARE WHAT WE ARE

1. Eric W. Sanderson, *Mannahatta: A Natural History of New York City* (New York: Abrams, 2009).

2. Daniel J. Boorstin, *The Americans: The Democratic Experience* (New York: Random House, 1973), pp. 288–90.

3. Dianne and Don Judd, *The Hamptons* (New York: Crescent Books, 1991).

4. *New York* magazine (USA), December 10, 2007.

5. T. B. Bottomore, *Classes in Modern Society* (England: George Allen & Unwin, 1978).

6. Joan Didion, *Where I Was From: A Memoir* (England: Harper Perennial, 2004), p. 128.

7. Correspondents of the *New York Times*, *Class Matters* (New York: Times Books, 2005), p. 75.

8. "Facts, Statistics, & Holidays," The Official State of Connecticut Web-

site, http://www.ct.gov/sots/cwp/view.asp?A=3188&Q=392592 (accessed May 4, 2010); *Insight Guide Florida* (Singapore: APA Publications, 1998), p. 15; *Complete Flags of the World* (England: Dorling Kindersley, 2008), p. 18.

9. Kate Fox, *Watching the English* (London: Hodder & Stoughton, 2005), p. 406.

10. Ibid., p. 73.

11. Ibid., p. 82.

12. William A. DeGregorio, *The Complete Book of U.S. Presidents* (Fort Lee, NJ: Barricade Books, 2009).

13. Barbara Cady, *Icons of the 20th Century* (New York: Overlook Press, 1998).

14. Alan Taylor, *American Colonies: The Settling of North America* (New York: Penguin, 2001), p. 139.

15. Ibid., p. 140.

16. Ibid., p. 157.

17. Ibid., pp. 137, 141, 181–85, 263–71, 336, 342, 355–57; Donald B. Kraybill, *The Puzzles of Amish Life* (Intercourse, PA: Good Books, 1998), p. 3; "Huguenot Society of South Carolina," www.huguenotsociety.org (accessed May 4, 2010); L. DeAne Lagerquist, *The Lutherans* (Westport, CT: Greenwood, 1999); Daniel J. Boorstin, *The Americans: The National Experience* (New York: Random House, 1965), pp. 62–65.

18. Taylor, *American Colonies*, p. 265.

19. Ibid., p. 317.

20. Robert J. McKeever and Philip Davies, *Politics USA* (England: Pearson Longman, 2009), p. 89.

21. *Commercial Appeal* (USA), October 8, 2003.

22. Reyner Banham, *Los Angeles: The Architecture of Four Ecologies* (Berkeley: University of California Press, 2009), p. xviii; *New York Times* (USA), February 27, 2008.

23. Paul Escott et al., eds., *Major Problems in the History of the American South: Documents and Essays*, vol. 2, *The New South* (Boston: Houghton Mifflin, 1999); *New York Times* (USA), September 30, 2007.

24. *New York Times* (USA), September 30, 2007.

25. Po Bronson, *Why Do I Love These People?* (New York: Vantage Books, 2005), p. 137.

26. Barack Obama, *Dreams of My Father* (England: Canongate Books, 2007), p. 305.

27. *National Geographic* magazine (USA), January 1988.

28. D. J. Waldie, *Where We Are Now: Notes from Los Angeles* (Santa Monica: Angel City Press, 2004), p. 13.

29. Tommy Hilfiger and George Lois, *Iconic America* (New York: Universe Publishing, 2007), pp. 84–85.

30. Smithsonian Institution, *Do All Indians Live in Tipis?* (New York: Harper, 2007), p. 18.

31. Edmund White, *My Lives: An Autobiography* (New York: Ecco Books, 2006), p. 272.

32. Charlie LeDuff, *US Guys* (New York: Penguin, 2006), p. 143.

33. Boorstin, *The Americans: The National Experience*, pp. 283–84.

34. Ibid., p. 285.

35. Walt Wolfram and Ben Ward, eds., *American Voices: How Dialects Differ from Coast to Coast* (Malden, MA: Blackwell, 2007), pp. 27, 45, 68.

36. Allan Metcalf, *How We Talk: American Regional English Today* (Boston: Houghton Mifflin, 2000), p. 20.

37. Ibid., p. 29 [emphasis added].

38. Robert J. McKeever and Philip Davies, *Politics USA* (England: Pearson Longman, 2009), p. 88.

39. LeDuff, *US Guys*, p. 202.

40. Ibid., p. 201.

41. "National Voter Turnout in Federal Elections: 1960–2008," www.infoplease.com/ipa/A0781453.html (accessed May 3, 2010).

42. McKeever and Davies, *Politics USA*, p. 126.

43. Ibid., p. 3; *Time* magazine (Holland), November 6, 2006.

44. Didion, *Where I Was From*, p. 147.

45. *National Geographic* magazine (USA), January 1988.

46. *Empire* magazine (England), March 2007.

47. *New York* magazine (USA), September 21, 2009.

48. *W* magazine (USA), November 2007.

49. Janet Shibley Hyde, *Understanding Human Sexuality* (New York: McGraw-Hill, 1979), p. 57.

50. Glenn Wilson and Qazi Rahman, *Born Gay: The Psychology of Sex Orientation* (England: Peter Owen, 2005); Bruce Bagemihl, *Biological Exuberance* (New York: St. Martin's Press, 2000).

51. McKeever and Davies, *Politics USA*, p. 127.

52. *BusinessWeek* (England), October 20, 2003.

53. Ethan Watters, *Urban Tribes: Are Friends the New Family?* (England: Bloomsbury, 2003), p. 39.

54. White, *My Lives*, p. 356.

55. Jon Katz, *The New Work of Dogs* (New York: Villard Books, 2003), p. 10.

56. Ibid., p. 17.

57. *New York Times* (USA), November 16, 2005.

58. *Vanity Fair* (England), November 2006; *Vanity Fair* (England), May 2006.

59. Andres Garrod and Robert Kelkenny, *Balancing Two Worlds* (Ithaca, NY: Cornell University Press 2007), p. 37.

60. *New York Times* (USA), November 17, 2007.

61. Rebecca Walker, *Black, White and Jewish: Autobiography of a Shifting Self* (New York: Riverhead, 2001); Haki R. Madhubuti, *YellowBlack* (Chicago: Third World Press, 2006).

62. Metcalf, *How We Talk*, p. 156.

63. *New York Times* (USA), October 26, 1998; McKeever and Davies, *Politics USA*, p. 3.

64. *Advocate* magazine (USA), August 29, 2006.

65. Pew Research Center's Forum on Religion and Public Life, *Religious Commitment Analysis* (Washington, DC: Pew Forum on Religion and Public Life, 2009).

66. *New York Times* (USA), July 17, 2007; *New York Times* (USA), March 28, 2010.

67. *Vanity Fair* (USA), June 7, 2006.

68. *New York Times* (USA), September 4, 2008.

69. *Advocate* magazine (USA), December 19, 2006.

70. *New York Times* (USA), July 26, 2009.

71. David Brooks, *Bobos in Paradise* (New York: Simon & Schuster, 2000), p. 37.

72. *Vanity Fair* (England), July 2009.

73. Robert Mondavi and Paul Chutkow, *Harvests of Joy: How the Good Life Became Great Business* (Boston: Harcourt, 1999).

74. Michael J. Silverstein and Neil Fiske, *Trading Up: The New American Luxury* (New York: Portfolio, 2003), pp. 183–89.

75. Ibid., p. 37.

76. Ibid., p. xii.

77. *Time* magazine (Holland), April 16, 2001.

78. *Advocate* magazine (USA), August 28, 2007.

79. Wilson and Rahman, *Born Gay*, pp. 13–27.

80. *Salon* (USA), July 22, 2002.

81. *Advocate* magazine (USA), December 19, 2006.

82. *Advocate* magazine (USA), December 19, 2006; *New York* magazine (USA), September 25, 2006.

83. *International Herald Tribune* (France), December 22, 2006.

84. *New York* magazine (USA), October 19, 2009.

85. *Time* magazine (Holland), June 15, 2009.
86. *Time* magazine (Holland), October 30, 2006.
87. *New York* magazine (USA), March 2, 2009.
88. Ibid.
89. *Time* magazine (Holland), October 26, 2009.
90. *New York* magazine (USA), October 19, 2009.

CHAPTER 3: ORGANIZED LIVING

1. *International Herald Tribune* (France), January 27–28, 2007.
2. Ibid.
3. Ibid.
4. Ibid.
5. *Vanity Fair* (England), March 2007.
6. David Brooks, *On Paradise Drive* (New York: Simon & Schuster, 2004), p. 76.
7. Ibid., p. 7.
8. "Things to Do on a Georgia Vacation: Auto Racing in Savannah, GA," Essortment, www.essortment.com/all/autoracingsava_nmg.htm (accessed May 3, 2010).
9. Po Bronson, *Why Do I Love These People?* (New York: Vintage Books, 2005), p. 35.
10. Michael J. Silverstein and Neil Fiske, *Trading Up: The New American Luxury* (New York: Portfolio, 2003), p. 5.
11. Rich Merritt, *Secrets of a Gay Marine Porn Star* (New York: Kensington Books, 2005), p. 20.
12. Donald B. Kraybill, *The Puzzles of Amish Life* (Intercourse, PA: Good Books, 1998), p. 4.
13. Kathleen McLary, *Amish Style* (Bloomington: Indiana University Press, 1993), p. 2.
14. Kraybill, *The Puzzles of Amish Life*, pp. 32–38; Ruth P. Rubinstein, *Dress Codes: Meanings and Messages in American Culture* (Boulder: Westview Press, 2001), p. 259.
15. Augusten Burroughs, *Dry: A Memoir* (New York: Picador, 2003).
16. Sam Fussel, *Muscle: Confessions of an Unlikely Bodybuilder* (England: Cardinal Books, 1991), p. 62.
17. Andrew Essex, *New York's 50 Hottest Night Spots* (n.p.: City & Company, 1997), p. 24.
18. J. C. Cooper, *An Illustrated Encyclopedia of Traditional Symbols*

(London: Thames & Hudson, 1978); Carl G. Liungman, *Dictionary of Symbols* (New York: Norton, 1991).

19. Walter Ong, *Orality and Literacy: The Technologizing of the Word* (England: Methuen, 1988).

20. *National Geographic* magazine (USA), January 1988.

21. *Complete Flags of the World* (England: Dorling Kindersley, 2008), p. 14.

22. Miranda Bruce-Mitford, *The Illustrated Book of Signs & Symbols* (New York: DK, 1996), p. 107.

CHAPTER 4: STYLISH COMMUNICATION

1. Kate Fox, *Watching the English* (England: Hodder & Stoughton, 2005), p. 39.

2. John Peacock, *The Chronicle of Western Costume* (London: Thames & Hudson, 1991).

3. Marilynn Brewer and Norman Miller, *Intergroup Relations* (England: Open University Press, 1996), p. 22.

4. *Vanity Fair* (USA), May 2010.

5. Paul Fussel, *Uniforms: Why We Are What We Wear* (New York: Houghton Mifflin, 2002), p. 78.

6. Ruth P. Rubinstein, *Dress Codes: Meanings and Messages in American Culture* (Boulder: Westview Press, 2001), pp. 257–59; Catherine Bell, *Ritual: Perspectives and Dimensions* (New York: Oxford University Press, 1997), p. 145; Donald Kraybill, *The Puzzles of Amish Life* (Intercourse, PA: Good Books, 1998).

7. Erling Bjøl, *USAs Historie* (Denmark: Gyldendal, 2005), p. 29.

8. Michael S. Kimmel, *Manhood in America: A Cultural History* (New York: Free Press, 1996), p. 148.

9. Ibid., pp. 150–51.

10. Joy S. Kasson, *Buffalo Bill's Wild West: Celebrity, Memory, and Popular History* (New York: Hill and Wang, 2001).

11. Ibid.

12. Rubinstein, *Dress Codes*, pp. 126–27.

13. H. W. Brands, *The Age of Gold: The California Gold Rush and the New American Dream* (New York: Anchor, 2003).

14. Bjøl, *USAs Historie*, p. 32.

15. Holly George-Warren and Michelle Freedman, *How the West Was Worn: A History of Western Wear* (New York: Abrams, 2001), pp. 130, 189–

90; M. Jean Greenlaw, *Ranch Dressing: The Story of Western Wear* (New York: Lodestar, 1993), pp. 7, 41–43; Colin McDowell, *McDowell's Directory of Twentieth-Century Fashion* (England: Muller, 1987); Henrik Vejlgaard, *Anatomy of a Trend* (New York: McGraw-Hill, 2008), pp. 121–30.

16. George-Warren and Freedman, *How the West Was Worn*, pp. 32, 34; Greenlaw, *Ranch Dressing*, pp. 12–13.

17. Greenlaw, *Ranch Dressing*, p. 47.

18. George-Warren and Freedman, *How the West Was Worn*, pp. 31–32; Greenlaw, *Ranch Dressing*, pp. 61–63.

19. Greenlaw, *Ranch Dressing*, pp. 64–65.

20. Stuart Miller and Geoffrey Moss, *The Biker Code: Wisdom for the Ride* (New York: Simon & Schuster, 2002), pp. 5, 15, 17.

21. Ralph "Sonny" Barger, *Hell's Angel* (England: Fourth Estate, 2001), pp. 28–29.

22. Mick Farren, *The Black Leather Jacket* (England: Plexus, 2008).

23. Barger, *Hell's Angel*, p. 21.

24. Nat Young, *History of Surfing* (Sydney: Palm Beach Press, 1996).

25. Ibid., p. 46.

26. International Surfing Museum, www.surfingmuseum.org/ (accessed May 1, 2010).

27. Young, *History of Surfing*, p. 75.

28. International Surfing Museum, www.surfingmuseum.org/.

29. Amy de la Haye and Cathie Dingwall, *Surfers, Soulies, Skinheads and Skaters* (England: V & A Publications, 1996); Ted Polhemus, *Street Style* (London: Thames & Hudson, 1994), pp. 48–49; *Textile View* (Holland), Winter 2005.

30. George-Warren and Freedman, *How the West Was Worn*, p. 72; Polhemus, *Street Style*, p. 28.

31. Vejlgaard, *Anatomy of a Trend*, pp. 159–61.

32. Ibid.

33. Chuck D. and Yusuf Jah, *Fight the Power: Rap, Race and Reality* (New York: Delacourte, 1998); Russell Simmons, *Life & Def: Sex, Drugs, Money and God* (New York: Three River Press, 2002); Polhemus, *Street Style*, pp. 106–108; Tommy Hilfiger with David A. Keeps, *All-American: A Style Book* (New York: Universe Publishing, 1997).

34. Bjøl, *USAs Historie*, p. 745.

35. *Vanity Fair* (England), November 2005.

36. Ibid.

37. Ibid.

38. Universal Zulu Nation, www.zulunation.com/ (accessed May 3, 2010).

39. Hilfiger and Keeps, *All American*; *W* magazine (USA), September 2001.

40. Lee Montgomery, *The Things Between Us: A Memoir* (New York: Free Press, 2006), pp. 7, 8.

41. Po Bronson, *What Should I Do with My Life?* (New York: Ballantine Books, 2005), p. 127.

42. Edmund White, *My Lives: An Autobiography* (New York: Ecco Books, 2006), p. 32.

43. *Vanity Fair* (England), February 2007.

44. *New York* magazine, August 3, 2009.

45. *Vanity Fair* (England), November 2006.

46. David Beckham, *My World* (London: Hodder & Stoughton, 2000), p. 93.

CHAPTER 5: TO BE OR NOT TO BE A TRIBE

1. Michael Cunningham and Graig Marberry, *Crowns: Portraits of Black Women in Church Hats* (New York: Doubleday, 2000), pp. 124, 132.

2. Bill Yenne, *Encyclopedia of North American Indian Tribes* (North Dighton, MA: JG Press, 1998), pp. 24, 119; Miranda Bruce-Mitford, *The Illustrated Book of Signs & Symbols* (New York: DK, 1996), p. 66; James D. Horan, *North American Indian Portraits* (New York: Crown, 1975).

3. Smithsonian Institution, *Do All Indians Live in Tipis?* (New York: Harper, 2007), p. 71; Alan Taylor, *American Colonies: The Settling of North America* (New York: Penguin, 2001), p. xii.

4. Douglas Brinkley, *The Wilderness Warrior: Theodore Roosevelt and the Crusade for America* (New York: HarperCollins, 2009).

5. Stephen Scott, *The Amish Wedding and Other Special Occasions of the Old Order Communities* (Intercourse, PA: Good Books, 1988).

6. David Beckham, *My World* (London: Hodder & Stoughton, 2000).

7. Terisa Green, *The Tattoo Encyclopedia* (New York: Simon & Schuster, 2003), pp. x–xi; *Iconoculture* newsletter (USA), Winter 1992/93; Vickie Abrahamson, Mary Meehan, and Larry Samuel, *The Future Ain't What It Used to Be* (New York: Riverhead Books, 1997), pp. 32–33.

8. *New York* magazine (USA), September 28, 2009.

9. Alison Lurie, *The Language of Clothes* (New York: Random House, 1981), pp. 85–86.

10. Ruth P. Rubinstein, *Dress Codes: Meanings and Messages in American Culture* (Boulder: Westview Press, 2001), p. 277.

11. Hal Fischer, *Gay Semiotics* (San Francisco: NFS, 1977), pp. 7, 13.

12. Richard Plant, *The Pink Triangle: The Nazi War against Homosexuals* (New York: Holt, 1986).

13. "The New Yellow Ribbon Tradition," The Library of Congress: The American Folklife Center, www.loc.gov/folklife/ribbons (accessed May 3, 2010).

14. *Economist* (England), December 23, 2006–January 5, 2007.

15. Yenne, *Encyclopedia of North American Indian Tribes*, p. 11.

16. Morton H. Fried, *The Notion of Tribe* (Menlo Park, CA: Cummings, 1975).

17. Corinne Hofmann, *The White Masai* (New York: Amistad, 2007).

18. David Miles, *The Tribes of Britain* (London: Weidenfeld & Nicolson, 2005), p. 7.

19. Yenne, *Encyclopedia of North American Indian Tribes*.

20. Rubinstein, *Dress Codes*, pp. 260–62.

21. "Front Porch: The Celebration Community Web Site," Celebration, Florida, www.celebration.fl.us (accessed May 3, 2010).

22. Fried, *The Notion of Tribe*, p. 85.

23. David Brooks, *On Paradise Drive* (New York: Simon & Schuster, 2004), p. 6.

24. Bill Bishop, *The Big Sort* (Boston: Houghton Mifflin, 2008), pp. 5–7.

25. Ted Polhemus, *Street Style* (London: Thames & Hudson, 1994), p. 64.

26. Thomas Powers, *Vietnam: The War at Home* (Boston: G. K. Hall, 1984), p. 201.

27. Ted Morgan, *Literary Outlaw: Life and Times of William S. Burroughs* (New York: Holt, 1986), p. 199.

28. David Hajdu, *Positively 4th Street* (New York: Farrar, Straus and Giroux, 2001), photo after p. 88.

29. Po Bronson, *What Should I Do with My Life?* (New York: Ballantine Books, 2005), p. 104.

30. *Vanity Fair* (England), August 2009.

31. Luc Reid, *Talk the Talk: The Slang of 65 American Subcultures* (Cincinnati: Writer's Digest Books, 2006).

32. Walt Wolfram and Ben Ward, eds., *American Voices: How Dialects Differ from Coast to Coast* (Malden, MA: Blackwell, 2007), p. 253.

33. Bruce-Mitford, *The Illustrated Book of Signs & Symbols*, p. 66.

34. Smithsonian Institution, *Do All Indians Live in Tipis?* (New York: Harper, 2007), p. 18.

35. Andrew Essex, *New York's 50 Hottest Night Spots* (n.p.: City & Company, 1997), pp. 44–45.

36. *International Herald Tribune* (France), December 14, 2007.

37. Chase Reynolds Ewald, *Cowboy Chic: Western Style Comes Home* (Salt Lake City: Gibbs Smith, 2000).

CHAPTER 6: DEVOTED TO A STYLE

1. Linda Chase and Laura Cerwinske, *In the Romantic Style* (London: Thames & Hudson, 2000); Judith Miller and Martin Miller, *Victorian Style* (England: Mitchell Beazley, 1997); editors of *Victoria* magazine, *Romantic Country Style* (New York: Hearst Books, 1999); Elizabeth Wilhide, *Bohemian Style* (New York: Watzon-Guptil Publications, 2001); Mary Schoeser, *More Is More: An Antidote to Minimalism* (England: Conran Octopus, 2001); Stephen Calloway, *Divinely Decadent* (England: Mitchell Beazley, 2001); Nancy Corzine, *Glamour at Home* (New York: Rizzoli, 2009); Kelly Weastler, *Modern Glamour: The Art of Unexpected Style* (New York: Regan Books, 2004); Chase Reynolds Ewald, *Cowboy Chic: Western Style Comes Home* (Salt Lake City: Gibbs Smith, 2000); Christine Mather and Sharon Woods, *Santa Fe Style* (New York: Rizzoli, 1986); Carol Sama Sheelan, *Mary Emmerling's American Country Classics* (New York: Clarkson Potter, 1990); Ann McArdle, *Natural Interiors* (Beverly, MA: Rockport Publishers, 2000); Stewart Walton and Sally Walton, *Eco Deco: Chic, Ecological Design Using Recycled Materials* (England: Aquamarine, 2000); Agnesa Reeve, *The Small Adobe House* (Salt Lake City: Gibbs Smith, 2001); Aurora Cuito, *Small Apartments* (New York: HarperCollins Design International, 2003); Quim Rosell, *Minimalist Interiors* (New York: HarperCollins Design International, 2003); Sally Walton, *White Home: Pure Simplicity for Tranquil Interiors* (England: Lorenz Books, 2002); Ann Stillman O'Leary, *Adirondack Style* (New York: Crown, 2002); Tricia Foley, *Sailing Style: Nautical Inspirations for the Home* (New York: Clarkson Potter, 2003); Anna Kasabian, *New England Style* (New York: Rizzoli, 2003); June Sprigg and David Larkin, *Shaker: Life, Work, and Art* (England: Cassel, 1987); Mary Trewby, *Simple Country Style: And How to Achieve It* (England: Conran Octopus, 1990); Henrietta Spencer-Churchill, *Classic Interior Design: Using Period Features in Today's Home* (USA: Rizzoli, 2003); Marion Haslam, *Retro Style: The '50s Look for Today's Home* (New York: Universe Publishing, 2000); Suzanne Trocme, *Retro Home* (New York: Rizzoli, 2000); Michael Webb, *Modernism Reborn: Mid-Century American Houses* (New York: Universe Publishing, 2001).

2. *Cool Hotels* (England: teNeues, 2003); Herbert Ypma, *Hip Hotels*

(London: Thames & Hudson, 1999); Herbert Ypma, *Hip Hotels: City* (London: Thames & Hudson, 1999); Herbert Ypma, *Hip Hotels: Ski* (London: Thames & Hudson, 2002); Herbert Ypma, *Hip Hotels: Escape* (London: Thames & Hudson, 2003); Herbert Ypma, *Hip Hotels: USA* (London: Thames & Hudson, 2003); Herbert Ypma, *Hip Hotels: Beach* (London: Thames & Hudson, 2004); Herbert Ypma, *Hip Hotels: Budget* (London: Thames & Hudson, 2004).

3. Julie Mundy, *Elvis Fashion: From Memphis to Las Vegas* (New York: Universe, 2004).

4. Graham M. Vaughan and Michael A. Hogg, *Introduction to Social Psychology* (Australia: Prentice Hall Australia, 1998), pp. 241–43.

5. Adrian C. North and Adam J. Lonsdale, *Musical Taste and Ingroup Favoritism* (England: *Group Processes & Intergroup Relations*, 2009), pp. 319–27.

6. Michael Silverstein and Neil Fiske, *Trading Up: The New American Luxury* (New York: Portfolio, 2003), p. 138.

7. Erling Bjøl, *USAs Historie* (Denmark: Gyldendal, 2005), p. 742.

8. "Luxury for the Masses," *Harvard Business Review*, April 2003.

9. *BusinessWeek* (England), December 13, 2002.

10. *BusinessWeek* (England), November 18, 2002; *BusinessWeek* (England), April 9, 2001.

11. Tim Sullivan, "Get Real Girl Steals the Limelight," Toy Directory Monthly, www.toydirectory.com/monthly/getrealgirls.asp (accessed May 3, 2010).

12. David Raizman, *History of Modern Design* (England: Laurence King, 2003), p. 134.

13. Ibid., pp. 211–12.

14. *BusinessWeek* (England), February 16, 2004; *Newsweek* (England), January 12, 2004.

15. Christopher Byron, *Martha Inc.* (New York: Wiley, 2003), pp. 136, 194–96.

16. *International Herald Tribune* (France), September 22, 2007.

17. *New York* magazine (USA), August 3, 2009.

CHAPTER 7: DESIGNED LIFE

1. *Vanity Fair* (England), June 2007.

2. Warren Belasco and Philip Scranton, eds., *Food Nations* (New York: Routledge, 2002), p. 26.

3. Jeremiah Tower, *California Dish: What I Saw (and Cooked) at the American Culinary Revolution* (New York: Free Press, 2003), pp. 118–19.

4. *New York Times* (USA), March 8, 2009.

5. Laura Cerwinske, *Miami Hot & Cool* (London: Thames & Hudson, 1990); *Insight Guide Florida* (Singapore: APA Publications, 1998), pp. 164–65.

6. Nat Young, *History of Surfing* (Sydney: Palm Beach Press, 1996); "History," Paskowitz: Professional Surf Training, www.paskowitz.com/history.html (accessed May 3, 2010).

7. *American Bicyclist* (USA), March/April 2009.

8. *New York Times* (USA), November 18, 2007.

9. *Time* magazine (Holland), April 23, 1979; *New York Times* (USA), October 31, 2007.

10. *New York Times* (USA), July 25, 2009.

11. *Time* magazine (Holland), August 24, 2009.

12. *Forbes Global* (England), 2001.

13. Stephen Slater, *The Illustrated Book of Heraldry* (London: Hermes House, 2005).

14. Anistatia R. Miller and Jared M. Brown, *What Logos Do and How They Do It* (Beverly, MA: Rockport Publishers, 2000); Wally Olins, *Corporate Identity* (London: Thames & Hudson, 1991); Bruce Chadwick and David M. Spindel, *The Bronx Bombers* (New York: Abbeville Press, 1992); Bruce Chadwick and David M. Spindel, *The Boston Red Sox* (New York: Abbeville Press, 1992).

15. Georgina O'Hara, *Encyclopaedia of Fashion* (London: Thames & Hudson, 1989); Jon Henderson, *The Last Champion: The Life of Fred Perry* (England: Yellow Jersey Press, 2009).

16. *International Herald Tribune* (France), August 31, 2007.

17. Terisa Green, *The Tattoo Encyclopaedia* (New York: Simon & Schuster, 2003), pp. x–xi; Ralph "Sonny" Barger, *Hell's Angel* (England: Fourth Estate, 2001), p. 72; Wakefield Poole, *Dirty Poole: The Autobiography of a Gay Porn Pioneer* (Los Angeles: Alyson Publications, 2000), pp. 183–84; Micha Ramakers, *Dirty Pictures* (New York: St. Martin's Press, 2000); Vickie Abrahamson, Mary Meehan, and Larry Samuel, *The Future Ain't What It Used to Be* (New York: Riverhead Books, 1997), pp. 32–33; *Iconoculture* newsletter (USA), Winter 1992/93.

18. *U.S. News & World Report* (USA), November 3, 1997.

19. Tommy Hilfiger and George Lois, *Iconic America* (New York: Universe Publishing, 2007), p. 320.

20. Abraham H. Maslow, *Motivation and Personality* (New York: Longman, 1970), pp. 56–61.

21. Ibid., p. 56.

22. Ibid., p. 7.

23. David G. Myers, *Psychology* (New York: Worth Publishers, 1998), p. 366.

24. H. W. Janson, *History of Art* (New York: Abrams, 1995), pp. 48–57.

25. Maslow, *Motivation and Personality*, p. 58.

26. Stephen Moore and Julian L. Simon, *It's Getting Better All the Time: 100 Greatest Trends of the Last 100 Years* (Washington, DC: Cato Institute, 2000), pp. 62–63.

27. Edward N. Wolff, *Top Heavy: The Increasing Inequality of Wealth in America and What Can Be Done about It* (New York: New Press, 2002).

28. *New York Times* (USA), citing the US Census Bureau, April 18, 2007.

29. *Time* magazine (Holland), October 26, 2009.

30. Ibid.

31. *Newsweek* (USA), May 12, 2003.

32. *Time* magazine (Holland), October 2009.

33. *International Herald Tribune* (France), August 4–5, 2007.

34. "Fashion Designers," GLBTQ: The World's Largest Encyclopedia of Gay, Lesbian, Bisexual, Transgender, and Queer Culture, http://www .glbtq.com/topic/arts_79.html (accessed May 3, 2010).

35. Heather A. Rupp and Kim Wallen, "Sex Differences in Viewing Sexual Stimuli: An Eye-Tracking Study in Men and Women," *Hormones and Behavior* 51 (2007): 524–33; John Gray, *Men Are from Mars, Women Are from Venus* (London: Thorsons, 1998), p. 16.

36. Rupp and Wallen, "Sex Differences in Viewing Sexual Stimuli."

37. William Mann, *Behind the Screen: How Gays and Lesbians Shaped Hollywood* (New York: Penguin, 2001), pp. 215–18, 227.

38. *Time* magazine (Holland), April 23, 1979.

39. *Village Voice*, August 8–14, 2001.

40. Henrik Vejlgaard, *Anatomy of a Trend* (New York: McGraw-Hill, 2007).

41. "The Buzz on Buzz," *Harvard Business Review*, November/December 2000; Katherine Sender, "'Business, Not Politics': Gays, Lesbians, Bisexuals, Transgendered People and the Consumer Sphere," department paper commissioned by GLAAD (Gay & Lesbian Alliance Against Defamation), University of Pennsylvania, 2002.

42. *Advocate* magazine (USA), December 20, 2005.

CHAPTER 8: SOCIETY REARRANGED

1. *Advocate* Magazine (USA), March 13, 2007.

2. David Myers, *Psychology* (New York: Worth Publishers, 1998), p. 583.

3. Michael Franzini, *One Hundred Young Americans* (New York: Collins Design, 2007), pp. 26, 199.

4. Mark Harris, *Pictures at a Revolution: Five Movies and the Birth of the New Hollywood* (New York: Penguin, 2008), pp. 102–103; *International Herald Tribune* (France), February 16–17, 2008.

5. *Vanity Fair* (England), July 2009.

6. *New York Times* (USA), June 1, 2009.

7. *BusinessWeek* (England), July 12, 2004.

8. Israel Zangwill, *The Melting-Pot: Drama in Four Acts* (n.p.: Biblio-Life, 2009).

9. Erling Bjøl, *USAs Historie* (Denmark: Gyldendal, 2005), p. 332.

10. Ronald Baylor, *Culture and Democracy in the United States* (Piscataway, NJ: Transaction Publishers, 1997).

11. Alvin Tofler, *PowerShift* (New York: Bantam Books, 1990), p. 244.

12. Arthur M. Schlesinger Jr., *The Disuniting of America: Reflections on a Multicultural Society* (New York: Norton, 1998).

13. Clotaire Rapaille, *The Culture Code* (New York: Broadway Books, 2006), pp. 33, 76.

14. Jacque Attali, *Millennium: Winners and Losers in the Coming World Order* (New York: Times Books, 1991), p. 27.

15. Henrik Vejlgaard, *Anatomy of a Trend* (New York: McGraw-Hill, 2008), pp. 114–16.

16. *International Herald Tribune* (France), December 26, 2006.

17. *Time* magazine (Holland), November 2, 2009.

18. Sarah Bradford, *America's Queen: The Life of Jacqueline Kennedy Onassis* (New York: Penguin, 2001); Michael J. Silverstein and Neil Fiske, *Trading Up: The New American Luxury* (New York: Portfolio, 2003), pp. xii, 37, 162; *Vanity Fair* (England), July 2009; Robert Mondavi and Paul Chutkow, *Harvests of Joy: How the Good Life Became Great Business* (New York: Harcourt Brace, 1999), p. 22.

19. *New York Times* (USA), November 2, 2007.

20. *New York Times* (USA), August 7, 2007.

21. *Time* magazine (Holland), August 17, 2009.

22. *Economist* (England), December 23, 2006–January 5, 2007.

23. Jean M. Greenlaw, *Ranch Dressing: The Story of Western Wear* (New York: Lodestar, 1993), p. 43.

24. Holly George-Warren and Michelle Freedman, *How The West Was Worn: A History of Western Wear* (New York: Harry N. Abrams, 2001), pp. 72–85.

25. Inga Wintzell, *Jeans och Jeanskultur* [with English summary] (Sweden: Nordiska Museet, 1985), p. 129.

26. Steven Gaines and Sharon Churcher, *Obsession: The Lives and Times of Calvin Klein* (New York: Carol, 1994), pp. 214–15, 250.

27. Vejlgaard, *Anatomy of a Trend*, pp. 121–30.

APPENDIX: CREATING THE STYLE MAP

1. Henrik Vejlgaard, *Forbrug i designersamfundet* (Denmark: Borsens Forlag, 2004).

2. Ibid.

INDEX